MW00785971

THE ART OF BANK

M&A

THE ART OF BANK M&A

Buying, Selling, Merging, and Investing in Regulated Depository Institutions in the New Environment

Alexandra Reed Lajoux

Dennis J. Roberts

New York Chicago San Francisco Athens London
Madrid Mexico City Milan New Delhi
Singapore Sydney Toronto

1 2 3 4 5 6 7 8 9 0 QFR/QFR 1 9 8 7 6 5 4 3

ISBN 978-0-07-179956-0
MHID 0-07-179956-7

e-ISBN 978-0-07-179957-7
e-MHID 0-07-179957-5

Library of Congress Cataloging-in-Publication Data

Lajoux, Alexandra Reed.
The art of bank M&A : buying, selling, merging, and investing in regulated depository institutions in the new environment / Alexandra Lajoux and Dennis J. Roberts.
pages cm
ISBN 978-0-07-179956-0 (hardback) — ISBN 0-07-179956-7 (hardback) 1. Bank mergers—United States. 2. Financial institutions—Law and legislation—United States. I. Roberts, Dennis J. II. Title. III. Title: Art of bank M and A.
HG1722.L29 2014
332.1068'1—dc23 2013034240

This publication is designed to provide accurate and authoritative information in regard to the subject matter covered. It is sold with the understanding that neither the author nor the publisher is engaged in rendering legal, accounting, securities trading, or other professional services. If legal advice or other expert assistance is required, the services of a competent professional person should be sought.

—From a Declaration of Principles Jointly Adopted by a Committee of the American Bar Association and a Committee of Publishers and Associations

McGraw-Hill Education books are available at special quantity discounts to use as premiums and sales promotions or for use in corporate training programs. To contact a representative, please visit the Contact Us pages at www.mhprofessional.com.

To the memory of Shirley Edwards Wilkinson,

whose excellence as a bank branch manager strengthened

her customers, encouraged her colleagues, and inspired her friends.

Alexandra Reed Lajoux

To the memory of Robin Ann Quattlebaum,

who after an epic struggle departed this life on July 5, 2013.

Dennis J. Roberts

CONTENTS

FOREWORD

A New World for Bank Mergers

By Heath P. Tarbert*

The first two decades of the twenty-first century represent a critical juncture in the history of the U.S. banking sector. Beginning in 1999, an unprecedented expansion into nonbanking activities combined with the emergence of new Internet-based technologies, a vibrant mortgage market, and financial innovations from Wall Street to Main Street to fuel the organic growth of banks, as well as an abundance of mergers and acquisitions (M&A) activity, for nearly a decade. Then came the global financial crisis. The entire U.S. banking industry plunged into an abyss of chaos not witnessed since the throes of the Great Depression. Bankruptcy or bailout became the limited menu of options offered to many financial institutions. In addition, the aftermath of the financial crisis triggered another significant series of events: a cascade of new laws and regulations and an era of increased scrutiny by government authorities, the media, and seemingly the public at large. The ultimate effects of these tumultuous changes may not be known for decades, particularly as policymakers continue to introduce new prudential measures and debate the role that banks should play in the marketplace. The overall trajectory of the U.S. banking sector—as well as prospects for further industry consolidation—hangs very much in the balance.

---

* Heath P. Tarbert is a partner at the law firm of Allen & Overy LLP, where he is recognized for his transactional and regulatory expertise involving U.S. and foreign banks, thrifts, credit unions, nonbank financial institutions, and holding companies. Earlier in his career, Mr. Tarbert served as special counsel to the U.S. Senate Banking Committee, associate counsel to the president of the United States, and a law clerk at the Supreme Court of the United States.

Tumultuous changes do, however, consistently yield opportunities for those willing to seize them. Despite the prevailing reluctance that has characterized the bank M&A market in recent years, a number of competitive and regulatory factors are generating a demand for acquisitions that simply cannot be ignored. At the outset, the United States has far more independent banks per capita than those of other developed nations. For example, the United Kingdom has 110 banks, while the United States has over 7,000, with a large portion of the latter figure comprising community banks.[1] While some may contend that Americans are "overbanked,"[2] the reality is that community banks remain vital to the fabric of American domestic and economic life. And although community banks account for a smaller portion of insured deposits than do megabanks, they have traditionally maintained a competitive advantage in lending to small and medium-sized businesses.[3] Notwithstanding this unique and important role in the U.S. economy, the typical community bank can be very small. Often these banks are family-owned enterprises that focus on serving several towns within one or more counties. The current environment of low interest rates, rising regulatory and compliance costs, and market-specific challenges have created a climate where community banks with assets of $1 billion or less are arguably "too small to succeed."[4] Out of necessity, these institutions may face only a binary set of choices in the near future: acquire or be acquired.[5]

On the other end of the spectrum, large money-center banks are facing challenges of a wholly different sort. Many critics in Washington, DC, and in the media assert that these institutions have become "too big to fail"—a pejorative term indicating that a given bank's distress or insolvency may threaten the stability of the financial system such that the government must bail out the institution before it fails. Despite passage of the sweeping Dodd–Frank Act and a host of capital and liquidity requirements, supplemental prudential measures, and activity restrictions now imposed on large financial institutions, the debate continues in Washington on whether these megabanks should be "broken up."[6] Many large U.S. banks are rethinking their business models and in some cases refocusing on core business lines responsible for their past successes. As a consequence, the nation's largest banks are expected to shed noncore businesses, as well as make modest acquisitions consistent with their long-term strategies.[7]

Between community banks and megabanks are regional banks and foreign banks that are poised to occupy various niches and subsegments within the U.S. banking sector. Indeed, many contend that regional banks—particularly institutions with approximately $10 billion to $50 billion in assets—are best positioned to grow through mergers and acquisitions.[8] Banks of this size that are well capitalized and well managed are unlikely to present systemic risk concerns for regulators in Washington. At the same time, federal and state banking supervisors may encourage the institutions to employ their superior financial and material resources to "roll up" smaller regional and community banks with less robust performance records. In addition, many large financial institutions based abroad now find themselves outside the U.S. banking sector looking inward. Some of these foreign banks—particularly those based in fast-growing regions such as Asia, Latin America, and the Middle East—are considering investing resources to establish a more robust presence in the United States.[9] Although some foreign banks have successfully pursued organic growth strategies by establishing branches and depositories in the United States, a number of others have made considerable gains through the acquisition of domestic banks with stable retail deposit bases.[10]

Pressures from nonbank competitors also are becoming more acute. Insurance companies, asset management firms, and even some nonfinancial commercial companies are finding ways to penetrate the lending and deposit-taking business or otherwise offer credit products that compete directly with the services offered by traditional banks. A number of life and casualty insurance companies already own thrifts, as do several independent investment advisory firms.[11] Finally, in order to build up the requisite capital to compete in the new competitive environment, banks of varying sizes may need to rely on new sources of equity and debt funding. Private equity firms, for example, could emerge as major players in the banking sector, although their influence on individual institutions may be circumscribed to some degree by regulatory barriers. In short, the competitive forces from outside the banking sector may be as strong as those coming from within.

All of these competitive and regulatory factors are expected to drive U.S. banking sector consolidation in the next decade, making a new book on bank M&A timely. The fundamental question for every CEO and his or her board is whether their bank is positioned to take advantage of the coming merger wave. If, as Seneca said long ago, "luck is what happens when preparation meets opportunity," then bank executives would do well to begin focusing on their preparation. *The Art of Bank M&A*—which answers more than 250 important questions on a range of highly relevant topics—will assist those working at and with financial institutions of all sizes in better understanding and navigating the new world of bank mergers rapidly taking shape.

PREFACE

> As long as I keep seeing people keep getting up and going to work every day, I will keep believing in the possibility of economic growth.
>
> —*David Ciccone*[1]

In the spring of 2011, when the journey of writing this tome began, the financial services industry was recovering from trauma. Following a meltdown in mortgage finance, Congress had passed a major financial reform bill, and bankers were facing the uncertainty of hundreds of rule makings. The trust of bankers in customers, and the trust of customers in bankers, had been shaken. Furthermore, many tried-and-true economic paradigms, such as the assumption that low interest rates bring economic growth, seemed to be broken. Yet one fact remained true, and it carried the authors of this book forward through completion: banks continue to play a vital role in the local, national, and world economy. We began this project anchored in the firm conviction that enlightened free enterprise can yield national and personal wealth and with respect for the financial professionals who help to safeguard and increase this wealth day by day.

This book applies these motivating values to the challenging subject of bank M&A.

As noted in the opening section, Setting, commercial banks play a critical role in the economic life of people and nations. Chapter 1 takes a broad look at this vital sector, explaining the importance of banks in the national and global economy and presenting basic statistics on bank mergers. Chapter 2 summarizes the major changes in banking law that have evolved over time, in the years since the financial crisis that began in 2007. Chapter 3 identifies regulatory issues unique to banks that fit this legal category.

Whatever regulatory setting may apply, banks have leeway to develop and apply their own rules for merger success—the focus of Section 2,

From Strategies to Standards. Chapter 4 defines these two values in relation to one another and explains how banks achieve them. The last two chapters in this section provide guidance for determining and confirming the value a given bank may bring to the entity acquiring it. This requires an increasing degree of diligence—from the preliminary phase of sizing up a transaction through initial valuation/evaluation, to the formal process that ensures the validity of these findings. Thus, Chapter 5 leads readers through the basic steps for determining a price range when buying a bank. Chapter 6 aims to help acquirers achieve an acceptable level of assurance on their findings right up to a transaction's closing.

The first two sections of this book explain the regulatory framework surrounding bank mergers, along with the strategies and standards that should inform them. The next section addresses the equally important topic of synergies, defined as the incremental value created through combination. Chapter 7 explains why and how banks combine their resources, processes, and responsibilities through mergers. Chapter 8 provides a brief but instructive example of success. Chapter 9 peers into the future of banking.

The final section of our book focuses on special situations that may face bankers as they expand. Chapter 10 presents trends and issues in transactions that involve banks from two or more countries. Chapter 11 takes the reader through the difficult journey of bank insolvency. Chapter 12 ends on a more positive note by broadening the horizons of this book. It contains guidance for all investors, both institutional and individual, interested in aligning a part of their investment portfolios—and thus an aspect of their own economic future—with commercial banks, domestic or foreign, solvent or distressed, as they face their ever-evolving economic destiny. The Appendix presents summaries of Landmark U.S. Supreme Court Cases in Banking, 1799 to 2013.

FINAL REFLECTIONS ON WEALTH

In closing, we would like to quote an inspiring passage from Jaron Lanier, a technologist cited earlier on the subject of bank insolvency. "To lose trust in the basic inception of wealth is to lose trust in the idea of human improvement. If all the value that can be already is, then market dynamics can only be about churn, conflict, and accumulation," says Lanier, adding: "In an expanding market, new value and new wealth are created.... Not all wealth is created from game-changing events like inventions or natural resource discoveries. Some of it comes from the ability of ordinary people to keep promises."[2]

Bankers are the ones who believe those promises and help to fulfill the dreams that inspired them. Therefore, we dedicate this book to them and wish them success as they serve their customers through continued service and innovation in banking now and in the future.

Alexandra Reed Lajoux
Dennis J. Roberts
Washington, D.C.

ACKNOWLEDGMENTS

This book reflects lessons and insights from careers spanning four decades. As such, it would be impossible to acknowledge all of the many insightful and informative individuals and institutions contributing to these pages.

In this brief page, we identify sources of indispensable help. Without them this book would not be possible.

First, thanks go to Heath P. Tarbert, Partner at Allen & Overy LLP, for suggesting this book in the first place, codeveloping the original outline, reviewing the regulatory chapters, and contributing a foreword. We also thank Todd Hinson, paralegal at the American Bankers Association, for his support in all these respects.

At McGraw-Hill Education, we thank Gary Krebs, former publisher; Mary Glenn, associate publisher; Zachary Gajewski, acquisitions editor; and Jennifer Ashkenazy, his predecessor. We also express thanks to Richard Rothschild and David Andrews of Print Matters, as well as copy editor Laura Daly, proofreader Greg Teague, and indexer Robert Swanson.

Finally, we also wish to express our gratitude to McGraw-Hill Education and its predecessor firms for supporting the Art of M&A series since its earliest days.

THE ART OF BANK
M&A

SECTION 1

SETTING

Commercial banks play a critical role in the economic life of people and nations, and this opening section paints this role with a broad brush. **Chapter 1, Banking: An Overview,** takes a panoramic look at this vital sector, explaining the importance of banks in the national and global economy and presenting basic statistics on bank mergers. **Chapter 2, The Bank Regulatory Environment,** summarizes the major changes in banking law that have evolved over time, in the years since the financial crisis that began in 2007. **Chapter 3, Special Issues for Bank Holding Companies,** identifies regulatory issues unique to banks that fit this legal category.

CHAPTER 1

Banking: An Overview

Banks properly established and conducted are highly useful to the business of the country.

—*President Martin Van Buren, State of the Union Address, December 5, 1837*

Burn the banks.

—*Title of YouTube video posted January 4, 2013*[1]

Banks—alternately praised and blamed over time for their unique economic role as financial caretakers—are as old as money itself.[2] Derived from the Latin term for a bench or counter, the word *bank* usually conjures images of a physical place. For some, this may be a landmark building in the middle of town where tellers take deposits and cash checks while a manager in a corner office makes loans. For others, the term may evoke a skyscraper in Lower Manhattan where teams of newly minted MBAs in suits run the numbers on global transactions involving complex derivative securities. Still others may hear the word *bank* and envision a financial system responsible for calibrating the money supply and interest rates in their country—or a financial exchange network that extends around the world. All of these can be called banks, and each has a vital role in the local, national, and/or world economy. Indeed, without banking, free enterprise and its benefits could not exist.

The word *bank*, as used in this book, unless otherwise specified, means a depository institution functioning as a commercial bank, or a financial institution that owns such banks. Commercial banks are one of the three major types of depository institutions in the United States: namely, commercial banks, thrifts (which include savings and loan associations and savings banks), and credit unions. These three types of institutions have become more like each other in recent decades, and their unique identities have become less distinct. They still differ, though, in specialization and emphasis, as well as in their regulatory and supervisory structures—as discussed more fully in the next chapter. They also differ in scope. Commercial banks are the traditional "department stores" of the lending and deposit-taking world. Thrift institutions and credit unions are more like specialty shops that, over time, have expanded their lines of business to better compete for market share.[3]

Some well-capitalized bank holding companies may engage in merchant banking, by making limited equity investments in companies, or investment banking, by dealing in the securities and M&A (mergers and acquisitions) and underwriting businesses, and which may have some commercial banking operations.[4]

There is also a group of lenders known as "nonbank financial companies," such as AIG, GE Capital, and Prudential. Like banks, these entities make loans, but they do not usually take deposits and as such are not heavily regulated by government unless they are considered to be "systemically important" under current banking laws.[5] Some of them, such as GE Capital, may even own a thrift. Unlike commercial banks, nonbank banks can be owned and operated by companies outside the commercial banking industry.

In recent years, all of these various kinds of financial institutions have been in the spotlight, not for their accomplishments, but rather for their failures. General resentment against "bankers," a general term used to cover any financial professional, has pulled commercial bankers into the same category as other financial professionals, blurring lines of responsibility.

The recent financial crisis and lingering recession (called the Great Recession by some[6]) can trace its roots to financial institutions; in particular, blame goes to the institutions (such as nonbank subsidiaries of bank holding companies) that made, securitized, and resold subprime mortgage loans in a convoluted process that obscured the credit risk posed by these instruments, causing what some have called a mortgage market meltdown.[7] While many others in the financial system were also to blame for the financial crisis of 2007–2009 and subsequent developments—from the borrowers who overpromised on the loans to the regulators who encouraged low credit standards in the first place—it is also true that commercial banks played some role in the crisis; it was not just the mortgage lenders and investment banks. For example, as noted in the final report of the *National Commission on the Causes of the Financial and Economic Crisis in the United States,* in the minority report section, Wachovia was a large insured depository institution supervised by the Fed, OCC, and FDIC, yet it experienced heavy losses stemming from poor-quality assets.[8] Wachovia's inventory included subprime mortgages, syndicated credits within collateralized loan obligations, and a large volume of commercial real estate credits that were acquired or originated for inclusion in commercial mortgage-backed securitizations.[9] This vulnerability led to its near failure and prompted its sale to Citicorp under favorable government conditions now contemptuously nicknamed "too big to fail."

Therefore, despite their importance and service to the economy, banks and bankers have become targets of criticism. Recent trading losses and the perceived manipulation of bank lending rates have contributed additional pressure to bank reputations.

This chapter will present the best and the worst of banking's story and explain the fundamentals of the industry and its merger activities.

ROLE OF BANKS AND THEIR MERGERS

Clearly, by employing financial professionals who store, process, and lend, banks help the business economy of the United States, but what are the numbers involved?

In the United States, banking is a $13 trillion industry employing approximately two million men and women.[10] While these banking employees engaged in banking form only a small part of the 143 million-strong workforce in America,[11] their role in the economy is crucial. Each year banks and related financial institutions in the United States make more than $2.4 trillion in business loans.[12] More than one-fourth of the amount ($578.8 billion) goes for loans of $1 million or less.[13]

Compared to other industries, banks have a stellar record of philanthropic giving. The most recent top 10 list published by the *Chronicle of Philanthropy* gave the number 1 spot to Wells Fargo, for giving more than $315 million to charity. Other financial institutions in the Top 10 list for 2012 were Goldman Sachs (which owns a commercial bank), ranking fourth; Bank of America, ranking sixth; JPMorgan Chase, ranking seventh; and Citigroup, ranking tenth. As a result, it is fair to say that half of the top 10 companies for corporate philanthropy in 2012 were banks.[14]

How many banks and thrifts are there today in comparison to the past?

As of June 30, 2013, there were only 6,048 commercial banks and 960 thrifts in the United States insured by the Federal Deposit Insurance Corporation (FDIC),[15] a regulator that insures banks and, in the event of bankruptcy, acts as their receiver.[16] This level was down from 6,472 in mid–2012,[17] from 14,000 in 1981, and from 30,812 in 1921, according to various government sources.[18]

The causes for this overall decline include both mergers—as regional banks buy up the more successful community banks—and insolvencies, as regulators take failed banks into receivership.

The decline in bank numbers would be even lower if it were not for new bank charters. Many of these are granted to investors relaunching failed banks under new management. But a rare and welcome few are genuine de novo banks, as local business leaders start banks and hire banking professionals to run them. These de novo banks, along with other types of banks, such as banking cooperatives (state-chartered savings associations located in Massachusetts, New Hampshire, Rhode Island, and Vermont), add to the diversity of banking choices.

Note, however, that the number of de novo banks in the United States has been declining for the past several years. Despite de novo shelf registration rules approved in response to the financial crisis, there still seems to be an "undeclared 'moratorium'" on de novo bank approvals the FDIC.[19] The application process involves extensive paperwork that rarely wins approval.[20] In recent years, the FDIC has approved only a few de novo banks per year, and many of these are applications to restart banks acquired out of bankruptcy by replacing or reinstating a charter they lost through insolvency. Actual startup banks are extremely rare.

The reduction in the number of banks has not been accompanied by a reduction in the number of branches, however. Based on the most recent-data available (from 2011, published in January 2013) there were 118,190 bank branches in the United States, or 379.3 per million adults, up from 362.0 per million in 2004, an increase of nearly 5 percent.[21] Although the overwhelming majority of U.S.-based branches are affiliated with domestic banks, it is worth noting that many foreign banks have established branches in major U.S. cities.

The total value of deposit accounts in 2011 in the U.S. was $1.5 trillion, or, $4,846 per person living in the country.[22] Globally, based on 23 countries studied, there were 730,735 branches during this same period, or 301.6 per million inhabitants, with a value of $6,989 per inhabitant.[23]

What exactly is a bank merger, and what percent of all mergers involve banks?

According to the Federal Reserve, a bank merger is the combination of two or more separate institutions into a single institution. Such combinations may take the form of statutory mergers, consolidations, acquisitions, or the purchase of assets and assumption of liabilities.[24] The single institution that is formed is called the merged institution or the survivor. The bank that is merged into the survivor is called the nonsurvivor.

In the first half of 2013, the financial sector accounted for one in ten dollars that changed hands through M&A. According to Thompson Reuters, they counted for 10.1 percent of the $996.8 billion in deal value and one in ten of the year's 16,808 announced deals.[25] In 2012, financial mergers accounted for 13 percent of 37,923 announced deals worldwide and 8.6 percent of their $2.6 trillion value.[26] This more than $200 billion in value in bank M&A globally—boosted by heavy deal volume and by an average 34.2 percent premium paid for nonsurvivors in these kinds of deals—gave financials a number 5 ranking for M&A activity out of 12 main sectors, ranging from the most active M&A sector, energy, to the least active, retail. In the United States, SNL Financial reported 230 acquisitions worth a total of $13.6 billion in 2012, compared to 150 transactions worth $17 billion in 2011. The average deal size has been decreasing as megabanks avoid transactions that might be challenged under new bank holding company regulations.[27]

What services do commercial banks provide?

Commercial banks today provide a wide range of services. Individuals and companies look to banks for loans, but they also depend on such banks to make and receive payments. Checks, electronic payments, and credit card payments provide valuable services to bank customers.[28] Also, in some cases, commercial banks provide trust services, which are regulated by the Office of the Comptroller of the Currency (OCC), the FDIC, and/or relevant state supervisors.[29] Under certain conditions, banks can hold and manage property on behalf of a client (a "grantor"), then pass it on to a beneficiary upon the grantor's death.

The following list shows the magnitude of some common commercial bank services in the United States versus worldwide for the most recent period measured,[30] as well as a comparison to nonbanks.

- Transferable deposits: $1.5 trillion average value in the United States, compared to $5.3 trillion globally[31]
- Credit cards issued: 857 million in the United States, compared to 1.7 billion globally[32]
- Bank-processed checks: 22.8 billion checks processed in a year in the U.S., compared to 34 billion globally.[33] The number of checks processed may decrease in the future due to the automatic clearing house (ACH) system now in effect.[34] Note that checks are processed with the help of a banking system managed by the nation's central bank—that is, the Federal Reserve System.

What exactly is a central bank?

A central bank is a banking authority that provides a central financial infrastructure for a nation. The first prototype in the United States, the Revolutionary-era Bank of the United States,[35] has evolved to become the Federal Reserve System (the Fed) today. Among other functions, the Fed

- Manages the nation's supply of money while providing nationwide banking services to banks such as electronic funds transfer and check-clearing
- Serves as the banker for the federal government by providing financial services for the U.S. Department of the Treasury
- Supervises and regulates a large share of the nation's banking and financial system[36]

LEARNING FROM PROBLEMS OF THE PAST

Banks continue to be targets of public criticism by regulators and in the media. What are the main issues?

In recent years there have been at least three major scandals associated with banking: the crisis in subprime mortgage lending; massive, unanticipated bank trading losses; and the manipulation of the London Interbank Offered Rate (LIBOR).

Regarding the subprime lending crisis, the majority report of the Financial Crisis Inquiry Commission (FCIC), an independent panel appointed by Congress to determine root causes of the financial crisis, concluded that "[t]he captains of finance and the public stewards of our financial system ignored warnings and failed to question, understand, and manage evolving risks within a system essential to the well-being of the American public."[37] Those risk-vulnerable leaders—all of whom sold securities based on default-prone mortgages—included not only government-sponsored enterprises known as Fannie Mae and Freddie Mac,[38] but also major financial institutions including AIG, Bank of America, Bear Stearns, Citigroup, Countrywide, Lehman Brothers, Merrill Lynch, Moody's, and Wachovia. The FCIC report states that "there was a significant failure of accountability and responsibility throughout each level of the lending system. This included borrowers, mortgage brokers, appraisers, originators, securitizers, credit rating agencies, and investors, and ranged from corporate boardrooms to individuals."[39]

To make matters worse for banks' public image, in 2008 major banks in Brazil (Aracruz), France (Société Générale), and the United

States (Morgan Stanley) sustained notable trading losses valued at $2.5 billion, $4.9 billion, and $9 billion, respectively. A period of pending regulation and financial austerity followed for traders, but by 2011 headlines resumed. UBS sustained a $2 billion loss that year from a rogue trader based in London. In May 2012, JPMorgan Chase sustained an unanticipated trading loss estimated to have cost $2 billion (later upgraded to nearly $6 billion), triggering both internal and regulatory investigations.[40]

But perhaps worse than any trading loss was the discovery that LIBOR was subject to manipulation by banks. LIBOR, then estimated by the British Bankers Association (BBA), was supposed to represent the rate of interest that banks charge each other, forming a seemingly solid floor for other lending around the world. This was an unsettling development for the financial world: if LIBOR rates are based on anything other than true interbank economics, this undermines the very basis of credit markets and, by implication, other financial markets as well.[41] As of May 2013, the BBA no longer sets LIBOR rates. As of June 2013, the new administrator is New York Stock Exchange Euronext Rate Administration Limited (NYSE-Euronext).

What impact will recent banking scandals and crises have on bank M&A going forward?

For banks acquiring institutions, a negative event at the target bank can trigger a clause common to all merger agreements, the material adverse change (MAC) clause, also called a material adverse effect (MAE) clause. The typical clause says that an acquirer may withdraw its bid following an event that has a material adverse change in (or material adverse effect on) the financial condition, results of operations, or business of such party and its subsidiaries taken as a whole. This clause is good, of course, for acquirers, as it gives them an out if they are not longer willing to pursue a transaction. It should be noted, however, that MAC clauses usually contain an escape clause for events beyond the control of the banks, such as a general economic downturn. In any climate of crisis, MAC clauses can act as a drag on transactions and can even spark litigation later, if acquirers do not exercise them.[42]

Past scandals at acquired banks can also trigger shareholder lawsuits against acquiring banks—which can be settled for large amounts—even years after the fact. As of late 2012, the credit crisis had triggered 55 settlements worth a total of $7.93 billion, and details are still being hammered out.[43]

More generally, banking scandals can lower the trust level between the management of the acquiring bank and the bank to be acquired, and between all bank senior managers and their stakeholders, including customers, employees, and the general public.

As a result of these possible impacts, managers of bank M&A transactions need to put more effort into proving that their institutions are worthy partners, that their transactions are worthy investments, and that the future institutions they form will merit continued commitment by constituencies.

What can an acquirer do to minimize the chances of a material adverse change in a bank M&A transaction?

The recent financial crises demonstrated the need for contingency planning, risk profiling, and attention to operational detail.

The need for contingency planning is self-evident. When banks seek to grow through acquisition, they need to ask a variety of "what if" questions and hedge against the contingencies they predict. Each new crisis or scandal in the world of banking adds to "what if" questions that acquirers can ask. This is not to say that headlines should dictate an acquirer's risk analysis. Every bank is different. Still, when looking at a banking scandal, it is best not to be complacent, thinking that could never happen here. It is wiser to believe, to paraphrase an old saying, there but for due diligence, go I.

Furthermore, as part of contingency planning, when engaging in M&A, commercial banks need to calibrate their risk profiles to their identity as institutions. Some financial strategies may be more suited to large investment banks than to traditional community banks.

As institutions that hold insured deposits, banks have a particular need to avoid high-risk schemes. Indeed, it was once said of commercial bankers that banking was "an industry whose motto could well have been, 'Never Do Something the First Time' and whose more progressive members probably would have responded, 'You have to do everything a first time but not now.'"[44]

That conservative approach changed when the lines between investment banks and commercial banks blurred under bank deregulation with the repeal of the Depression-era Glass–Steagall Act with passage of the Financial Services Modernization Act of 1999, known as Gramm–Leach–Bliley Act after its sponsors. In less than a decade, as the FCIC report noted, "[t]he strategies of the largest commercial banks and their holding companies came to more closely resemble the strategies of investment banks."[45]

The crisis also showed that the senior management of banks large and small need to monitor details of bank operations, especially following mergers. According to the FCIC report,

> We conclude [that] dramatic failures of corporate governance and risk management at many systemically important financial institutions were a key cause of this crisis.... Many of these institutions grew aggressively through poorly executed acquisition and integration strategies that made effective management more challenging. The CEO of Citigroup told the Commission that a $40 billion position in highly rated mortgage securities would "not in any way have excited my attention," and the cohead of Citigroup's investment bank said he spent "a small fraction of 1%" of his time on those securities. In this instance, too big to fail meant too big to manage.

What exactly does "too big to fail" mean, and what implications does this have for bank mergers?

The phrase "too big to fail" originated in 1984 with U.S. Rep. Stewart B. McKinney (R-CT), speaking about the Continental Illinois bank, which received a government bailout in 1984 to avoid insolvency. Rep. McKinney said, with apparent sarcasm, "We have a new kind of bank. It is called too big to fail, TBTF, and it is a wonderful bank." Years later, a more pointed statement was made by Alan Greenspan, the former chairman of the Fed, speaking of some major financial institutions, "If they're too big to fail, they're too big. In 1911 we broke up Standard

Oil—so what happened? The individual parts became more valuable than the whole. Maybe that's what we need to do."[46]

In the case of financial institutions today, a breakup of a large bank would mean unwinding combinations of different kinds of financial institutions blended under one company name, such as JPMorgan Chase, a bank holding company that owns both a large commercial bank (Chase) and a large investment bank (JP Morgan). (For more on bank holding companies, see Chapter 3.)

BANKING FUNDAMENTALS

Are there different kinds of commercial banks?

Yes. Commercial banks may be national banks or state banks. In the United States, a national bank is a bank that has a charter to operate nationally and is under the supervision of the Office of the Comptroller of Currency.[47]

A state bank is any bank that is engaged in the business of receiving deposits and that is incorporated under the laws of any state or other U.S. jurisdiction.[48] Most commercial banks in the United States, including the top 50 commercial banks, are state banks.

U.S. regulators have set forth many rules that apply to both banks and "non-bank financial institutions," including merger-related rules. What exactly is the difference between the two kinds of entities?

The U.S. Code, which contains all federal laws, defines a bank as a financial institution that is chartered by a state or the federal government and empowered to take deposits. This definition is found in Title 12 of the U.S. Code, dedicated to Banks and Banking.[49] Title 26 of the U.S. Code, which is the Internal Revenue Code (also known as the tax code), expands on this definition, identifying a bank as an institution that must devote a substantial part of its business to taking deposits and making loans.[50] This federal definition describes what is commonly referred to as a commercial bank, which accepts insured deposits and makes loans,[51] as opposed to an investment bank, which provides various financial services but does not get involved with both deposits and loans.

A nonbank, by contrast, can make loans but can only accept uninsured deposits. Also, whereas a commercial bank is exclusively engaged in financial activities, the nonbank financial company need only be predominantly engaged in them.

A nonbank financial company, as defined in Title I of the Dodd–Frank Act, now part of Title 12 of the U.S. Code, is a company, domestic or foreign, that is "predominantly engaged in financial activities" in the United States, other than bank holding companies and certain other types of firms.[52] In subsequent rule making, "company" is defined broadly (in connection with Section 113 of the Dodd–Frank Act), to include any corporation, limited liability company, partnership, business trust, association (incorporated or unincorporated), or similar organization.

What exactly does "predominantly engaged in financial activities" mean?

A company is "predominantly engaged" in financial activities if either

- The annual gross revenues derived by the company and all of its subsidiaries from financial activities, as well as from the ownership or control of insured depository institutions, represent 85 percent or more of the consolidated annual gross revenues of the company; or
- The consolidated assets of the company and all of its subsidiaries related to financial activities, as well as related to the ownership or control of insured depository institutions, represent 85 percent or more of the consolidated assets of the company.

"Financial activities" are defined in a June 2013 rule[53] based largely on the list of activities that appear in previous laws for bank holding companies electing to engage in nonbanking activities under the Gramm–Leach–Bliley Act,[54] including more than 30 discrete areas ranging from the most obvious (e.g., lending, insuring, and brokering) to areas that some might not consider to be financial services (e.g., providing services as an auditor, consultant, or courier).

We have listed all these "financial activities" in Appendix 1-A to drive home an important point. Any company that buys firms in the above industries might wind up being considered a "nonbank financial company" and come under a whole set of financial regulations—if the revenues or assets weigh in at 85 percent of the total and if that company is designated as being "systemically important" by the Financial Stability Oversight Council established under Title I of the Dodd–Frank Act.

Why does it matter how regulators define "activities that are financial in nature"?

It matters because of public policy. If an activity is considered financial in nature, then it may fall under one or more of the banking laws that presumably protect the public interest. This is an important issue for regulators because they perceive banks as trying to diversify away from regulation. As Sen. Sherrod Brown (D-OH) claimed in July 2013 hearings on bank holding companies, large bank holding companies are extremely diverse.

> While the United States once separated banking from traditional commerce, today's banks are now allowed to engage in a variety of nonfinancial activities, such as owning oil pipelines and tankers, electricity power plants and metals warehouses. Today, the six largest U.S. bank holding companies have 14,420 subsidiaries, only 19 of which are traditional banks.[55]

Whether or not this statistic is true, the fact is that banks are diverse. The new definition of "financial" activities attempts to broaden the definition to include such diverse activities—but at the same time creating the possible risk of regulatory overreach.

BANKING DATA

Looking at banks' balance sheets, what is the size and type of assets and liabilities held by commercial banks in the United States?

As of August 2, 2013, according to the Fed, banks and other insured depository institutions in the United States held more than $13.5 trillion in assets and more than $12 trillion in liabilities, with a residual (assets minus liabilities) of nearly $1.5 trillion.[56]

- Assets included in the Fed's total are bank credit, interbank loans, cash assets (cash held in the bank vault), and trading assets (derivatives).
- Liabilities included in the total are deposits, borrowings, and trading liabilities.

A substantial portion of these assets and liabilities are held by the 10 largest banks, due to consolidation over the past three decades.[57]

What is the ideal balance of assets and liabilities for a bank, and who determines that?

This is not exactly the question to ask about banks. Bank financial health is seen through the lens of capital and liquidity—factors that are correlated to assets and liabilities but not identical to them. This is a complex, technical area that undergoes continual recalibration by authorities. The main global authority for bank capitalization is the Basel Committee on Banking Supervision, under the Bank for International Settlements, author of the Basel series, currently at Basel III, titled "A Global Regulatory Framework for More Resilient Banks and Banking Systems."[58]

Basel sets requirements for capital and liquidity, among other standards. As noted by Douglas J. Elliott of the Brookings Institution in his commentary on Basel, capital represents the portion of a bank's assets that have no associated contractual commitment for repayment, while liquidity refers to the ability to convert an asset to cash without excessive cost—with cash having the highest liquidity.[59] Capital is therefore available as a cushion in case the value of the bank's assets declines or its liabilities rise. Having more capital may mean having more liquidity, but it can also depress profits, since returns on accessible cash are by definition lower than returns on invested funds held as debt or equity securities.

This in turns gives rise to the notion of risk-based capital—a concept that began with the first Basel accord in 1988. Risk-based capital means basing the amount of capital that must be maintained (e.g., equity or perpetual debt issued) on the riskiness of the assets the bank supports (e.g., quality of the loan portfolio). Before 1988, neither banks nor bank regulators identified specific amounts of capital needed to support specific types of assets.

In the United States, a new capital adequacy standard is currently being developed by the three main bank regulators—as mentioned, the Fed, the OCC, and the FDIC.[60] (For more about these regulators, see Chapter 2.) The new capital adequacy standard is expected to be compliant with Basel III. While some bankers have criticized it for being too stringent, there is general agreement that banks need to have high standards for capital and liquidity as a buffer against the major internal and external risks seen in recent years.

Obviously, if a bank's liabilities become too great in relation to its assets, the bank becomes insolvent. What happens to deposits if a bank is declared insolvent?

Deposits in FDIC-insured banks are insured up to $250,000 per depositor. Most depositors have accounts with balances lower than this limit. So clearly with this kind of limit in force, depositors can receive back their funds if needed. However, insolvency is not a simple matter of liquidating a bank and having the FDIC pay back the short fall. If a bank fails, it goes into receivership with the FDIC, under the Federal Deposit Insurance Act, as amended under Dodd-Frank. Under this federal law, as soon as possible after the default of an insured depository institution, the FDIC may "organize a new national bank or Federal savings association in the same community as the insured depository institution in default to assume the insured deposits of such depository institution in default. . . ."[61]

In most cases, the assets and deposits are transferred to another, solvent bank through an FDIC-facilitated "purchase and assumption" transaction. (For more on bank insolvency, see Chapter 11.)

CONCLUDING COMMENTS

Commercial banks are indispensable to the modern economy—safeguarding cash, providing liquidity, lending money, and providing other financial services, such as credit cards and investing. Given their importance, banks are highly regulated. At the same time, they are vulnerable to the challenges of crisis and scandal. Any merger professional involved in the banking sector, and any banking professional involved in mergers, can benefit by understanding the role that banks play in society, a role heavily influenced by regulation—the focus of our next chapter.

APPENDIX 1-A

Definition of "Predominantly Engaged in Activities That Are Financial in Nature or Incidental Thereto"

A Final Rule of the Federal Deposit Insurance Corporation June 10, 2013[62]

Under this rule, the term "financial activity" has a very broad meaning, including:

(i) Lending, exchanging, transferring, investing for others, or safeguarding money or securities.

(ii) Insuring, guaranteeing, or indemnifying against loss, harm, damage, illness, disability, or death, or providing and issuing annuities, and acting as principal, agent, or broker for purposes of the foregoing, in any state.

(iii) Providing financial, investment, or economic advisory services, including advising an investment company (as defined in section 3 of the Investment Company Act of 1940).

(iv) Issuing or selling instruments representing interests in pools of assets permissible for a bank to hold directly.

(v) Underwriting, dealing in, or making a market in securities.

(vi) Engaging in any activity closely related to banking or managing or controlling banks. This section lists 21 specific areas:

- Extending credit and servicing loans.
- Activities related to extending credit—including real estate and personal property appraising, arranging commercial

real estate equity financing, check-guaranty services, collection agency services, credit bureau services; asset management, servicing, and collection activities; acquiring debt in default; and real estate settlement servicing.

- Leasing personal or real property under certain circumstances.
- Operating nonbank depository institutions.
- Trust company functions.
- Financial and investment advisory activities.
- Agency transactional services for customer investments.
- Investment transactions as principal.
- Management consulting.
- Support services including certain courier services.
- Insurance agency and underwriting.
- Community development activities.
- Money orders, savings bonds, and traveler's checks.
- Data processing—if the data to be processed, stored, or furnished are financial, banking, or economic.
- Providing administrative and other services to mutual funds.
- Owning shares of a securities exchange.
- Acting as a certification authority for digital signatures and authenticating the identity of persons conducting financial and nonfinancial transactions.
- Providing employment histories to third parties for use in making credit decisions and to depository institutions and their affiliates for use in the ordinary course of business.
- Check cashing and wire transmission services.
- Services offered in connection with banking services such as, in connection with offering banking services, providing notary public services, selling postage stamps and postage-paid envelopes, providing vehicle registration services, and selling public transportation tickets and tokens.
- Real estate title abstracting.

(vii) Other actions usual in connection with the transaction of banking such as:

- Providing management consulting services,
- Operating a travel agency in connection with financial services,
- Organizing, sponsoring, and managing a mutual fund,
- Commercial banking and other banking activities.

(viii) Acting as a finder in bringing together one or more buyers and sellers of any product or service for transactions that the parties themselves negotiate and consummate (described in detail).

(ix) Directly or indirectly acquiring or controlling, shares, assets, or ownership of a company or other entities if involved in insurance.

(x) Directly or indirectly acquiring or controlling, shares, assets, or ownership of a company or other entities if involved in investment banking.

(xi) Lending, exchanging, transferring, investing for others, or safeguarding financial assets other than money or securities.

(xii) Providing any device or other instrumentality for transferring money or other financial assets.

(xiii) Arranging, effecting, or facilitating financial transactions for the account of third parties.

(xiv) Ownership or control of one or more depository institutions.

CHAPTER 2

The Bank Regulatory Environment

> A large, fragmented regulatory structure with numerous regulators remains. This requires regulators to coordinate actions and try to reconcile or balance differing approaches to ensure that regulated entities are subject to appropriate scrutiny.
>
> —*Report of the U.S. Government Accountability Office on Financial Regulatory Reform, January 23, 2013*

While many in the United States blame banking deregulation for the recent financial crisis, it is notable that U.S. banks are heavily regulated—arguably more so than their foreign counterparts.[1] In the United States and in other countries, banking and government regulation are inseparable, and for good reason. The business of banks is money—something few individuals or enterprises can function without. By storing funds securely and lending them prudently, banks make possible our modern postbarter economy—and its potential for prosperity. No government sanctioned by its people can reasonably ignore this critical sector.

This chapter takes on the ambitious task of summarizing the regulatory framework for U.S. banking by looking at primary bank regulators, landmark banking laws (listed in Appendix 2-A), bank housing loans, bank examinations, nonbank subsidiaries, systemically important financial institutions (SIFIs), antitrust considerations, and matters of legal interpretation and jurisdiction.

PRIMARY BANK REGULATORS

Who are the main federal banking regulators in the United States?

There are three main federal banking regulators in the United States: the Board of Governors of the U.S. Federal Reserve System (the Federal

Reserve, or Fed for short), the Office of the Comptroller of the Currency (OCC), and the Federal Deposit Insurance Corporation (FDIC).[2] These are covered in the first three chapters of Title 12 of the U.S. Code of Federal Regulations.[3] In addition to the triumvirate, there is the National Credit Union Administration (see Exhibit 2.1).

All of these can be influenced by the oversight activities of the Consumer Financial Protection Bureau (CFPB), the new agency formed in 2010 after the financial crisis. A depository financial institution may be impacted by one or more of these entities, depending on the type of charter it chooses—commercial bank, savings association, or credit union. An institution can obtain charters at the federal level or choose from among regulators for the 50 states.

Exhibit 2.1 Federal Prudential Regulators and Their Basic Functions

OFFICE OF THE COMPTROLLER OF THE CURRENCY (OCC)

Charters and supervises national banks and federal savings associations.

BOARD OF GOVERNORS OF THE FEDERAL RESERVE SYSTEM

Supervises state-chartered banks that opt to be members of the Federal Reserve System, bank holding companies, thrift holding companies and the nondepository institution subsidiaries of those institutions, and nonbank financial companies designated for enhanced supervision by the Financial Stability Oversight Council.

FEDERAL DEPOSIT INSURANCE CORPORATION (FDIC)

Supervises FDIC-insured state-chartered banks that are not members of the Federal Reserve System, as well as federally insured state savings associations; insures the deposits of all banks and thrifts that are approved for federal deposit insurance; and resolves all failed insured banks and thrifts; has been given the authority to resolve large bank holding companies and certain nonbank financial companies that are subject to supervision by the Board of Governors of the Federal Reserve System and subject to enhanced prudential standards.

NATIONAL CREDIT UNION ADMINISTRATION

Charters and supervises federally chartered credit unions and insures savings in federally and most state-chartered credit unions.

Source: OCC, Federal Reserve, FDIC, and National Credit Union Administration, chart published by Government Accountability Office, 2013, http://www.gao.gov/assets/660/651401.pdf, p. 4.

Exhibit 2.2 Status of Regulators' Efforts to Implement Dodd–Frank

Total number of provisions: 236
Total number of related rule makings: 398
Percent of rules final: 40.5 percent
Percent of rules pending: 29.1 percent
Percent of rules still to be issued: 30.4 percent

Source: Analysis of data from Davis Polk Wardwell and the Government Accountability Office.

All of the prudential regulators were affected by the Dodd–Frank Act of 2010, which, in addition created the CFPB as an extra layer of oversight. Dodd–Frank implementation was still a work in progress more than two years after enactment, as noted in a January 2013 report from the U.S. Government Accountability Office[4] (see Exhibit 2.2 for details as of October 1, 2013).

The Federal Reserve Board

What is the role of the Fed, and how does it affect bank M&A?

As mentioned in Chapter 1, the Fed has four main roles. It manages the nation's supply of money and credit (e.g., interest rates), makes possible the interstate banking services offered by private banks, provides financial services to the U.S. Department of the Treasury, and acts as a supervisor and regulator to bank holding companies—including their M&A activity.

The Fed's first role, in money supply and interest rates, makes it the focus of attention for all businesses, not just banks.

Looking at that first role, how does the Fed help direct the nation's supply of money and credit?

The basic role of the Fed, under the Federal Reserve Act of 1913, is to help member banks manage their cash, and more broadly to help the nation manage its money supply. Its three main tools are bank reserve requirements, open market operations, and the discount rate.

- The Fed sets bank reserve requirements, meaning how much cash banks must have on hand to satisfy any demands made by their depositors. (Regular bank accounts are called "demand deposits" for this reason.) The reserve is set as a percentage of deposits, determined in groups or tranches. Under current U.S. regulations, banks with more than $12.4 million and up to and including $79.5 million must set aside 3 percent of their capital, and banks with more than $79.5 million must set aside 10 percent. Banks with $12.4 million in capital or less are exempt from these requirements.[5] To make sure they meet the reserve requirements, banks have accounts with the Fed and may take out loans from the Fed to make up any shortfall between cash on hand and cash needed by their demand depositors.

- The open market operations of the Fed's Open Market Committee are the Federal Reserve's principal tool for implementing monetary policy. The committee buys and sells U.S. Treasury bonds and other federal securities (e.g., the loans of the Small Business Administration), and these transactions largely determine the federal funds rate—the interest rate at which depository institutions lend balances at the Fed to other depository institutions overnight. The federal funds rate, in turn, affects monetary and financial conditions (e.g., interest rates charged or paid by financial institutions), which ultimately influence employment, productivity, and the overall level of prices.
- The discount rate is the interest rate charged to commercial banks and other depository institutions on the fully secured loans banks receive from their regional Fed bank's lending facility, the so-called discount window. Discount rates are established by each regional Fed's board of directors, subject to the review and determination of the board of governors of the Fed's board itself. There are three levels of loans (and credit rates) in the Fed system: primary, secondary, and seasonal. Primary credit loans are extended overnight or for another very short period to banks in sound financial condition. The rate charged on these loans is sometimes called the Fed's discount rate, as it is the main one used by the Fed.[6] If banks are not sound enough to qualify for these loans, they can get secondary credit at a higher discount rate for their short-term liquidity

needs. The third type of loan, seasonal credit, goes to depository institutions with performance that varies predictably by season; it is an average of selected market rates.

How does the Fed make possible the interstate banking services offered by private banks?

As the main regulator of bank holding companies, the Fed has a major role in interstate banking. The Fed has an inspection program for conducting inspections of bank holding companies and their nonbank subsidiaries. The supervisory objectives of the program are to ascertain whether the financial strength of the bank holding company is being maintained on an ongoing basis and to determine the effects or consequences of transactions between a holding company or its nonbanking subsidiaries and its subsidiary banks. For more about the Fed's role in interstate banking, see Chapter 3.

What financial services does the Fed provide to the Treasury?

As fiscal agents of the United States, the Reserve Banks function as a bank for the U.S. government, performing a variety of services for government agencies, including the Treasury, as well as some government-sponsored enterprises and international organizations. These services are the same as or similar to services that the Reserve Banks provide to the private-sector banking system. They include maintaining the Treasury's bank account, processing payments, and issuing, safekeeping, and transferring Treasury securities.[7]

What about the Fed's power to approve mergers?

The Fed has power to approve bank mergers when the resulting institution would be a state member bank. The Bank Merger Act of 1960 (as amended) sets forth the factors to be considered, namely

- *Monopolization.* The agency cannot approve a proposed transaction that would result in a monopoly, or that would be in furtherance of any combination or conspiracy to monopolize or to attempt to monopolize the business of banking in any part of the United States.

- *Anticompetitiveness.* The agency cannot approve a proposed transaction the effect of which in any section of the country may be substantially to lessen competition, or to tend to create a monopoly or otherwise restrain trade.
- *Traditional banking factors.* The agency must take into consideration the financial and managerial resources and the future prospects of the existing and proposed institutions, along with the convenience and needs of the community to be served. In addition, the responsible agency must take into consideration in every case the effectiveness of any insured depository institution involved in the proposed merger in combating money-laundering activities, including in overseas branches.[8]

When a company (or individual) wants to acquire a bank, in most cases it is necessary to inform a Federal Reserve Bank in the jurisdiction or the Fed Board itself. The Fed then publishes the details and invites comments from the general public. Apart from bank mergers involving state-chartered member banks, the Fed also has the authority to approve acquisitions by bank holding companies of banks and nonbanks under Sections 3 and 4 of the Bank Holding Company Act.

For more details, see Chapter 3.

What is the Volcker Rule?

The so-called Volcker Rule relates to a provision of Dodd–Frank inspired by former Fed chairman Paul Volcker. The provision makes it illegal for banks to trade securities on their own behalf or to sponsor a hedge fund or private equity fund. Some liken this provision to the Glass–Steagall Act of 1933, which separated commercial and investment banking prior to its repeal in 1999. The provision became effective July 21, 2012, with a grace period of two years for full conformity. As of October 2013, none of the federal agencies charged with implementing it, including the Fed, have agreed on final rules.

The Office of the Comptroller of the Currency

Moving on to the second main bank regulator, what is the role of the OCC?

The role of the OCC is to charter, regulate, and supervise the nation's 1,500 national banks and approximately 50 U.S. branches of foreign banks, as well as federal savings associations, an oversight area added in 2011 when the OCC took over the function of the former Office of Thrift Supervision (OTS) in this area.

The relationship between federal and state regulation of national banks is in legal flux. In *Watters v. Wachovia Bank,* 550 U.S. 1 (2007), the U.S. Supreme Court affirmed the general supremacy of OCC jurisdiction in bank regulatory matters. However, the high court made exceptions to this authority in the more recent case of *Cuomo v. Clearing House Association,* 557 U.S. 519 (2009), when a closely divided court declared that the OCC does not have the power to preempt state fair lending laws.

Can you summarize the regulatory powers of the OCC as compared to the Fed and FDIC?

The OCC is responsible for the general oversight and supervision of the national banking system. As stated in the OCC handbook, *The Bank Supervision Process,*[9] the OCC seeks to ensure a banking system in which national banks

- Soundly manage their risks,
- Maintain the ability to compete effectively with other providers of financial services,
- Meet the needs of their communities for credit and financial services,
- Comply with laws and regulations, and
- Provide fair access to financial services and fair treatment of their customers.

National banks must receive a full-scope, on-site examination from an OCC examiner at least once during each 12-month period, with certain exceptions for some smaller banks, which may be examined on an 18-month cycle.

The Federal Deposit Insurance Corporation

Moving now to the third main regulator, what is the role of the FDIC?

The FDIC has three roles. First, it insures bank deposits. Second, it can take control of a bank that is declared, or is in danger of becoming, insolvent.[10] Third, the FDIC is the primary federal bank regulator and supervisor for state-chartered banks that are not members of the Federal Reserve System. This includes substantial authority over the approval of M&A transactions.

According to the FDIC manual for trust examiners, "mergers, acquisitions, and transfers are predominantly a safety and soundness issue."[11] Several statutes may govern such transactions, depending on individual case-specific circumstances.

Does the FDIC sue directors and officers of banks?

Yes. As of January 15, 2013, according to its own website, the FDIC authorized suits in connection with 95 failed institutions against 788 individuals for directors and officers (D&O) liability over the preceding five years. This included 45 filed D&O lawsuits (4 of which have settled and 1 of which resulted in a favorable jury verdict) naming 355 former directors and officers. The FDIC also authorized 46 other lawsuits for fidelity bond, insurance, attorney malpractice, appraiser malpractice, accounting malpractice, and residential mortgage-backed securities claims stemming from the financial crisis. In addition, 163 residential mortgage malpractice and fraud lawsuits were pending as of January 2013, consisting of lawsuits filed and inherited (see Exhibit 2.3).

Exhibit 2.3 Authorized Defendants in FDIC Lawsuits, January 1, 2009 to September 21, 2013

2009	11
2010	98
2011	264
2012	369
2013	265

Source: FDIC.gov, September 21, 2013, 2013. http://www.fdic.gov/bank/individual/failed/pls/

Other Banking Regulators

What are the other main banking regulators, other than the Fed, OCC, and FDIC?

There are two more of note:

- The National Credit Union Administration is the federal agency that charters and supervises federal credit unions and insures savings in federal and most state-chartered credit unions.
- The Consumer Protection Financial Bureau cuts across various regulator areas by focusing on individual consumers (as opposed to businesses) as recipients of financial services. The agency conducts financial rule making, engages in financial supervision, and enforces federal consumer financial protection laws across the board.
- Last but not least, state banking regulators play a vital role in banking regulation, working on the front lines locally to ensure compliance with state banking laws and supporting compliance with federal banking laws. The main champion of the state banking system, and a voice for state banking regulators, is the Conference of State Bank Supervisors (www.csbs.org).

What are the main federal banking laws in the United States enforced or supported by these regulators?

There are more than 30 federal laws that have impacted banking, and they are often referenced by name. (For a list of these laws, see Appendix 2-A.)

Those seeking to understand banking law tend to focus on the specific laws passed by Congress. This is only natural, given the great amount of attention that goes to these legislative acts, with their often colorful titles, eloquent sponsors, and immediate impact on banking practice.

For a more systematic view of banking law, however, it is useful to look at Title 12 of the U.S. Code. Every law passed by Congress becomes part of, or is "codified" in, the U.S. Code, expanding it, revising it, or repealing it in part. There is also a U.S. Code of Federal Regulations, containing all the regulations from the agencies, a massive set of rules that implement the broader statutes contained in the U.S. Code. To see the full extent of banking regulations, go to ecfr@nara.gov.

BANK HOUSING LOANS

One of the main functions of lenders is to make housing loans. What is current federal housing policy regarding these loans, and what lessons were learned about it in the financial crisis?

Current federal housing policy intends to foster equal access to housing, including home ownership, through access to bank loans. The cornerstone of the policy is the Community Reinvestment Act of 1977 (CRA), which encourages bank loans in economically disadvantaged communities. CRA is a title within the original Housing and Community Development Act of 1977 (HCDA), a law that has had numerous legislative revivals since its enactment.

What exactly does the CRA require of banks?

The CRA, first made into law in 1977 as a response to alleged redlining of certain neighborhoods or groups, has been modified or amplified by almost constant legislation right up until the recent 2007 financial crises.

With some teeth it encourages commercial banks and savings associations to help meet the needs of borrowers in all segments of their communities, including low- and moderate-income neighborhoods, consistent with "safe and sound operation."[12]

Specifically, the CRA requires that all banks insured by the FDIC must be evaluated by federal banking agencies to determine if the banks and savings and loans to offer credit in all communities in which they are chartered to do business and in which they take deposits. This requirement is meant to discourage redlining, the practice of denying credit in certain neighborhoods without regard to creditworthiness.

The term "community" is defined very specifically under the statute and related rules. Under the CRA regulations, a depository institution is obliged to designate an "assessment area delineation" to serve as the areas within which the federal bank regulators will measure the institution's performance in helping to meet the lending needs of its "community." The critical "assessment area delineation" is chosen by the institution itself, although the institution must make this designation of its community according to "principles" enunciated by the federal bank regulators. These "principles" that a depository institution must follow in designating its assessment area delineation require that an assessment area must be one or more metropolitan statistical areas (MSAs) as defined by the Office of Management and Budget, or one or more contiguous political subdivisions; and that the assessment area delineation must include the "geography" (defined as a census tract, or a block numbering area) in which the institution has its main office, any branches or deposit-taking ATMs, as well as surrounding geographies in which the institution has originated or purchased a substantial portion of its loan portfolio.

Federal regulatory agencies examine banking institutions for CRA compliance and take this information into consideration when approving applications for new bank branches or for mergers or acquisitions. Banks get CRA scores based on their records of local reinvestment.

Some believe that bank response to the CRA and HCDA contributed to the 2008–2009 financial crisis by giving lenders and borrowers alike incentives to participate in toxic debt, or loans that could not be repaid. This was the conclusion of the minority report of the Financial Crisis Inquiry Commission (FCIC). As stated in that report, "the *sine qua non* of the financial crisis was U.S. government housing policy, which led to the creation of 27 million subprime and other risky loans—half of all mortgages in the United States—which were ready to default as soon as the massive 1997–2007 housing bubble began to deflate."[13] The majority report, however, concluded that the CRA was "not a significant factor in subprime lending or the crisis"[14] and instead placed most blame on banks and their chief regulator, the Fed.

What about the "CRA commitments" that banks make–often after mergers?

Pending mergers often put a bright spotlight on CRA compliance. Commercial banking is often a very local business.[15] Consequently, many banks make community reinvestment part of their culture at all times—not just when they merge. After all, contributing to the prosperity of local communities means contributing to bank prosperity as well, in the long run. Yet some groups want banks to do more for local communities, and they can and do take advantage of merger announcements to take concerted action on this front.

The National Community Reinvestment Coalition, a group formed to raise awareness of the CRA, urges members to "monitor bank mergers, acquisitions and expansions to identify strategic opportunities to encourage banks in [a] local area to improve their community reinvestment records."[16] If a bank's CRA performance record does not stand up to scrutiny when financial institutions are engaged in a merger or acquisition (e.g., if the bank received a low CRA score on its last exam), then federal regulators may delay or deny the proposed transaction.[17] In advance of this response from regulators, banks may work with community stakeholders to develop a community reinvestment plan that can be a part of the merger plan. In the first 10 years following CRA's enactment, banks made more than $4.5 trillion in such pledges.[18]

BANK EXAMINATIONS

Since all three of the main regulators conduct bank examinations, this raises a question of interest to bank acquirers interested in clean bills of health. Do all three regulators have a consistent approach to their examinations?

Ideally, they should take a uniform approach, but they can vary. That is why there is a Federal Financial Institutions Examination Council (FFIEC), an interagency body empowered to prescribe uniform principles, standards, and report forms for the federal examination of financial institutions by the Fed, OCC, and FDIC, as well as the National Credit Union Administration and the Consumer Financial Protection Bureau, the new agency formed after the financial crisis. The FFIEC makes recommendations to promote uniformity in the supervision of financial institutions. In 2006 the State Liaison Committee (SLC) was added to the council as a voting member. The SLC includes representatives from the Conference of State Bank Supervisors, the American Council of State Savings Supervisors, and the National Association of State Credit Union Supervisors.

BANK SUBSIDIARIES

Some commercial banks have subsidiaries or affiliates that engage in other types of financial activities. What regulations apply to these entities?

As explained in more detail in Chapter 3, a national bank may control a financial subsidiary, or hold an interest in one, if the activities of the subsidiary are permitted for national banks. Under Section 4(k) of the Bank Holding Company (as modified under the Gramm–Leach–Bliley Act), a financial holding company may engage in any activity, and may acquire and retain the shares of any company engaged in any activity, that the Federal Reserve Board determines to be "financial in nature" or "incidental" or "complementary" to financial activity and does not pose a substantial risk to the safety or soundness of depository institutions or the financial system generally.

There is a catch, though:

- These activities may not include real estate development or investment, or most types of insurance (life, disability, health, or loss); however, they may include real estate lending.[19]
- Also, the bank must meet certain criteria. For example, the national bank and each depository institution affiliate of the national bank must be well capitalized and well managed; the aggregate consolidated total assets of all financial subsidiaries of the national bank cannot exceed 45 percent of the consolidated total assets of the parent bank, or $50 billion, whichever is less.
- Finally, the bank must have received the approval of the Office of the Comptroller of the Currency for the financial subsidiary to engage in the activities.

SYSTEMICALLY IMPORTANT FINANCIAL INSTITUTIONS

What about Federal Reserve power over nonbank financial companies?

Section 113 of Dodd–Frank authorized a new entity, the Financial Stability Oversight Council (FSOC), to be chaired by the Secretary of the Treasury, to determine whether or not a nonbank financial company will be supervised by the Fed and will therefore be subject to "prudential standards" in accordance with Title I of the Dodd–Frank Act. In essence, the FSOC oversees a systemic risk regime. The FSOC has authority to determine if material financial distress at the nonbank financial company, or the nature, scope, size, scale, concentration, interconnectedness, or mix of the activities of the nonbank financial company, could pose a threat to the financial stability of the United States.[20]

What are the general powers of the FSOC?[21]

Title I of Dodd–Frank established the FSOC to monitor sources of systemic risk and to promulgate rules for implementation by the various financial regulators represented on the FSOC. Among other things, the law vested in the FSOC the authority to

- Designate—by supermajority vote—certain companies as SIFIs
- Require and empower the Fed to impose measures to regulate core financial aspects of large bank holding companies (with $50 billion or more in assets) and nonbank SIFIs, such as measures involving capital, leverage, and liquidity, as well as risk management protocols[22]
- Permit—by supermajority vote—the Fed to order SIFIs to divest assets to avert a "grave threat" to financial stability
- Collect information from financial regulators to monitor the financial system
- Identify regulatory gaps and other potential threats to financial stability

- Facilitate greater coordination and conversation among financial regulators
- Resolve disputes among member agencies over a particular entity, product, or activity

Title VIII of Dodd–Frank also authorizes the FSOC to designate certain other financial activities for supervision by the Fed, the Securities and Exchange Commission (SEC), or the Commodity Futures Trading Commission (CFTC), namely, entities that engage in systemically important payment, clearing, or settlement activities—so-called financial market utilities (FMUs).[23]

What financial institutions has the FSOC designated as SIFIs so far?

So far, the SIFI designation is limited to companies with assets of more than $50 billion that predominantly engage in financial services. In April 2013 the Federal Reserve published rule making defining this term.[24] As of mid–2013, the FSOC had not yet designated any nonbank SIFIs under Title I of Dodd–Frank, but it has been publicly reported that several large U.S. nonbanks were under consideration for designation. The SIFI designation can potentially extend to thrifts and their holding companies, broker-dealers, investment advisers (potentially including managers of hedge funds and private equity funds), investment banks, and other asset management firms. The FSOC has designated several FMUs.

How do resolution plans, or "living wills," for SIFIs work?

The resolution plans of SIFIs required under Dodd–Frank (Title I) must explain how the SIFI can achieve a rapid and orderly resolution in the event of material financial distress. Along with nonbanks designated as SIFIs by the FSOC, all bank holding companies and foreign banks with over $50 billion in worldwide assets must file living wills. Nine of the largest banks submitted their initial resolution plans on July 1, 2012. Rule making is ongoing. For more on living wills, see Chapter 11.

In early 2012, the Fed published a proposed rule to implement the enhanced prudential standards required of SIFIs under Title I (in addition to living wills)—including single counterparty credit limits, a risk committee requirement, leverage limits, and so-called stress testing—a close look at financial indicators with financial worst cases in mind. Most SIFIs have passed stress testing successfully to date.[25]

In addition, bank regulators have been releasing new rules that include revisions to the capital adequacy framework that reflect the implementation of Basel III in the United States.[26]

ANTITRUST CONSIDERATIONS

How do antitrust laws apply to bank mergers?

Depending on size, bank mergers may need to be reported to and scrutinized by the Antitrust Division of the Department of Justice (DOJ). The DOJ screens hundreds of bank mergers every year, the majority of which involved competitive analysis based on local market concentration.[27] In 2012 DOJ received 1,429 premerger notifications under Hart–Scott–Rodino, the 1976 law that established the federal premerger notification program providing the Federal Trade Commission (FTC) and the DOJ with information about large mergers and acquisitions before they occur. Although only a small percentage of these involved transactions involving commercial banks,[28] the DOJ screened 519 bank mergers that year, the highest since 2008, but lower than in previous years (see Exhibit 2.4). It investigated 44 of these transactions. Only one resulted in a divestiture order[29] (see Chapter 7 for a discussion of this case).

Exhibit 2.4 General Antitrust Activities of the Department of Justice Antitrust Division, 2003–2012

Hart-Scott-Rodino (HSR) Premerger Notifications	**2003**	**2004**	**2005**	**2006**	**2007**	**2008**	**2009**	**2010**	**2011**	**2012**
	1,014	1,428	1,675	1,768	2,201	1,726	716	1,166	1,450	1429
Participation in Bank Merger Proceedings (not all HSR related)										
Total screenings	994	1,127	943	1,048	1,030	656	463	379	428	519

Source: U.S. Department of Justice, http://www.justice.gov/atr/public/workload-statistics.html.

How do bank regulations define "local" or "community" for banks?

They consider community in two different ways. For urban areas, they define a metropolitan statistical area (MSA), and for rural areas, they use county lines.

Is banking becoming more concentrated?

Yes. Between 1985 and 2010, the overall share of assets commanded by the top 10 banks tripled, to take approximately half of market share.[30]

Looking at local areas, the average three-firm concentration ratio (market share controlled by the three largest banks) in the most recent year analyzed was 61.2 percent for urban areas and 85.5 percent for rural counties.[31]

Can the DOJ force bank divestitures?

Yes. For example, in fiscal year 2011 (ending September 2011), the Antitrust Division investigated two bank merger transactions for which divestiture was required prior to the consummation. In one case (Hancock Holding Company and Whitney Holding Corporation), the DOJ required the merging parties to divest eight Whitney branch offices in Louisiana and Mississippi. The divestiture included Whitney's entire branch network in the Biloxi and Gulfport area in Mississippi and a branch in Washington Parish, Louisiana. The division advised the Fed, whose final approval of the merger was required, that with these divestitures, the merger would not have an adverse effect on competition in local markets for retail banking or small business banking services.[32] The DOJ took similar action in the case of Berkshire Hills Bancorp Inc. and Legacy Bancorp Inc., requiring a divestiture of four Legacy branch offices in Berkshire County, Massachusetts.

INTERPRETATION AND JURISDICTION ISSUES

Suppose a law is ambiguous. Does the agency charged with administering the law have an absolute say on what Congress intended, or do courts have a role in interpretation?

Courts do have a role in interpreting the law beyond what agencies say. The U.S. Supreme Court ruled on this matter in *Chevron U.S.A. Inc. v. Natural*

Resources Defense Council, 467 U.S. 837 (1984). This case gave a two-part process for determining whether an agency's interpretation of a statute is lawful—a result known as the "*Chevron* deference."

- First the court determines "whether Congress has directly spoken to the precise question at issue," and "[i]f the intent of Congress is clear, that is the end of the matter; for the court, as well as the agency, must give effect to the unambiguously expressed intent of Congress." Congressional intent may be discerned from the plain terms of the statute and by employing the traditional rules of statutory construction.[33]
- If the statute is silent or ambiguous, however, the court must decide "whether the agency's answer is based on a permissible construction of the statute." For example, it cannot be "arbitrary, capricious, or manifestly contrary to the statute."[34]

Not all agency rules qualify for *Chevron* deference. As the Supreme Court clarified in *United States v. Mead,* 533 U.S. 218 (9th Cir. 2001), *Chevron* deference is due only "when it appears that Congress delegated authority to the agency generally to make rules carrying the force of law, and that the agency interpretation claiming deference was promulgated in the exercise of that authority."

What about agency rules that are ambiguous? Can courts weigh in on those?

Yes, the courts have a role in interpreting unclear agency rules. Agencies are due some deference in rule making, said the U.S. Supreme Court in *Auer v. Robbins,* 519 U.S. 452 (1997). But a new twist came in *Christopher et al. v. SmithKline Beecham Corp.,* 132 S. Ct. 2156 (2012), which stated:

> Although *Auer* ordinarily calls for deference to an agency's interpretation of its own ambiguous regulation … this general rule does not apply in all cases. Deference is undoubtedly inappropriate, for example, when the agency's interpretation is "plainly erroneous or inconsistent with the regulation." … And deference is likewise unwarranted when there is reason to suspect

> that the agency's interpretation "does not reflect the agency's fair and considered judgment on the matter in question." ... This might occur when the agency's interpretation conflicts with a prior interpretation ... or when it appears that the interpretation is nothing more than a "convenient litigating position," ... or a "*post hoc* rationalizatio[n] advanced by an agency seeking to defend past agency action against attack."[35]

What are some examples of jurisdiction issues in lawsuits against bank directors and officers?

Recently, U.S. District Courts in the 7th Circuit (Chicago, Illinois) and the 11th Circuit (Atlanta, Georgia) have opined on jurisdiction for cases against bank officers and directors. In *FDIC v. Steven Skow, et al.,* regarding Integrity Bank of Alpharetta, Georgia, and *FDIC v. John M. Saphir, et al.,* regarding Heritage Community Bank, of Glenwood, Illinois, the courts defined the legal grounds on which the FDIC's bank failure claims against D&Os may be litigated, especially in the early motion stage.

CONCLUDING COMMENTS

This review of regulators and laws in various areas has focused on several major issues, including housing loans, bank examinations, nonbank subsidiaries, SIFIs, antitrust, and matters of legal interpretation and jurisdiction. As Appendix 2-A shows, these bank regulations have a long and continuing history.

APPENDIX 2-A

Landmark U.S. Banking Laws

The following list shows important laws that have affected the banking industry in the United States over the past century and a half:[36]

- *National Bank Act of 1864* (Ch. 106, 13 Stat. 99). Established a national banking system and the chartering of national banks.
- *Federal Reserve Act of 1913* (Pub. L. 63-43, 38 Stat. 251, 12 U.S.C. § 221). Established the Federal Reserve System as the central banking system of the United States.
- *Amendment to the National Banking Laws and the Federal Reserve Act* (Pub. L. 69-639, 44 Stat. 1224). Also known as the McFadden Act of 1927. Prohibited interstate banking.
- *Banking Act of 1933* (Pub. L. 73-66, 48 Stat. 162). Also known as the Glass–Steagall Act. Established the FDIC as a temporary agency. Separated commercial banking from investment banking, establishing them as separate lines of commerce.
- *Banking Act of 1935* (Pub. L. 74-305, 49 Stat. 684). Established the FDIC as a permanent agency of the government.
- *Federal Deposit Insurance Act of 1950* (Pub. L. 81-797, 64 Stat. 873). Revised and consolidated earlier FDIC legislation into one act. Embodied the basic authority for the operation of the FDIC. A title under this law was called the Bank Merger Act; it is under this act that the Interagency Bank Merger Application is promulgated.[37]
- *Bank Holding Company Act of 1956* (Pub. L. 84-511, 70 Stat. 133). Required Federal Reserve Board approval for the establishment of a bank holding company. Prohibited bank holding companies headquartered in one state from acquiring a bank in another state.

- *Truth in Lending Act, Title I of the Consumer Credit Protection Act of 1968* (Pub. L. 90-321, 82 Stat. 146). Required meaningful disclosure of credit terms so that consumers will be able to compare more readily the various credit terms available to them and avoid the uninformed use of credit, and to protect consumers against inaccurate and unfair credit billing and credit card practices.
- *Bank Secrecy Act of 1970* (Pub. L. No. 91-508, 84 Stat. 1114 to 1124). Required businesses (including banks) to keep records and file reports that are determined to have a high degree of usefulness in criminal, tax, and regulatory matters. Specifically, it required banks to report cash transactions over $10,000 via the Currency Transaction Report (CTR). The documents filed by businesses under the Bank Secrecy Act requirements are heavily used by law enforcement agencies, both domestic and international, to identify, detect, and deter money laundering—transfers of money disguised as legitimate but furthering some unlawful activity whether it is in furtherance of a criminal enterprise, terrorism, tax evasion, or other unlawful activity. The Bank Secrecy Act has led to other money laundering acts,[38] as follows:
  - *Money Laundering Control Act of 1986.* Criminalized the act of money laundering, prohibited structuring transactions to evade CTR filings, and introduced civil and criminal forfeiture for BSA violations.
  - *Money Laundering Prosecution Improvement Act of 1988.* Expanded the definition of financial institution to include businesses such as car dealers and real estate closing personnel and required them to file reports on large currency transactions; and required the verification of identity of purchasers of monetary instruments over $3,000.
  - *Bank Fraud Prosecution and Taxpayer Recovery Act of 1990 (Crime Control Act).* Updated the FDIC Statement of Policy issued pursuant to Section 19 of the Federal Deposit

Insurance Act that prohibits, without the prior written consent of the FDIC, any person from participating in banking who has been convicted of a crime of dishonesty or breach of trust or money laundering or who has entered a pretrial diversion in connection with such an offense.

- *Annunzio–Wylie Money Laundering Suppression Act of 1992.* Added Section 18(w) to the Federal Deposit Insurance Act, which provides for the revocation of federal deposit insurance of institutions convicted of certain money laundering crimes; required Suspicious Activity Reports and eliminated criminal referrals; and required verification and record keeping for wire transfers.
- *Money Laundering Suppression Act of 1994.* Required banking agencies to develop anti–money laundering examination procedures and streamlined the CTR exemption process.
- *Money Laundering and Financial Crimes Strategy Act of 1998.* Required banking agencies to develop anti–money laundering training for examiners, required Treasury and other agencies to develop a National Money Laundering Strategy, and created the High Intensity Money Laundering and Related Financial Crime Area Task Forces in high intensity financial crime areas (HIFCAs).
- *Uniting and Strengthening America by Providing Appropriate Tools to Restrict, Intercept, and Obstruct Terrorism Act of 2001*
- Pub. L. No. 107-56, 115 Stat. 272 through 402 (USA PATRIOT Act). Required government–institution information sharing and voluntary information among financial institutions, required verification of customer identity program, required enhanced due diligence programs, and required anti–money laundering programs across the financial services industry. It required the federal bank regulatory agencies to consider the effectiveness of a financial institution's anti-money laundering activities when reviewing bank mergers and bank holding company acquisitions.

- *International Banking Act of 1978* (Pub. L. 95-369, 92 Stat. 607). Brought foreign banks within the federal regulatory framework. Required deposit insurance for branches of foreign banks engaged in retail deposit taking in the United States.
- *Financial Institutions Regulatory and Interest Rate Control Act of 1978* (Pub. L. 95-630, 92 Stat. 3641). Also known as FIRIRCA. Created the Federal Financial Institutions Examination Council. Established limits and reporting requirements for bank insider transactions. Created major statutory provisions regarding electronic fund transfers.
- *Depository Institutions Deregulation and Monetary Control Act of 1980* (Pub. L. 96-221, 94 Stat. 132). Also known as DIDMCA. Established NOW accounts. Began the phase-out of interest rate ceilings on deposits. Established the Depository Institutions Deregulation Committee. Granted new powers to thrift institutions. Raised the deposit insurance ceiling to $100,000.
- *Depository Institutions Act of 1982* (Pub. L. 97-320, 96 Stat. 1469). Also known as Garn–St. Germain. Expanded FDIC powers to assist troubled banks. Established the Net Worth Certificate program. Expanded the powers of thrift institutions.
- *Competitive Equality Banking Act of 1987* (Pub. L. 100-86, 101 Stat. 552). Also known as CEBA. Established new standards for expedited funds availability. Recapitalized the Federal Savings and Loan Insurance Corporation (FSLIC). Expanded FDIC authority for open bank assistance transactions, including bridge banks.
- *Financial Institutions Reform, Recovery, and Enforcement Act of 1989* (Pub. L. 101-73, 103 Stat. 183). Also known as FIRREA. FIRREA's purpose was to restore the public's confidence in the savings and loan industry. FIRREA abolished the FSLIC, and the FDIC was given the responsibility of insuring the deposits of thrift institutions in its place. The FDIC insurance fund created to cover thrifts was named the Savings Association Insurance Fund

(SAIF), while the fund covering banks was called the Bank Insurance Fund (BIF). FIRREA also abolished the Federal Home Loan Bank Board. Two new agencies, the Federal Housing Finance Board (FHFB) and the Office of Thrift Supervision (OTS), were created to replace it. Finally, FIRREA created the Resolution Trust Corporation (RTC) as a temporary agency of the government. The RTC was given the responsibility of managing and disposing of the assets of failed institutions. An oversight board was created to provide supervisory authority over the policies of the RTC, and the Resolution Funding Corporation (RFC) was created to provide funding for RTC operations.

- *Crime Control Act of 1990* (Pub. L. 101-647, 104 Stat. 4789). Title XXV of the Crime Control Act, known as the Comprehensive Thrift and Bank Fraud Prosecution and Taxpayer Recovery Act of 1990, greatly expanded the authority of federal regulators to combat financial fraud. This act prohibited undercapitalized banks from making golden parachute and other indemnification payments to institution-affiliated parties. It also increased penalties and prison time for those convicted of bank crimes, increased the powers and authority of the FDIC to take enforcement actions against institutions operating in an unsafe or unsound manner, and gave regulators new procedural powers to recover assets improperly diverted from financial institutions.
- *Federal Deposit Insurance Corporation Improvement Act of 1991* (Pub. L. 102-242, 105 Stat. 2236). Also known as FDICIA. FDICIA greatly increased the powers and authority of the FDIC. Major provisions recapitalized the Bank Insurance Fund and allowed the FDIC to strengthen the fund by borrowing from the Treasury.

  The act mandated a least-cost resolution method and prompt resolution approach to problem and failing banks and ordered the creation of a risk-based deposit insurance assessment scheme. Brokered deposits and the solicitation of deposits were restricted, as were the nonbank activities of insured state banks.

FDICIA created new supervisory and regulatory examination standards and put forth new capital requirements for banks. It also expanded prohibitions against insider activities and created new Truth in Savings provisions.

- *Housing and Community Development Act of 1992* (Pub. L. 102-550, 106 Stat. 3672). Established regulatory structure for government-sponsored enterprises (GSEs), combated money laundering, and provided regulatory relief to financial institutions.
- *Riegle Community Development and Regulatory Improvement Act of 1994* (Pub. L. 103-325, 108 Stat. 2160). Established the Community Development Financial Institutions (CDFIs) Fund, a wholly owned government corporation that would provide financial and technical assistance to CDFIs. Contains several provisions aimed at curbing the practice of "reverse redlining," in which nonbank lenders target low- and moderate-income homeowners, minorities, and the elderly for home equity loans on abusive terms. Relaxed capital requirements and other regulations to encourage the private sector secondary market for small business loans. Contains more than 50 provisions to reduce bank regulatory burden and paperwork requirements. Required the Treasury Department to develop ways to substantially reduce the number of currency transactions filed by financial institutions. Contains provisions aimed at shoring up the National Flood Insurance Program established in 1968.
- *Riegle–Neal Interstate Banking and Branching Efficiency Act of 1994* (Pub. L. 103-328, 108 Stat. 2338). Permitted adequately capitalized and managed bank holding companies to acquire banks in any state one year after enactment. Concentration limits apply, and CRA evaluations by the Federal Reserve are required before acquisitions are approved. Allowed interstate mergers between adequately capitalized and managed banks, subject to concentration limits, state laws, and CRA evaluations. Extended the statute of limitations to permit the FDIC and RTC to revive lawsuits that had expired under state statutes of limitations.

- *Economic Growth and Regulatory Paperwork Reduction Act of 1996* (Pub. L. 104-208, 110 Stat. 3009). Modified financial institution regulations, including regulations impeding the flow of credit from lending institutions to businesses and consumers. Amended the Truth in Lending Act and the Real Estate Settlement Procedures Act of 1974 to streamline the mortgage-lending process. Amended the Federal Deposit Insurance Act to eliminate or revise various application, notice, and record-keeping requirements to reduce regulatory burden and the cost of credit. Amended the Fair Credit Reporting Act to strengthen consumer protections relating to credit-reporting agency practices. Established consumer protections for potential clients of consumer repair services. Clarified lender liability and federal agency liability issues under the Comprehensive Environmental Response, Compensation, and Liability Act of 1980 (CERCLA), known as Superfund. Directed FDIC to impose a special assessment on depository institutions to recapitalize the SAIF, aligned SAIF assessment rates.
- *Gramm–Leach–Bliley Act of 1999* (Pub. L. 106-102, 113 Stat. 1338). Repealed the last vestiges of the Glass–Steagall Act of 1933. Modified portions of the Bank Holding Company Act to allow affiliations between banks and insurance underwriters. While preserving the authority of states to regulate insurance, prohibited state actions that have the effect of preventing bank-affiliated firms from selling insurance on an equal basis with other insurance agents. Created a new financial holding company under Section 4 of the Bank Holding Company Act authorized to engage in underwriting and selling insurance and securities, conducting both commercial and merchant banking, and investing in and developing real estate and other "complimentary activities." Limited the kinds of nonfinancial activities in which these new entities may engage. Allowed national banks to underwrite municipal bonds and restricted the disclosure of nonpublic customer information by financial institutions. All financial institutions must provide customers the

opportunity to "opt out" of the sharing of customers' nonpublic information with unaffiliated third parties. The act imposed criminal penalties on anyone who obtains customer information from a financial institution under false pretenses.

Amended the Community Reinvestment Act to require that financial holding companies cannot be formed before their insured depository institutions receive and maintain a satisfactory CRA rating. Required public disclosure of bank–community CRA-related agreements, granted some regulatory relief to small institutions in the shape of reducing the frequency of their CRA examinations if they have received outstanding or satisfactory ratings, and prohibited affiliations and acquisitions between commercial firms and unitary thrift institutions.

Made significant changes in the operation of the Federal Home Loan Bank System, easing membership requirements and loosening restrictions on the use of Federal Home Loan Banks funds.

- *International Money Laundering Abatement and Financial Anti-Terrorism Act of 2001* (Pub. L. 107-56). See the Bank Secrecy Act of 1970. Legislation designed to prevent terrorists and others from using the U.S. financial system anonymously to move funds obtained from or destined for illegal activity. Authorized and required additional record keeping and reporting by financial institutions and greater scrutiny of accounts held for foreign banks and of private banking conducted for foreign persons.

  Required financial institutions to establish anti–money laundering programs and imposes various standards on money-transmitting businesses. Amended criminal anti–money laundering statutes and procedures for forfeitures in money-laundering cases and required further cooperation between financial institutions and government agencies in fighting money laundering.

- *Sarbanes–Oxley Act of 2002* (Pub. L. 107-204). Established the Public Company Oversight Board to regulate public accounting firms that audit publicly traded companies. Prohibited such firms from providing other services to such companies along with the audit. Required that chief executive officers and chief financial officers certify the annual and quarterly reports of publicly traded companies. Authorized, and in some cases required, that the Securities and Exchange Commission issue rules governing audits.

The law requires that insiders may no longer trade their company's securities during pension fund blackout periods. It mandates various studies, including a study of the involvement of investment banks and financial advisers in the scandals preceding the legislation. Also included are whistle blower protections and new federal criminal laws, including a ban on alteration of documents.

- *Fair and Accurate Credit Transactions Act of 2003* (Pub. L. 108-159). Amended the Fair Credit Reporting Act. Designed to improve the accuracy and transparency of the national credit reporting system, prevent identity theft, and assist victims. It contains provisions enhancing consumer rights in situations involving alleged identity theft, credit scoring, and claims of inaccurate information. It requires use of consumer reports to provide certain information to consumers who are offered credit on terms that are materially less favorable than the offers that the creditor makes to a substantial portion of its consumers. Companies that share consumer information among affiliated companies must provide consumers notice and an opt out for sharing of such information if the information will be used for marketing purposes.
- *Dodd–Frank Wall Street Reform and Consumer Protection Act of 2010* (Pub. L. 111-203, H.R. 4173). Expanded governmental oversight of financial institutions and public companies in general. Introduced sweeping changes to regulation of banks, thrifts, holding companies, and related institutions. The reforms to the banking industry are largely embodied in several separate statutes: the Financial Stability Act of 2010, the Enhancing Financial Institution Safety and Soundness Act of 2010, and the Bank and Savings Association

Holding Company and Depository Institution Regulatory Improvements Act of 2010 (incorporated into the law). Among other topics, Dodd–Frank addressed regulatory reorganization, the Volcker Rule, derivatives for banks, securitizations, the credit rating industry, insurance, consumer financial protection, and mortgage lending.[39] The law contains several important provisions governing bank M&A deals.[40]

CHAPTER 3

Special Issues for Bank Holding Companies

Not all bank holding companies are created equal.

—Amanda Alix[1]

Like companies in other industries, commercial banks can use a holding company structure to accomplish their business goals. Bank holding companies, however, more than their peers, have attracted special public and regulatory attention, given the importance of finance to the economy. The result has been a vast set of regulations that make legal compliance challenging for banks, especially in the area of mergers. Bankers involved in holding company M&A, whether as buyers or sellers, can benefit from knowing the basic elements of this regulatory maze.

BANK HOLDING COMPANIES: DEFINITIONS

What is a bank holding company?

Basically, a bank holding company is a legal entity that owns one or more subsidiary banks. A bank holding company may also own subsidiaries apart from banks. This distinguishes it from a commercial bank that provides only banking services through a single entity with no parent company, such as a small, local community bank.

All bank holding companies in the United States are regulated under the Bank Holding Company Act of 1956 and supervised by the Federal Reserve Board (the Fed).

Technically, a bank holding company is any company that directly or indirectly owns, controls, or has the power to vote 25 percent or more of any class of the voting shares of a bank; controls in any manner the election of a majority of the directors or trustees of a bank; or is found to exercise a controlling influence over the management or policies of a bank.

There can be a kind of "Russian doll" structure: a bank holding company may own another bank holding company, which in turn may own another bank. The bank at the top is called the top holder.

What is a financial holding company?

Banking regulations use the term *financial holding company* to refer to bank holding companies that diversify beyond traditional commercial banking by owning or controlling nonbank activities. Well-known examples include Bank of America, Wells Fargo, and Citigroup.

Prior to 1999, a bank holding company was permitted to engage only in the business of banking or "activities closely related to banking."[2] As authorized by the Gramm–Leach–Bliley Act (a landmark law discussed in Chapter 2), the Fed's regulations now allow a bank holding company or a foreign banking organization to become a financial holding company and engage in an expanded array of financial activities if the company meets certain capital, managerial, and other criteria. Financial holding companies can underwrite and deal in securities, serve as an insurance agent and underwriter, and engage in merchant banking. Financial holding companies also may engage to a limited extent in a nonfinancial activity if the Fed determines that the activity is complementary to one or more of the company's financial activities and would not pose a substantial risk to the safety or soundness of its subsidiary banks or the financial system.[3]

Is a holding company structure common in banking? How many bank holding companies are there?

Yes, it is common for banks to organize using a holding company structure. As of June 30, 2012, the United States had nearly 4,700 bank holding companies, compared to nearly 6,500 banks at the time.[4] The bank holding companies together had more than $17 trillion in assets, compared to $129 billion for banks.[5] The top five bank holding companies hold half of these assets (see Exhibit 3.1).[6]

Exhibit 3.1 Top Five U.S. Bank Holding Companies

Name and Headquarters	Number of Subsidiaries	Assets (in billions)
JPMorgan Chase & Co. (New York)	3,391	$2,389
Bank of America Corporation (Charlotte)	2,019	$2,176
Citigroup Inc. (New York)	1,645	$1,882
Wells Fargo & Company (San Francisco)	1,366	$1,437
The Goldman Sachs Group, Inc. (New York)	3,115	$ 959

Source: National Information Center of the Federal Financial Institutions Examination Council (assets in billions as of June 30, 2013), with number of subsidiaries provided by Federal Reserve Bank National Information Center as of July 2012, cited by the Federal Reserve Bank of New York.

How can bank holding companies as a group hold more assets than all banks as a group when there are far more banks than bank holding companies?

This is because not all bank holding company assets are held by their subsidiary banks. In fact, assets held in nonbanking subsidiaries or directly by the BHC parent are accounting for an increasingly larger percentage of bank holding company assets over time.[7] The largest bank holding companies exemplify this trend, and as mentioned they hold half of all bank holding company assets.

How can a business become a bank holding company?

A company must apply to the Federal Reserve Board for any of the following:

- To become a bank holding company
- To acquire ownership or assets of a bank or bank holding company
- To acquire control of or power to vote shares of a bank or bank holding company

Applications are published in the *Federal Register*, the daily journal of the U.S. government, with a comment period that is facilitated by technology. Comments may be sent via email and even broadcast through social media.

The *Federal Register* site (federalregister.gov) has links to social media, including Facebook and Twitter.[8]

Bank holding companies can be complex due to their subsidiaries in differing financial industries. What kind of resources can help bankers and analysts assess their performance?

Many banks retain expert analysts to assess their own performance and those of peers. At the same time, there are free resources for analysis. The Fed publishes the *Bank Holding Company Performance Report*, along with a user's manual.[9] For each bank holding company, it presents earnings and profitability, asset quality, liquidity and funding, capitalization, growth, and parent company condition. In addition, this report presents the dollar amounts of year-to-date average assets, net income, and the number of companies in the bank holding company's peer group. Note that some bank holding companies are better than others in estimating losses associated with acquired banks.[10] As additional guidance, the Federal Financial Institutions Examination Council (FFIEC), introduced in Chapter 2, publishes a report on bank holding company peer groups, with summary data by peer group, listing peer group members for closer analysis.[11]

How can I check the status of a bank holding company merger or acquisition?

The Fed's weekly "Notice of Formation and Mergers of, and Acquisitions by, Bank Holding Companies; Change in Bank Control," which is updated at least every three days, provides the most recent list of bank holding company M&A.[12]

MERGER APPROVALS

Beyond approving applications, what is the role of the Federal Reserve Board in bank holding company regulations, especially mergers?

The Fed has broad authority over bank holding companies, and the banking system in general, based on the aforementioned Bank Holding Company

Act, as well as the Bank Merger Act of 1960, the Change in Bank Control Act of 1978, and the Dodd–Frank Act of 2010.[13]

The Bank Holding Company Act of 1956 gave the Fed primary responsibility for regulating bank holding companies. Through this law, Congress wanted to prevent holding companies from gaining monopoly power and to continue the separation of banking and business as under previous law (the Glass–Steagall Act of 1933). For example, the act requires Fed approval for any company to acquire any bank or bank holding company, or for any bank holding company to merge or consolidate with another bank holding company or to acquire 5 percent or more of the voting securities of any other bank or bank holding company. The Gramm–Leach–Bliley Act changed the rules of the game for bank holding companies. As mentioned earlier, a bank holding company that qualifies to become a financial holding company is permitted to engage in a broad range of financial activities, including securities underwriting and dealing, some types of insurance underwriting and sales, and merchant banking.

As such, the nature of Fed oversight of bank holding company mergers has changed. As mentioned in Chapter 2, the Fed approves bank mergers based on a variety of factors. Rather than focusing solely on issues of antitrust (which is also the province of the Department of Justice), the Fed focuses on financial soundness and other matters. A bank holding company seeking financial holding company status due to an acquisition of a nonbank company[14] must file a statement with the Fed certifying that the company meets the capital, managerial, and other requirements to be a financial holding company permitted under Gramm–Leach–Bliley.

When considering applications to acquire a bank or a bank holding company, the Fed is required to consider not only the likely effects of the acquisition on competition, but also the convenience and needs of the communities to be served, the financial and managerial resources and future prospects of the companies and banks involved, and the effectiveness of the company's policies to combat money laundering.[15]

These factors are similar to those that must be considered in reviewing bank acquisition proposals by banks that are not holding companies. To ensure that all merger applications are evaluated in a uniform manner, the Fed must request reports from the Department of Justice and from any other agency addressing the competitive impact of the transaction.

What if a proposed bank acquisition crosses state lines? Are there additional considerations?

In mergers crossing state lines, the Federal Reserve must also consider market share metrics. Specifically, under the Riegle–Neal Interstate Banking and Branching Efficiency Act of 1994, the Fed may not approve the deal if the resulting organization would control more than 10 percent of all deposits held by insured depository institutions or more than 30 percent of insured deposits in any one state. (Clearly, controlling $1 out of every $10 deposited in the country, or $3 out of $10 in every state, would constitute a heavy market concentration and make the nation's finances too dependent on one institution.)

For an example of an approved interstate merger, see the case of Trustmark Corporation's acquisition of BancTrust Financial, holding company for BankTrust as explained in Chapter 8.

What additional regulations are imposed on bank acquisitions by the Change in Bank Control Act of 1978?

The Change in Bank Control Act of 1978 authorizes the federal agencies that regulate banks to deny proposals by a single individual, group, or entity to acquire control of an insured bank or a bank holding company. The Fed is responsible for approving changes in the control of bank holding companies and state member banks (i.e., state banks that are members of the Federal Reserve System[16]), and the Federal Deposit Insurance Corporation (FDIC) and the Office of the Comptroller of the Currency (OCC) are responsible for approving changes in the control of insured state nonmember and national banks, respectively.

In considering a proposal under this law, the Fed must review several factors, including the bank's financial condition; the competence, experience, and integrity of the acquiring person or group of persons; the effect of the transaction on competition; and the adequacy of the information provided evaluating the merger by the acquiring party.

What about foreign acquisitions?

Foreign banks have a restriction similar to the interstate restrictions described above. In addition, when a foreign bank seeks to acquire a U.S. bank, the Fed considers the quality of supervision that bank receives in its home jurisdiction and will generally place restrictions on the activities of the acquirer. (For more on this topic, see Chapter 10.)

GETTING APPROVAL FOR FINANCIAL SUBSIDIARIES

What special requirements must a bank parent company meet in order to have financial subsidiaries?

It is possible for a bank (and not just a bank or financial holding company) to have a financial subsidiary of its own. A national bank may control a financial subsidiary, or hold an interest in one, only if the financial subsidiary engages solely in activities that are financial in nature (or incidental to a financial activity) and that are permitted for national banks to engage in directly.[17]

The activities engaged in by the financial subsidiary may not include many forms of insurance, such as insuring, guaranteeing, or indemnifying against loss, harm, damage, illness, disability, or death, with certain exceptions.[18] Also, generally speaking, financial subsidiaries may not provide or issue annuities that produce taxable income (as in whole life insurance),[19] nor may they develop or invest in real estate unless expressly authorized by law.

In addition to these restrictions on its financial activities, any bank that seeks to own subsidiaries, as well as each depository institution that is affiliated with the bank, must be well capitalized and well managed, and it must meet certain size criteria.

In most cases, a bank that wishes to engage in these activities will do so by having its parent bank holding company elect to become a financial holding company and operate through a nonbank subsidiary.

How does federal law define a "well-capitalized" and "well-managed" bank?

The key to capitalization is proportion; the parent bank cannot be smaller than the subsidiary. As of January 2013, to be well capitalized means that the aggregate consolidated total assets of all financial subsidiaries of the bank, as parent, may not be more than 45 percent of the consolidated total assets of the parent bank, or more than $50 billion, whichever is less, with certain exceptions permitted by the OCC.[20] To be well managed, the bank should have and use managerial resources that the appropriate federal banking agency determines are satisfactory, and/or have received a rating of 1 or 2 in a bank examination.[21]

What are the size criteria that banks must meet in order to hold financial subsidiaries?

A national bank may have financial subsidiaries if (in addition to meeting other criteria) the bank is one of the nation's 100 largest insured banks and has at least one issue of outstanding debt that meets standards of credit-worthiness or other criteria that the OCC and Fed may jointly establish. Bank size is determined based on consolidated total assets at the end of each calendar year.

Can an investment bank or financial company convert to a bank holding company?

Yes, by simply buying a bank. Indeed, this has been a recent trend. When Goldman Sachs and Morgan Stanley, as the last of Wall Street's major investment banks, made the transition in 2008, some hailed this movement from investment banking toward commercial banking as the end of the Wall Street era.[22] The investment banks entered the ranks of financial corporations, alongside the likes of American Express, Charles Schwab, and Discover.

In converting to bank holding companies, these organizations and others like them have come under the stricter regulations of the Fed, FDIC, and/or OCC, but they have also gained access to greater liquidity—for example, by being able to borrow money from the Fed.

MERCHANT BANKING

What is merchant banking, and how can bank holding companies get involved in it?

Merchant banking, also known as private equity, is not directly defined under U.S. banking laws, but it generally means the acquisition of unregistered equity stakes in other companies.[23]

Section 4(k) of the Bank Holding Company Act authorizes a financial holding company to acquire or control any amount of shares, assets, or ownership interests of a company or other entity that is engaged in any activity not otherwise authorized for the financial holding company under that law. This is referred to as a "merchant banking investment," and it enables a company to hold an ownership interest in a company that is engaged in commercial activities beyond those traditionally in the banking or financial services arena.

The law sets forth conditions under which a financial holding company may directly or indirectly acquire or control a merchant banking investment. That is, the acquisition or control of shares, assets, or ownership interests are not permitted unless they are part of a "bona fide underwriting or merchant or investment banking activity."

What types of merchant banking ownership interests may a bank holding company acquire?

A comprehensive variety of interests are allowed, including shares, assets, or ownership interests of a company or other entity. These include any debt or equity security, warrant, option, partnership interest, trust certificate, or other instrument representing an ownership interest in the company or entity, whether voting or nonvoting.

In practice, these types of investments are done directly or indirectly through the formation of one or more private equity funds. The latter activities are now restricted due to the Volcker Rule under the Dodd–Frank Act.

What exactly is the Volcker Rule, and how does it impact bank holding company M&A activity?

The Volcker Rule is the name for a section of Dodd–Frank (Section 619 in Title VI) named after the former Federal Reserve chairman Paul Volcker.

This section of the law prohibits banking entities from investing in, sponsoring, or having certain relationships with a hedge fund or private equity fund, subject to certain exceptions. Nonbank financial companies that are supervised by the Fed that engage in such activities may be subject to additional capital requirements, quantitative limits, or other restrictions, but unlike banking entities, they are not precluded from investing in, or sponsoring, a hedge fund or private equity fund. For more on the Volcker Rule, see Chapter 2.[24]

Regarding assets, are there restrictions on how a financial holding company may acquire these?

Yes, there are restrictions. A financial holding company may not acquire or control assets, other than debt or equity securities or other ownership interests in a company, unless

- The assets are held by or promptly transferred to a portfolio company.
- The portfolio company maintains policies, books and records, accounts, and other indicia of corporate, partnership, or limited liability organization and operation that are separate from the financial holding company and limit the legal liability of the financial holding company for obligations of the portfolio company.
- The portfolio company has management that is separate from the financial holding company to the extent required by law.

Again, this restriction is there to ensure that the financial holding company does not engage in commercial activities but limits its merchant banking activities to purely financial investments.

What exactly is a portfolio company?

In most industries, a "portfolio company" is a company in which an investment fund has an interest. However, in banking, due to restrictions on the kinds of companies commercial banks may own or control, this term has a specific meaning.

In banking law, a portfolio company is any company or entity engaged in any activity not authorized for the financial holding company under the Bank Holding Company Act of 1956.[25] The term also refers to any of such company's shares, assets, or ownership interests that are held, owned, or controlled directly or indirectly by the financial holding company, including through a private equity fund that the financial holding company controls.

As such, the portfolio company designation gives commercial banks a way to get involved in nonfinancial activities without violating the Bank Holding Company Act. Although banks are not permitted to control companies that have nonfinancial activities, they are permitted to control funds that invest in such companies.

Can a commercial bank acquire these interests directly, or must it be through another part of the bank holding company?

A bank may not engage in merchant banking directly; it must work through the holding company structure. A financial holding company may not acquire or control merchant banking investments on behalf of the bank or a depository institution or subsidiary of a depository institution; however, a holding company or a subsidiary (other than a depository institution or subsidiary of a depository institution) may acquire or control merchant banking investments if it does so through an affiliate.

What type of affiliate is required for a financial holding company to make merchant banking investments?

A financial holding company may acquire or control merchant banking investments if it qualifies under at least one of the following:

- *Securities affiliate.* The financial holding company is or has an affiliate that is registered under the Securities Exchange Act of 1934 as a broker or dealer, or as a municipal securities dealer (including a separate department or division of a bank that is registered as a municipal securities dealer).

- *Insurance affiliate with an investment adviser affiliate.* The financial holding company controls an insurance company that is predominantly engaged in underwriting life, accident and health, or property and casualty insurance (other than credit-related insurance), or providing and issuing annuities; and a company that is registered with the Securities and Exchange Commission as an investment adviser and provides investment advice to an insurance company.

May a financial holding company manage a portfolio company?

No. A financial holding company or any of its banking subsidiaries[26] may not "routinely manage or operate" any portfolio company. The regulations spell out at great length what this means because this ban is critical in both policy and practice to preserve the long-standing separation of banking and financial services and general commercial activities. For example, a holding company is not allowed to have a holding company officer serve as an officer of the portfolio company or to have agreements with the portfolio company that would restrict the company's ordinary business operations. This kind of routine management would not be allowed except for a limited period of time (no more than nine months unless notice is given) to obtain a reasonable return on its investment or to avoid significant loss.

This said, a financial holding company can exercise some oversight of a portfolio company. It may select any or all of the directors of a portfolio company or have one or more of its directors, officers, or employees serve as directors of a portfolio company as long as the portfolio company employs officers and employees responsible for routinely managing and operating the company.

As for agreements, it is acceptable for the financial holding company to place restrictions on the portfolio company regarding events outside the ordinary course of business, such as acquisition, change in auditors, change in accounting methods, changes in officers, new securities issuances, bylaw changes, or major change of control transactions (sale, merger, consolidation, spin-off, recapitalization, liquidation, dissolution, or sale of substantially all of the assets of the portfolio company or any of its significant subsidiaries). Also, officers or employees of the financial holding company, with some restrictions spelled out by law, may provide financial, investment, and management consulting advice to a portfolio company; help with the underwriting or private placement of its securities; and provide oversight and advice with respect to the portfolio company's performance or activities.

DODD–FRANK M&A PROVISIONS

What does the Dodd–Frank Act of 2010 say about bank acquisitions?

Sections 163 and 604 of the Wall Street Reform and Consumer Protection Act of 2010, known as Dodd–Frank, affect bank acquisitions.[27] Specifically, they amend relevant provisions in the federal banking laws relating to mergers and acquisitions to include systemic risk or "financial stability" as a factor that federal regulators may use to block transactions.

- Section 163, which expands the scope of bank holding company law to apply to any nonbank financial company supervised by the Fed, states that a bank holding company with assets equal to or more than $50 billion or a nonfinancial company overseen by the Fed shall not acquire any company, other than an insured depository institution, with assets of $10 billion or more, without providing notice. The section also says that in approving an acquisition, the Fed will "consider the extent to which the proposed acquisition would result in greater or more concentrated risks to global or United States financial stability or the United States economy."
- Section 604, amending the Bank Holding Company Act, requires the Fed, when evaluating a proposed bank acquisition, merger, or consolidation, to consider "the extent to which [the] proposed acquisition, merger, or consolidation would result in greater or more concentrated risks to the stability of the United States banking or financial system." It also requires the Fed to consider financial stability concerns when reviewing notices by bank holding companies to engage in nonbanking activities.

In addition, Section 165 of Dodd–Frank expands the list of enhanced prudential standards for bank holding companies with more than $50 billion in assets by asking the Fed to consider whether the firm owns an insured depository institution.[28] The section also requires regulators to also consider the nonfinancial activities and affiliations of the firm—both of these are considered additional risk factors when it comes to assessing systemic risk.

Subsection d of Section 165 additionally requires that these large bank holding companies publish plans for resolution—so-called living wills—in the event that they should become insolvent. (For more on living wills, see Chapter 11.)

As of March 2013, neither the Federal Reserve Board nor any other banking regulator had blocked a transaction on systemic risk grounds. Nonetheless, the Fed has made it clear that it will not be friendly to giant mergers. Fed Governor Daniel K. Tarullo has stated that he would "urge a strong, though not irrebuttable, presumption of denial for any acquisition by any firm that falls in the higher end of the list of global systemically important banks developed by the Basel Committee for purposes of assessing capital surcharges."[29]

What impact have Dodd–Frank and other banking laws and regulations had on bank mergers involving holding companies?

The expanded scope of Fed review has arguably discouraged major mergers while encouraging smaller ones. As noted in Chapter 1 of this book, SNL Financial reported a recent rise in bank mergers along with a decline in their value.[30] The rise in the number of mergers is a return to precrisis levels; from 2008 through 2011, bank mergers dropped from previous levels in the decade.[31] The drop in average size is also fairly new. Until recently, regulators had been concerned about "megamergers."[32] This concern seems to have abated, with fewer very large mergers being proposed. Larger banks have grown so much through acquisitions over the past decades that many are close to the deposit cap under the Riegle–Neal Interstate Banking Act.[33] Meanwhile, smaller banks have found the regulatory burden of Dodd–Frank particularly onerous and feel a pressure to combine. [34]

Fortunately for them, bankers seeking smaller mergers have gotten a green light from federal regulators. The Fed has indicated that there may be a safe harbor from antitrust scrutiny when an acquisition involves less than $2 billion in assets or results in a firm with less than $25 billion in total assets.[35]

CONCLUDING COMMENTS

Bank holding companies, by definition, arose due to merger activity. For some bank holding companies, however, the era of large mergers may be over. Despite the benefits that larger bank size can deliver, public concern about bank size is not likely to abate in the near future.[36] The next section of this book will address bank strategy and standards in the new regulatory environment.

SECTION 2

FROM STRATEGIES TO STANDARDS

Whatever regulatory setting may apply to them, banks have leeway to develop and apply their own strategies and standards for merger success. This next section, **Chapter 4, Bank Strategies for Growth and Value,** defines these two values in relation to one another and explains how banks achieve them. The last two chapters in this section provide guidance for determining and confirming the value a given bank may bring to the entity acquiring it. This requires an increasing degree of diligence—from the preliminary phase of sizing up a transaction through initial valuation/evaluation, to the formal process that ensures the validity of these findings. Thus, **Chapter 5, Preliminary Valuation for Deal Pricing,** leads readers through the basic steps for determining a price range when buying a bank. **Chapter 6, Confirmatory Bank Due Diligence,** can help acquirers achieve an acceptable level of assurance on their findings right up to a transaction's closing.

CHAPTER 4

Bank Strategies for Growth and Value

Shareholders don't really care about how big you are. They care about what happens to their stock. Customers don't care about how big you are. They care about the service that you give them.

—*John Medlin, Wachovia Bank*[1]

Every banker knows that being bigger does not always mean being better. Nonetheless, like their counterparts in other industries, many bankers strive to grow their enterprises from the de novo stage if for no other reason than to stave off the inevitable erosion that time and change can bring. In a very real sense, banks must "grow or die"—not merely to get bigger, but to keep from disappearing.

Furthermore, banks have a bias toward growth. Larger banks tend to have more sustainable profits than do their smaller peers because they have greater capacity to handle regulatory burdens and to sell more ancillary products to bigger clients.[2]

All banks must keep finding new customers to replace the ones they are losing. On the retail side, no customer lives forever, and on the business side, no business is guaranteed perpetual existence either. Growth is the converse of this decline.

Banks strive to continue in business by bringing in new deposits, which generates fees and supports loans to more borrowers, bringing in more loan repayments. Net profits from these activities increase the size of bank assets and provide funds to invest back into the bank by hiring more talent, upgrading technology, or pursuing innovations in products and services. These improvements in turn can attract more depositors and borrowers, and so it continues. In a philosophical sense, growth is more about the journey than the destination.

For some banks, efforts to grow are matched or exceeded by attrition, so bank size remains stable or declines. For most other banks, however, growth efforts cause an increase in size—dramatically so for banks that expand rapidly through acquisition.

At the same time, bankers know that all their growth-oriented activity does not necessarily generate returns to shareholders. Growth in size must also bring growth in sustainable value, or it can hasten the result all banks hope to avoid: insolvency.

While a government may declare from time to time that a bank is "too big to fail" and must be supported in its reorganization—or in layperson's terms, bailed out—the converse is also true: a bank can become too big to succeed. This can happen unless the bank's strategies are based in value as well as growth.

This chapter will discuss growth and its limitations, then explore the relevance of growth to three kinds of banks: community banks, regional banks, and megabanks. A concluding note on value will refer to later chapters.

TWO KINDS OF GROWTH

Let's start right out by facing the issue of bank growth. What exactly is it, and how can banks achieve it?

Bank growth generally refers to an increase in some basic indicator of bank size. As discussed below in the section on bank size, these indicators may be assets, deposits, number of branches, or other measures such as "sum of total transaction accounts, savings deposits, and small time deposits," used by the Fed for the purpose of deposit reporting.[3] Generally speaking, growth in one of these areas will cause growth in others.

However one defines its size, there are two major paths a bank can follow in the pursuit of growth—"organic" or "internal growth" and "growth by acquisition." This is not to say that these two paths cannot be pursued simultaneously; indeed, they often are.

Both organic and acquisition growth may include the addition of new products and services, new markets (geographically speaking), improved delivery of current services, new nontraditional banking services that go beyond simply collecting deposits and making loans, and improved economies of scale and/or scope. Economies of scale occur when average costs decline as bank products or services are provided in larger quantities. Economies of scope happen when costs drop because the products or services are produced jointly with another product or service.[4]

Furthermore, growth by acquisition may be seen as having either of two possible components or motivations. The term *bolt-on acquisition* is usually used to describe simply adding more of the same to a basic platform the acquirer already has, whereas the term *strategic acquisition* is often used to describe the acquisition of new or different products and services. Either way, it is important for the acquirer to know what it is buying (the focus of the next two chapters).

What are the pros and cons of these two types of growth?

There are various arguments for and against these two types of growth, but in sum they usually take a position on one side or the other of the famous tortoise and hare of Aesop's Fables. Go slow or go fast.

Slower organic growth, "steady as she goes," is considered less risky and more manageable, the primary risk being that the world will leave the tortoise behind. Faster growth by acquisition has many inherent risks for the hare. These may include bad deal choices, poor integration, and loss of focus. No matter how well done, no significant acquisition will be easily integrated and will consume huge amounts of management time just trying to get it right post deal—as explained in Chapter 7.

How do banks themselves measure growth?

Measuring bank growth is always a question of beauty being in the eye of the beholder. There are many measures. For example

- Growth in assets (left side of the balance sheet)
- Growth in deposits (right side of the balance sheet)
- Growth in profits (income statement)

These are the big three, but without growth in profitability, the first two matter little. The only way to get growth in profits is by measured growth in assets and deposits. Well done, growth is a finely tuned choreography of these. But these are strategic, especially growth in assets and deposits, and growth in profits is a result.

Tactical growth, by contrast, would be growth in

- Market share
- Market capitalization (for publicly held banks)
- Branches
- Services
- Number of employees

Furthermore, in the post-Dodd–Frank era, there is a new indicator of size, and that is systemic importance. Systemically important financial institutions (SIFIs) is now a technical term under Title I of Dodd–Frank, as explained in Chapter 2. The rough proxy for SIFI is size, but as this legal concept is tested, other elements may come into play.

What is the most common measure of all of these?

The most commonly used indicator of bank growth is the rate of growth in deposits. Demand deposits, as mentioned earlier, are a core business for banks. Although lending relationships are also a significant source of profit for banks, deposits remain important. Indeed, growth can be considered, as defined by one source, as "all the new money flowing into the deposit portfolio—including capitalized interest added to balances."[5] According to this source, most of this growth (some 80 percent) comes from existing customers.

Yet measuring deposit growth is no simple calculation. Indicators of deposit growth can include some or all of the following:

- Increase in the number of new customers and associated balances
- Increase in new products sold and associated balances
- Increase in the level of deposits overall (including existing deposits)[6]

Some banks use the concept of "deposit acquisition" (new accounts) or "product acquisition" (new purchases of services) to describe growth, but bankers need to look beneath the surface of "growth" to see what is really going on.

When customers new or old bring in money from outside the bank, this is growth. However, when customers merely switch from one product to another, this does not cause net growth (although, depending on circumstances, it may increase the rate of growth). This is a substitution within one side of the balance sheet that results in no change to the customer portfolio balances overall, for example, in converting a term deposit to savings or vice versa.

If an existing depositor takes out a loan, this does cause growth. This increases bank assets, another way to measure bank size.

What are bank growth rates?

Usually when analysts speak of bank "growth rates," they are not talking about growth in the size of the bank measured by assets or by market value. Rather, they are talking about growth in key financial elements, or growth in ratios based on the elements.

The elements are either from the income statement (revenues, earnings) or balance sheet (deposits, assets, equity).

The key ratios for bank analysts include

- Return on assets (net operating income/total assets)
- Return on equity (net income/average stockholders' equity)
- Return on equity after dividends (net income minus dividends/average common stockholders' equity)

In two otherwise identical banks, the one with greater dividends is not necessarily producing a lower return on equity; it is just paying higher dividends. This may in fact be an efficient use of capital. If it earns the same profit but pays it out in dividends, thereby reducing equity, it will actually have a higher return on equity.

Ratios are used in financial analysis, including bank analysis, because they do not usually rely on one type of financial statement (i.e., one financial perspective) alone. They typically combine two or more statements, or views. For example, in the previous ratios, the numerators of these ratios are from the income statement; the denominators are from the balance sheet. In general, superior value of a bank, regardless of bank size, is measured by performance in key ratios, rather than the elements that the ratios compare. Furthermore, beneath the ratios are the actions of the employees who drive those numbers, so bank operations are key to value.[7]

How do bank examiners view bank growth?

The FDIC requires examiners to study, among other factors listed in its *Risk Management Manual of Examination Policies*, prospects and plans for growth, as well as past experience in managing growth. The agency defines growth as growth in assets, cautioning that this should be supported by growth in capital.

> Management's ability to adequately plan for and manage growth is important with respect to assessing capital adequacy. A review of past performance and future prospects would be a good starting point for this review. The examiner may want to compare asset growth to capital formation during recent periods. The examiner may also want to review the current budget and strategic plan to review growth plans. Through this analysis, the examiner will be able to assess management's ability to both forecast and manage growth.[8]

BANK GROWTH AND THE ECONOMY

How is bank growth affected by the general economy?

As an industry, banking is highly sensitive to economic conditions, doing well during periods of economic growth and poorly during periods of economic decline. Conversely, the general economy is relatively sensitive to the financial sector, partly because it now occupies such a large percentage of the gross national product (GNP)—today at more than 8 percent, the highest level in recorded U.S. history.[9]

The National Bureau of Economic Research (NBER) defines "recession" as a "significant decline in economic activity spread across the economy, lasting more than a few months, normally visible in real gross domestic product (GDP), real income, employment, industrial production, and wholesale-retail sales." This affects banks. When existing retail customers lose income or employment, or when commercial customers experience lower productivity and sales (the scenarios occurring in any recession), banks see shrinking deposits and defaulting loans. Banks are forced to call in loans or repossess collateral—and when borrowers go bankrupt or collateral loses value, banks cannot get repaid.

This has been true during the most recent U.S. recession, which historians date from December 2007 to June 2009 (although its effects still linger now a half decade later). This lingering period has been referred to as a balance sheet recession for companies. According to this theory (developed by Richard Koo of Nomura Research), in a balance sheet recession, the value of company assets, such as stocks and real estate, declines, but company debt stays constant or grows. Rather than focusing on maximizing profits, companies try to reduce debt; they stop borrowing. At the same time, their economic distress makes them unattractive to lenders; it is harder for bank to find creditworthy customers. So lending, a key activity for banks, declines.

What impact do interest rates have on bank value?

Low interest rates—say 1 percent for the purpose of illustration—make it harder for banks to make a return. If a bank has to promise a 1 percent return on a savings account, but borrows at almost the same rate, this is hardly enough to make a profit after servicing the account. For loans, the situation is worse because not only does the bank only get back only $1 on $100, but there is risk of default.[10]

How is inflation calculated, and what impact does it have on bank growth?

Inflation is a general increase in the overall price level of the goods and services in the economy. To calculate the inflation rate, several indicators are used. The Fed uses several price indexes and calculates an overall inflation rate as well as a "core" inflation rate that excludes the most volatile items, such as gasoline and food.[11]

For banks, as for companies in every industry,[12] inflation means that $1 today—whether as a deposit or promised as loan repayment—is worth less than $1 held or received tomorrow. A significant percentage of the assets held by banks is in currencies, which by their nature suffer a continual loss of value through inflation that may not be compensated by interest earned through loans. In fact, factoring in inflation, interest rates in any given period can approach or even dip below zero. As Ben Bernanke noted in a March 2013 speech during his Federal Reserve Bank chairmanship, "The expected average of the short-term real rate over the next 10 years has gradually declined to near zero over the past few years."[13]

Research is mixed on how bad inflation is for banks. A fairly recent study by Batterymarch Financial management suggests that commercial banking may be better than other industries in handling it as long as it is stable.[14] But two previous studies by John Boyd of the University of Minnesota and coauthors claimd that inflation has a dramatically *negative* impact on the profitability of banks as well as their willingness to extend credit.[15] As one of the Boyd studies notes, various measures of bank profitability—net interest margins, net profits, rate of return on equity, and value added by the banking sector—all decline in real terms as inflation rises, after controlling for other variables. So even at fairly modest inflation rates, the real net interest margin turns negative. Such low real rates of return suggest that the incentives to expand bank operations (organic growth by doing more of same) simply are not as strong as inflation rises.[16]

And an earlier Boyd study showed that at low to moderate rates of inflation, there is less lending by the financial sector to the private sector, a lower level of bank assets, and a lower level of liabilities issued by banks—in other words, the opposite of growth: "Predictable inflation can exacerbate informational frictions and impede financial sector performance with negative repercussions for economic activity."[17] The study also demonstrated that at low to moderate rates of inflation, there is less stock market liquidity and trading volume. As inflation rises, financial sector performance falls. So during inflationary periods, banks may sit back and wait. On the other hand, the presence of profit-eating inflation creates an incentive to find new ways to generate profits.

Therefore, like their peers in other industries, bankers must add to any dollars they may hold (to make up for the ravages of time), and the only way to do that is to grow in some way, shape, or form.

Could you explain what you mean by saying that banks must "grow" to compensate for inflation?

As mentioned, bankers have an intrinsic bias toward asset growth because the dominant incoming asset for banks is money, which is continuously facing loss of value through inflation. Consider that, according to the Department of Labor Statistics, it takes $126 today (2013) to buy what cost only $100 in 2003.[18] Any cash that the bank generates for itself through fees or repayment of loans should not be left alone; it must be converted into loans or securities, or it will lose value. Yet these loans and securities in turn are vulnerable to loss of value through default (in the case of loans) and price declines (in the case of securities). These show up on the balance sheet. In other industries, there is also erosion of asset value (asset depreciation), reflected on the balance sheet, but in these industries there is not as much focus on the balance sheet when it comes to valuation.

It is not surprising, then, that banks seek growth in asset size through means beyond their own day-to-day management, namely, through acquisition of other banks. But whether banks grow organically or through acquisition, they must strive to increase value. This is true whether they are community banks, regional banks, or very large banks—also known as megabanks.

BANK SIZE

How do regulators define large, medium, and small banks?

The very largest banks are defined as systemically important financial institutions. As explained in Chapter 2, the Federal Reserve has the authority to define SIFIs, and so far, the SIFI designation is limited to companies with assets of more than $50 billion that predominantly engage in financial services.

Another size category arises in the reporting area, where banks must report more than annually if they pass a certain size threshold. Banks involved in foreign investment—so-called Edge Act banks—must report weekly, irrespective of size (see Chapter 10).

Otherwise, frequency of reporting to the Fed depends a lot on size. The size threshold changes periodically, but currently, as we go to press, it is triggered if there is a sum of total transaction accounts, savings deposits, and small time deposits equal to or more than $1.628 billion, or if net transaction accounts (i.e., total transaction accounts minus any amounts due from other depository institutions and minus cash items in the process of collection) are greater than $12.4 million.[19]

Within these categories, some banks are weekly reporters, and some are quarterly reporters. In this case, banks' size is measured by the sum of total transaction accounts, savings deposits, and small time deposits. The weekly reporters hold $290.5 million or more, and the quarterly reporters hold less than $290.5 million. There is an additional exempt category for institutions that may report less frequently. A Reserve Bank may require a depository institution to report on a more detailed or more frequent basis prior to the annual determination of reporting categories if the institution begins to exhibit faster-than-normal growth in its total transaction accounts, savings deposits, and small time deposits.

In addition to the regulatory definitions discussed above, there is the notion of community banks and regional banks.

COMMUNITY BANKS

What exactly is a community bank?

There is no technical legal definition of a community bank per se, but according to a definition proposed by the Federal Deposit Insurance Corporation (FDIC), to be a community bank, an institution must

- Make loans and have core deposits
- Have no more that 10 percent of assets as foreign
- Have no more than 50 percent of assets in nonbanking specialties, such as credit card specialists

- Have less than $1 billion in assets, or, if greater than $1 billion, then a loan-to-asset ratio greater than 33 percent; core deposits-to-assets ratio greater than 50 percent; 75 or fewer offices; no more than two large metropolitan serviceareas with offices (based on metropolitan statistical areas discussed in Chapter 2); no more than three states with offices; and no office with more than $5 billion in assets.[20]

What is the value of a community bank?

In every nation, small community banks play a vital role. The local banker can be a pillar of the community—someone who knows and is known by the citizenry. The effective local banker can make judicious lending decisions, build goodwill, and integrate harmoniously with the community in ways that would be more challenging for large national banks. Local banks may also have a greater propensity to support local charities—although regional and megabanks may do the same, in order to build long-term value by enhancing their local reputations and therefore market appeal. As Richard Brown, chief economist for the FDIC, said in a speech in June 2013, "Without community banks, many rural areas, small towns, and urban neighborhoods would have little or no physical access to mainstream banking services."[21]

How many community banks are there in the United States?

Estimates vary, but the general consensus is that there are more than 6,500 community banks,[22] which comprise the vast majority of all banks in the United States. Their numbers are declining, in part through merger, leaving more room for midsize and large banks to grow larger.[23]

This is evident in a number of indicators, including market share held by small versus large banks, number of small versus large banks, and revenue growth rate of small versus large banks. Meanwhile, small banks are more vulnerable to failure than large ones; their size makes it difficult for them to support regulations. Conversely, the largest banks can afford compliance activities (due to economies of scale) and have a special immunity from failure known as "too big to fail," discussed earlier.

How do the earnings of community banks compare to that of larger banks?

According to the FDIC, community banks derive 80 percent of their revenue from net interest income (because of their focus on traditional lending and deposit gathering), compared with about two-thirds at noncommunity banks. In years past they have had an advantage in generating net interest income, but in recent years the net interest margin (the spread between asset yields and funding costs) has narrowed. This has depressed the earnings of community banks.[24]

REGIONAL BANKS

What is the technical definition of a regional bank?

There is no technical definition of this term, but it is generally understood to be a lending and depository institution that serves one or more broad geographic regions. It can also be defined by what it is not. A regional bank is not a community bank; it serves a broader market. Nor is it an SIFI; its market (and thus its impact) is narrower.

Some economists believe that regional banks are the best of both worlds, being able to service local communities (often through community banks they acquired and merged into their operations) yet at the same time having a larger network and infrastructure.[25] Nonetheless, when a regional bank acquires a community bank, there can be backlash from the community. Local citizens may be concerned about a variety of postmerger effects:

- Loss of employment due to a net loss in the number of local branches
- Customer inconvenience due to various aspects of change (new branch locations, new banking hours, changes to checking account details)
- Greater difficulty in obtaining loans if known, local loan officers are replaced

What is the current growth trend with regard to regional banks?

As we go to press, regional banks appear to be doing well in comparison to smaller and larger banks. They do less trading than megabanks, so they have not been hit by the trading problems that have affected the larger global banks. On the other hand, they are not limited by the economic situations of single communities, but can spread their activities more broadly, thus reducing their level of risk.[26]

For an example of how a regional bank built itself through acquisition, see Appendix 4-A.

MEGABANKS

What is a megabank?

A megabank is the slang term for a large global bank. The technical term now, as mentioned earlier, is SIFI. This is a high-end subcategory of the noncommunity banks (defined as having $10 billion or more in assets).

The ratio of assets for noncommunity banks versus community banks has grown during the years. The average asset size of a noncommunity bank today is $26.4 billion. This is 74 times larger than the average community bank, which has assets of just $290 million. A quarter century ago, the average noncommunity bank was only 12 times larger than the average community bank.[27]

What is the basic argument for the megabank? What value is there in having a high level of assets?

One argument is convenience. Banks store and move money for individuals and institutions; it is the commodity they manage. Theoretically, at least, the fewer transfer costs charged in the movement of money, the less expensive the movement is.

Another argument is the intrinsic value of a large asset base. More generally, money is a valued asset and score keeper in all industries. But in the case of banks, money has a particular significance: banks are centered on it because they deal in money as their main commodity.

DOWNSIZING THE BIGGEST BANKS

I'm suggesting they be broken up so that the taxpayer will never be at risk, the depositors won't be at risk [and] the leverage will be something reasonable.

Sandy Weill, quoted in Steve Schaeffer, "Father of the Financial Supermarket Sandy Weill Says Break Up the Big Banks," *Forbes,* July 25, 2012

IN DEFENSE OF THE MEGABANK

We can do a $20 billion bridge loan overnight for a company that's about to do a major acquisition. Size lets us build a $500 million data center that speeds up transactions and invest billions of dollars in products like ATMs and apps that allow your iPhone to deposit checks. We move $2 trillion a day, and you can see it by account, by company. These aren't, like, little things. And they accrue to the customer. That's what capitalism is.

Jamie Dimon, quoted in Steve Schaeffer, "Here's Why Banks Should Be So Big," *Forbes*, August 13, 2012

We move trillions a day in and out of JPMorgan in 156 countries . . . If big banks are broken up, I don't know who can do this.

Laban Jack, interviewed by Jeffrey Cunningham, The National Association of Corporate Directors' annual conference, October 13, 2013.

As for communities, this is a complex issue. Considered in and of itself, a bank's growth can have a positive impact on communities.[28] The challenge is that if a bank grows in size by taking over another bank, which in turn declines in size as the acquirer sheds branches, employees and communities can suffer, as mentioned earlier.

Is there a natural economic limit to effective bank size?

There is no known natural limit to bank size, but there is some evidence that economies of scale operate only to a point, beyond which there are diseconomies, as the bank becomes too large and unwieldy to manage well. The point seems to be above $100 billion[29] (see Exhibit 4.1).

Larger banks would do well to keep in mind the wisdom of Wachovia's John Medlin, who pointed out that for shareholders and customers alike, stock appreciation and customer service trump size any day.[30]

What have policymakers done to limit bank size?

Over the years, policymakers have tried to limit bank size. As mentioned in Chapter 2, Dodd–Frank (Section 622) prohibits a financial company from merging or consolidating with, or acquiring, another company if the resulting company's consolidated liabilities would exceed 10 percent of

Exhibit 4.1 Economies of scale (implicit subsidy-adjusted)

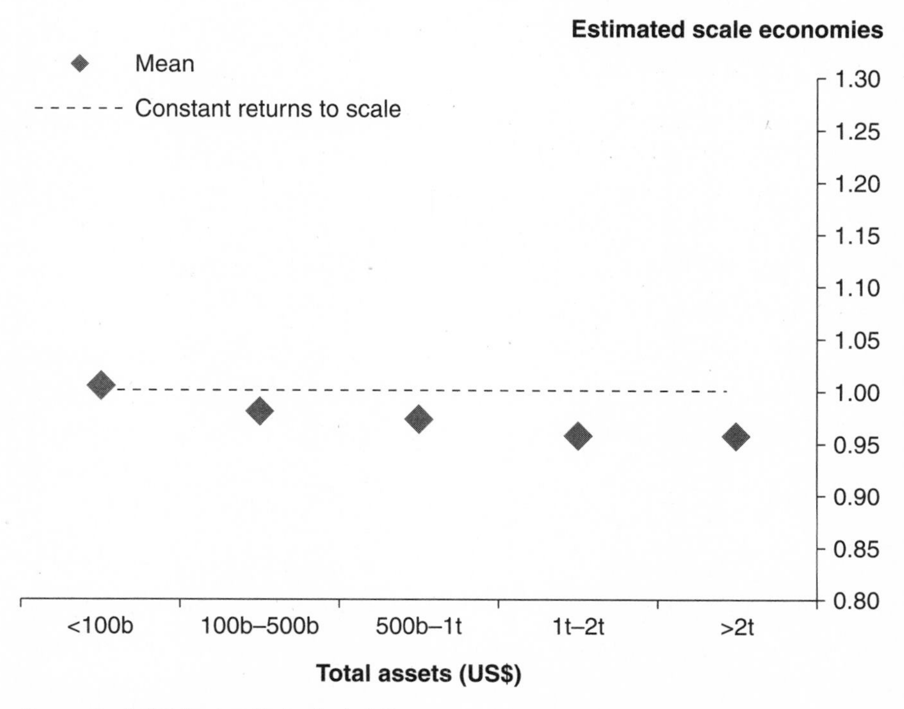

Source: Capital IQ, Bank of England calculations

the market (defined as the aggregate consolidated liabilities of all financial companies). This in effect closed a loophole in the 10 percent deposit cap under Riegle–Neal, because it counts not only deposits but also nondeposit liabilities and off-balance sheet exposures. Recently, a number of legislators have proposed limiting bank size as a percentage of GDP.[31]

Will big banks keep getting bigger?

There are signs that the era of the megabank is waning. In recent years, a number of megabanks have downsized their workforces dramatically. Some observers predict that banks will downsize in a more structural way, through divestitures.[32]

COMPARATIVE GROWTH STRATEGIES BY SIZE

Which banks are more likely to grow through acquisition—community banks, regional banks, or megabanks?

Acquisition has not been an important source of asset growth for community institutions, according to a recent study by the FDIC.[33] From 1984 to 2011, relative to their numbers, community banks reporting in 2011 to the FDIC accounted for far fewer direct and, especially, indirect acquisitions than did noncommunity banks. The assets of institutions directly acquired by community banks during the period amounted to only around 15 percent of all assets held by community banks in 2011. Thus, according to FDIC studies, acquisition and consolidation were far less important to charter growth among community institutions.

By contrast, for noncommunity banks (with assets greater than $10 billion) growth in assets came about largely on the strength of charter acquisition. The 558 noncommunity banks operating at year-end 2011 directly acquired or consolidated 2,401 charters during the period with assets of $6 trillion, an amount equal to just over one-half of the assets held by noncommunity banks in 2011. Moreover, the 2,401 institutions directly acquired by noncommunity banks had already acquired or consolidated 8,490 other charters since the beginning of the period in 1984. In this way, institutions reporting as noncommunity banks in 2011 directly or indirectly absorbed 71 percent of the charters that exited the industry between 1984 and 2011 (see Exhibit 4.2).

Exhibit 4.2 Acquisitions Were Instrumental in the Rapid Growth of Assets at Noncommunity Banks Between 1984 and 2011

		As of Year-End 2011		Between 1984 and 2011			
				Number of Charters Acquired		Assets of Charters Directly Acquired ($ Million)	Assets Acquired as Percent of 2011 Total Assets
	Group	Number of Charters	Total Assets ($ Million)	Directly	Indirectly		
Community Banks	Reported at Year-End 1984	5,057	$1,436,786	2,573	567	$217,204	15.1%
	New Charter After 1984	1,742	$535,952	454	103	$65,641	12.3%
	Total	6,799	$1,972,737	3,027	670	$282,844	14.3%
Noncommunity Banks	Reported at Year-End 1984	314	$10,129,136	2,111	8,147	$5,494,491	54.2%
	New Charter After 1984	244	$1,790,372	290	343	$514,868	28.8%
	Total	558	$11,919,507	2,401	8,490	$6,009,360	50.4%
	Total	**7,357**	**$13,892,245**	**5,428**	**9,160**	**$6,292,204**	**45.3%**

Source: FDIC Community Banking Study, December 2012, http://www.fdic.gov/ regulations/resources/cbi/report/cbi-full.pdf.

CONCLUDING COMMENTS

With the decrease in the number of banks in the U.S., and with relatively weak profits during this economic period, it may seem as though days of banking growth are behind us. But this view would be overly pessimistic. The global professional services firm Deloitte Touche Tohmatsu Ltd. has made some sensible predictions on retail banking growth. The advisory firm notes that deposits and lending are no longer dominant avenues for growth. Instead, the future of banking, until at least 2020, will lie in services such as asset management, annuities, and defined contribution management. "Several leading banks are already responding to these attractive growth trends—and their potential for fee-based revenues—for example, by acquiring securities firms and/or organically building their existing investment activities," notes Deloitte.[34] Chapter 8 highlights a case in point.

Regarding community banks, community bankers participating in a recent roundtable hosted by the FDIC predicted they would see more consolidation in the coming years, but there would still be significant numbers of survivors.[35] Some believe that consolidation is more likely because there are an increasing number of bankers who will decide to leave the industry. Reasons cited by bankers included lower earnings potential for community banks due to insufficient demand for loans and interest rate risk, among other factors; decreased stature of profession ("demonization" of bankers); fatigue due to economic stress and regulatory requirements; frustrations with perceived regulatory burden; unfair competition (usually from large banks and/or credit unions); changing technology needs; and concerns about attracting new investors.[36] Even so, many bankers will remain in the field to meet these and other challenges, including the challenge of bank M&A valuation and due diligence, the subject of the next two chapters.

APPENDIX 4-A

BB&T's Purchases of Banks and Thrifts, 1931–2012

BB&T is a regional financial holding company. BB&T has maintained a long-term focus on a strategy that includes expanding and diversifying the BB&T franchise in terms of revenues, profitability and asset size. This strategy has encompassed both organic growth and acquisitions of complementary banks and financial businesses. During the 1990s and through the mid-2000s, BB&T's growth resulted largely from mergers and acquisitions as the economics of business combinations were compelling. Since that time, BB&T has focused more on organic growth, but is well positioned for strategic opportunities.[37]

Company Name	Year	Exchange Ratio*
Bank Atlantic	2012	
Colonial Bank	2009	
Haven Trust	2008	
Coastal Financial Corporation	2007	0.385
First Citizens Bancorp	2006	1.30
Main Street Banks Inc.	2006	0.6602
Republic Bancshares, Inc.	2004	0.81
Equitable Bank	2003	1.00
First Virginia Banks	2003	1.26
AREA Bancshares	2002	0.55
MidAmerica Bancorp	2002	0.7187
Regional Financial Corporation/		
First South Bank	2002	
Century South Banks	2001	0.93

(Continued)

Company Name	Year	Exchange Ratio*
Community First Banking Co.	2001	0.98
F&M National Corporation	2001	1.09
FCNB Corp.	2001	0.725
FirstSpartan Financial	2001	1.00
Virginia Capital Bancshares	2001	0.5109
BankFirst Corp.—Common	2000	0.455
BankFirst Corp.—Preferred	2000	1.406
First Banking of Southeastern Georgia	2000	0.74
Hardwick Holding Company	2000	0.932
One Valley	2000	1.28
Premier Bancshares—Common	2000	0.5155
Premier Bancshares—Preferred	2000	2.2945
First Citizens Corp. of Newnan, Georgia	1999	1.079
First Liberty Financial Corp.	1999	0.87
Mainstreet Financial Corp.	1999	1.18
Mason Dixon	1999	1.30
Matewan Bancshares Inc.—Common	1999	0.67
Matewan Bancshares Inc.—Preferred	1999	0.8375
Franklin Bancorporation	1998	0.35
Life Bancorp of Norfolk	1998	0.58
Maryland Federal Bancorp	1998	1.2078
Fidelity Financial Bankshares Corp.	1997	0.7137
UCB	1997	1.135
Virginia First	1997	0.32645
Southern National Preferred	1996	1.4767
Commerce Bank of Virginia	1995	1.305
Southern National Corp.	1995	1.45
First Savings Bank	1994	0.855
Home Federal Savings Bank	1994	2.57717
LSB Bancshares Inc. of South Carolina	1994	1.2593
Regency Bancshares, Inc.	1994	1.81197
1st Home Federal	1993	

Company Name	Year	Exchange Ratio*
Carolina Savings Bank	1993	
Citizens Savings	1993	0.9389
Citizens Savings Bank	1993	
East Coast Savings Bank Inc.	1993	
Edenton Savings & Loan Association	1993	
FedFirst Bancshares, Inc.	1993	2.3443
First Fincorp	1993	2.76
Mutual SSB	1993	
Old Stone Bank of North Carolina	1993	
Security Financial Holding	1993	0.7822
First Security Federal Savings Bank	1992	
Peoples Federal Savings Bank	1992	
Workmen's Bankcorp Inc.	1992	1.50
Albemarle Savings & Loan Association	1991	
Gate City Federal	1991	
Home Savings & Loan Association	1991	0.4686
Preferred Savings Bank	1991	
Southeastern Federal Savings Bank	1991	
Carolina Bancorp (First Federal of the Carolinas)	1990	0.816
First Federal of Pitt County	1990	1.75
Mutual Federal Savings	1990	1.15603
Western Carolina Savings	1990	1.91724
American Bank & Trust Co.	1989	1.27109
Community Bank of South Carolina	1987	1.30
Liberty National	1987	
Union National Bank	1987	4.5284
Capital Bank & Trust	1986	2.46984
First Palmetto State Bank & Trust Company, Inc.	1986	0.64222
Horry County	1986	3.50
Anson County Bank & Trust	1984	2.0355

(*Continued*)

Company Name	Year	Exchange Ratio*
Carolina Bank of Sanford	1984	2.068
Cherryville National	1984	4.50
Community Bank of Greensboro	1984	0.83
City National Bank	1983	
Forsyth Bank & Trust Company	1982	0.77965024
Independence National Bank	1981	2.00
Edgecombe Bank & Trust Co.	1980	
Carolina State Bank	1979	
Lafayette Bank	1977	
Bank of Matthews	1976	1.175
Citizens Bank of Warrenton	1976	3.75
Bank of Charlotte	1970	
Bank of Statesville	1970	
Bank of Varina	1969	
Bank of Halifax	1968	
First National Bank in Henderson	1968	
Bank of Davie	1967	
Bank of Mayodan	1967	
The Bank of Mount Gilead	1967	
First National Bank of Leaksville	1966	
First National Bank of Whiteville	1966	
The Farmers Bank & Trust Company	1965	
The National Bank of Sanford	1965	
Bank of Rowland	1964	
Citizens Bank	1961	
Planters Bank	1959	
Wilson Industrial Bank	1958	
Toisnot Banking Company	1931	

* Not available on all transactions.

Source: BB&T 2013, as posted on the bank's website September 28, 2013, http://www.bbt.com/bbtdotcom/about/investor-relations/shareholder-services/merger-history.page#Bankthrifts. This list does not include BB&T's insurance acquisitions.

CHAPTER 5

Preliminary Valuation for Deal Pricing

Any banker will tell you that successfully managing the due diligence and acquisition process is not easy.

—*Jim Wilkson,*
President and CEO, BankSmart,
Petersburg, Florida[1]

The valuation and evaluation of banks in connection with a contemplated bank M&A transaction generally occur in the preliminary phase of sizing up a transaction. This preliminary due diligence is the main subject of this chapter. The concepts of preliminary due diligence and valuation/evaluation are inextricably intertwined and, if satisfactory, set the pattern for confirmatory due diligence, the subject of Chapter 6.

Preliminary due diligence (the evaluation phase) includes by necessity the more formal valuation of the target. Confirmatory due diligence involves the additional critical but following step of digging deeper and ultimately proving and verifying the assumptions made in the preliminary due diligence stage. One might consider this second phase the audit and confirmation stage. This latter stage is when the accountants, attorneys, technology, and other subject matter experts take over, although analysts may vary in the degree of emphasis placed on verification work as opposed to accepting what the target bank has presented in order to take a preliminary estimate of value and risk in the two phases of due diligence.

While the emphasis on preliminary acceptance versus verification may be different from analyst to analyst, these two phases broadly speaking always take place more or less in that order.

PRELIMINARY DUE DILIGENCE: THE BASICS

Why does due diligence come in two phases?

No bank, whether seeking to buy or to be bought, will want to suffer the business disruption and the significant expense involved in confirmatory due diligence without at least knowing what the likely deal terms are, valuation (a fair price based on circumstances) being the most important. This is the reason why a letter of intent to purchase a bank is usually not binding, although it sometimes may be binding as to a limited number of items. The letter of intent ordinarily follows preliminary due diligence and precedes confirmatory due diligence. Only after confirmatory due diligence will the final legally binding merger and acquisition agreements conclude the process.

As we will discuss in Chapter 6, actual or confirmatory due diligence covers areas such as legal status, contractual agreements, final deal documents, accuracy of financial records, regulatory concerns, technology, operating risk, and so forth. But at the beginning there is price and valuation to be more or less determined before these auditing and confirming steps can be or even should be taken. And price and valuation are in turn inextricably related to an overall evaluation of the target, especially in the case of banks.

This is not to imply that there is an overly bright line between the confirmatory and preliminary due diligence phases, as typically some of the items that will later be verified in confirmatory due diligence are of course also being seriously considered during preliminary due diligence. Nonetheless, it is useful to think of them this way as an organizational approach to the two stages of the due diligence function, preliminary and confirmatory, and this book takes that approach.

How can one determine how much a given bank is worth?

Decision makers may ask this question to support a variety of business actions, including setting a share price for an initial or secondary public offering, making a partial investment, determining bank CEO pay, or settling a dispute with a minority owner who wants to sell back shares—just to name a few scenarios that might require bank valuation. Valuation methods and therefore results vary based on context. This chapter will ask the question in a very specific context: preliminary due diligence and valuation/evaluation for deal pricing of a target bank in an M&A transaction. Appropriate valuation and evaluation of a target bank for preliminary deal pricing is, of course, one of the major goals in the setting of bank M&A. The end goal is to consummate a desirable deal at the right price. It is impossible to value a bank (ultimately a quantitative measurement) without simultaneously evaluating a bank's processes in managing its on- and off-balance-sheet activity (a more qualitative measurement). In other words, the question is not only what is the value of a target bank, but how well does the management of the bank maintain it and protect it against future risk? These two considerations are codependent. It is well to keep in mind that valuation is in the final analysis more about judgment than it is about mathematical formulas and methods. As the saying goes, "Garbage in, garbage out."

There are numerous texts written on the methods of valuing a business generally and a few on bank valuation specifically. The books on bank valuation typically run 400 to 800 pages. It would be outside the intended scope of this book to devote that much coverage to a subject adequately covered in the literature. This chapter will approach the subject by starting with only a necessary general overview of business valuation concepts, then focus mainly on those areas that make the valuation and evaluation of banks unique.

How is bank valuation similar to yet unlike other business valuation?

The valuation of banks and financial institutions is in many ways distinct from other business valuation and conceptually more difficult, as banking is a unique industry and requires unique approaches. This is perhaps the reason why relatively little has been written about bank valuation specifically.

In the valuation of most commercial business and economic assets, the value of the target is its ability to produce income in the future. To be more precise, it is the present value of that future income-earning ability. This reliance on the target enterprise's income statements, both historic and projected, usually accounts for the bulk of the valuation calculation, and so it is for banks, although the synergies unique to a particular buyer (investment value, see below) are also taken into consideration.

The interplay of the various and more or less complex features of a bank's balance sheet (on-balance-sheet activities) and their enormous sensitivity to various types of contextual factors adds another dimension. Among these are interest risk, default risk, timing and matching of funds flows, and liquidity issues. The interplay and mix of these factors cause the balance sheet to be of significantly greater importance than in the typical nonbank commercial business valuation. In the commercial arena, balance sheets are usually fairly straightforward and not overly complex, consisting of (1) working capital assets (cash and other short-term assets, e.g., inventory and accounts receivable, less short-term debt), *plus* (2) non–working capital assets, *less* (3) long-term debt.

In the case of banks, one might say the "balance sheet is the business." Indeed, a bank balance sheet can also be seen as a cash flow statement showing the source and use of funds—the source of bank funds constituting most of its liabilities, especially deposits, and the use of bank funds constituting most of its assets, especially loans. So the balance sheet plays a special role in banking.

Are valuation approaches different for community banks than for large banks?

Yes. It is important to distinguish community banks from larger regional banks. Community banks, especially small ones, are often essentially privately held, often having only a small number of shareholders, with the market for the shares being relatively inefficient. Sometimes shares are traded "across the president's desk" or by small market makers who may somewhat arbitrarily control the buy and sell stock price quotes (not totally arbitrarily, though, as there are rules for market makers). For this reason, valuing larger banks may rely more on the market approach described below (i.e., the trading values of shares of the target in the stock market), whereas community banks may often be more accurately valued by in effect starting from scratch, examining underlying assets and financial data, while somewhat ignoring the thin market for their shares.

Also, M&A transactions involving community banks are usually not mergers but more typically acquisitions where a more dominant party is clearly taking over. As mentioned previously, community banks are usually defined as banks with less than $1 billion in assets—a small amount on the balance sheet of larger banks. Indeed, community banks comprise about 90 percent of the banks in the United States while controlling only about a quarter of the banking assets.[2] Even in larger bank transactions the term *merger* can be misleading, as there usually is a dominant party. Much of the use of the term *merger* as opposed to *acquisition* is simply public relations gloss. It looks better from the point of view of the acquired bank to claim a "merger with" rather than an "acquisition by."

VALUATION APPROACHES

What are valuation standards that might apply to banks?

In recent years various standards of value, often differing from each other only subtly, have proliferated—some adding clarity to the mix and others sowing confusion. Much of the variation depends on the analyst's purpose. This chapter will set forth the most common standards as they apply to banks, namely, the potential applications of fair market value, fair value, and investment value standards in a transaction involving a bank and/or bank assets.

How does fair market value apply to banks?

Fair market value (FMV), sometimes known as market value, is probably the most widely known standard of value. Put simply, it is the objective cash price that would be arrived at between parties dealing at "arm's length" (i.e., independently), each possessed of equal information and subject to no special compulsion to transact. In theory, all skilled and objective valuators would arrive at the same FMV conclusion, although in real life they rarely exactly agree and often widely disagree. Typically, FMV is used as a hypothetical standard for litigation, tax planning, and other similar situations. It is important to note that it is hypothetical and does not involve a real transaction. Therein lies its weakness and generally inapplicability to M&A activity, which involves real transactions between real parties, often partly not in cash, with different levels of information and the necessarily subjective perspectives of value by each party and each transaction.

How does fair value apply to bank M&A?

Fair value is essentially an accounting concept and somewhat of a blend between investment value (discussed below) and FMV. Like FMV, it is hypothetical in nature, but unlike FMV, fair value takes into consideration the respective advantages or disadvantages that each party might gain from a transaction. Fair value is also sometimes used synonymously with investment value (see below) when undertaking due diligence in corporate transactions, and where particular synergies between two parties may mean that the price between them is higher than the price that might be obtainable on the wider market. Fair value is typically used only in retrospect, after the fact of a concluded transaction when it may come into play for the accountants recording the transaction or by litigants challenging it.[3] Otherwise, it is of little concern in a preliminary valuation in contemplation of a bank M&A.

How does investment value apply to bank M&A?

Investment value may differ widely from observer to observer, buyer to buyer. It is of most importance to and is usually calculated by the acquirer. This is the "Beauty is in the eye of the beholder" approach and usually results in a transaction or at least an offer made to acquire. Because this chapter focuses on valuation, we are primarily concerned here with the importance of investment value to an acquirer or dominant merger partner that might arise from an actual bank M&A transaction. (Investment value to individuals will be discussed in Chapter 12.) Beauty is always unique to individual buyers possessed of different synergies and advantages that might be uniquely available to it arising from a transaction, such as increased market share, new geographical presence, new lines of business, and costs savings from economies of scale.

What are the principal valuation methods (as opposed to valuation standards) used for banks?

In general, in all business valuations and appraisals, including that of banks, there are three broad approaches (with several subvariations), noted as follows: the income approach, the market approach, and the asset approach.

How does the income approach apply to the valuation of banks?

The income approach estimates the present value (in other words, how much a buyer should pay now) of the target bank's ability to earn future income. This is mainly based on either explicit or implicit projections of future income, and it may be determined in two different ways.

The capitalization of earnings approach is an implicit approach and is really a shortcut method (with all of the dangers inherent in shortcut methods) of projecting the investment value of future earnings. It is determined by simply multiplying the actual (normalized to eliminate unusual activity) recent historical or assumed base earnings (usually net income) by a multiple that represents a capitalization rate (e.g., for a capitalization rate of 20 percent, base earnings of $5 million times a multiple of 5 = a value of $25 million). A multiple that is applied to the base income is essentially and virtually synonymous with a capitalization rate (which is divided into the base period income rather than multiplied by it). Either approach will give the same result (i.e., a multiple of 5 is synonymous with a capitalization rate of 20 percent, a multiple of 4 with a capitalization rate of 25 percent, and so on). Following the earlier example, a capitalization rate of 20 percent applied to base earnings of $5 million is $25 million ($5 million divided by 20 percent). The danger in this approach is that insufficient attention may have been given to future fluctuations in earnings. It is also rarely used for any purpose other than an analyst's brief initial impression (preliminary valuation), in as much as banks, as dependent as they are on the nature of their balance sheet accounts, are not truly susceptible to this approach.

An alternative approach, but one that is also a part of the income approach and more sound, is discounted future earnings (DFE), in which a fair amount of detail and effort goes into projecting year-by-year earnings for some future periods. It is this discipline that makes the DFE approach more desirable than the capitalization of earnings approach. Once the future earnings are projected, the value of those earnings is then determined, as of the present time, by assuming the rate of return the analyst desires or believes appropriate (i.e., the present value today of $110 one year from now at a required or desired 10 percent rate of return for one year is $100).

There are numerous books written on the use of the DFE approach, and it would be redundant and not within the scope of this book to repeat the information here. It is worth noting, though, that the approach involves relatively simple arithmetic: principal × rate × time = amount of return; in our example, $100 × 10 percent × 1 (for one year) = $10, so the present (or today's) value of $110 (a year from now) is $100.

How does the market approach apply to the valuation of banks?

The second broad approach is the market approach. There are two types. The first version, the comparable transaction market approach, is calculated by having the analyst look at similar completed M&A transactions where available. This method should be considered preliminary and only useful to that extent, as truly comparable transactions are hard to find, and the data available typically are too limited to be of other than preliminary value.

In the second version, the guideline public company market approach, the value of a target bank is estimated by comparing it to similar entities. This approach would usually be more applicable to larger noncommunity banks (e.g., assets in excess of $1 billion) than to smaller, lightly traded community banks. In this approach, the subject bank's apparent valuation is calculated by considering its stock's trading value in relation to its earnings and then to that of similar public banks. This is also known as the income-to-total market cap ratio. Its stock's trading value may also be compared to its book value. This is known as the market value-to-book value (MBV) ratio.

Both of these approaches can indicate whether or not the market value of the target bank's stock makes sense when compared to similar banks and might be used as a reasonable proxy for its value. For example, in the guideline public company market approach, by using the MBV ratio of similar publicly or semipublicly traded banks, an estimate of value can be made. If the market value of a share is, say, $10, and the book value of the same share is $5, then it follows that the MBV ratio is 2 to 1 ($10 divided by $5). Many experts feel this is the most reliable preliminary approach for at least larger bank transaction valuation, while conceding that the problem here is that either book value or market value may be temporarily distorted due to either the whimsicality or fickleness of the public markets or the under- or overstatement of book value of the subject bank due to elements such as inadequate or excessive and pessimistic reserves against the book value of assets. Over reasonable time periods, though, this ratio can be fairly accurate if used cautiously and in conjunction with other methods, especially a careful analysis of the subject banks' balance sheet (assets and liabilities).

How does the asset approach apply to the valuation of banks?

The third approach, the asset approach, is not often encountered in the valuation of a commercial business or a bank except in a liquidation, implying the assets may be worth more liquidated than used in the operation of the bank. In this approach the assets are individually and in the aggregate valued as if they were being sold, collected, or wound down. However, it is generally useful and important to apply at least some of the same concepts of the asset approach in the valuation of any bank, even a solvent one. This is not because of an assumption of an actual liquidation per se but primarily due to the high degree of sensitivity of a bank's balance sheet to its value. This sensitivity results largely from a combination of (1) reserve requirements (see Chapter 10, discussion of the Basel Committee), (2) the relatively low equity-to-asset ratios maintained by a bank as compared to other commercial enterprises (7 to 10 percent as compared to double or triple that in other businesses) and the concordant risk of financial insolvency with only relatively slight reductions in asset value, (3) the interrelatedness of timing of collections and repaying of deposit liabilities, (4) interest rate fluctuations that a bank is uniquely exposed to on its balance sheet accounts, and (5) asset concentrations (loans and investments carried on its balance sheet) that may be subject to macroeconomic fluctuations and other customer/industry concentration dangers.

What are some common indicators of bank value and performance used by reporting services?

The well-regarded investment bank Sheshunoff & Co. Investment Banking highlights several key indicators of bank value, using the SNL Financial database of more than 20,000 U.S. financial institutions, including all publicly traded banks and thrifts, privately held institutions, and credit unions.[4] The indicators are health and robustness (performance) factors that can be used by other banks for comparison with their peers. These include

- Median bank price to tangible book value (MBV ratio, as discussed above)[5]
- Median bank price to last 12 months (LTM) earnings[6] (price-to-earnings ratio, as discussed above)
- Median bank tangible common equity over tangible assets (simply the ratio of equity to assets, a health indicator more than a true valuation)
- Median bank LTM return on average assets (again, more an evaluation of health and robustness than a valuation)[7]

This information is reported by region for banks headquartered in the Mid-Atlantic, Midwest, New England, Southeast, Southwest, and West.

What is the Texas ratio?

The Texas ratio was developed in the state of Texas during the 1980s' bank financial crisis. Although other states experienced bank failures, the problem was particularly acute in Texas, due to a large banking sector making many large nonperforming loans to energy and real estate. The ratio is the book value of all nonperforming tangible assets (including other real estate owned) divided by equity capital plus loan-loss reserves.[8] It was developed to measure a bank's likelihood of failure by comparing its bad assets to its available capital. When this ratio exceeds 100 percent, a bank lacks the capital needed to absorb potential losses from troubled assets. According to the Federal Reserve Bank of Dallas, the ratio does seem to be a good early indicator of bank failures, but it tends to overpredict the number of problem institutions.[9]

What is the efficiency ratio?

This is the ratio of expenses to net interest income (the amount yielded by loans and securities less the amount paid for deposits and other borrowings). The lower it is, the more efficient the bank. The *American Banker* magazine periodically lists the most efficient bank holding companies.[10] Interestingly, megabanks rarely make the top 100.[11]

BALANCE SHEET DUE DILIGENCE

What should an acquirer look for when conducting preliminary due diligence on a bank balance sheet?

Preliminary due diligence on a bank involves not only projecting its future earnings but also understanding the quality of its assets and the nature of its liabilities. In the sense mentioned above, "a bank's balance sheet is the business," more so than in most other types of business. In a normal business, the balance sheet reflects a snapshot at a particular point in time of the assets and liabilities accumulated on any given date as a result of the external operations of the business. In the case of a bank, the balance sheet reflects more than just the cumulative results of operations as they affect assets and liabilities; it reflects all of the bank's core financial operating factors. As such, it is the starting point for evaluating any target bank and its future prospects.

Operationally, it is a fact that most banks are quite similar. They make loans, take deposits, keep some cash on hand, pursue customers and (usually) open branches. Indeed, despite banks' efforts to distinguish themselves by their cultures (as discussed in Chapter 7), it has long been a problem for bankers to distinguish themselves in such a commodity business. Financially, however, banks do vary. Every bank balance sheet is different. If you want to know a bank, know its balance sheet. This is not to say that there are no other important factors, such as the number of branches, the types of business lines, the quality of management, and the geographical location. Nor is it good to neglect the importance of discounted future earnings—another important aspect of bank valuation. But the balance sheet is the natural starting point for determining the degree of actual collectability of the assets as well as the future timing of interest income, collections of assets, and repayment of liabilities. It is also the starting point for future income projections and provides valuable input into the DFE approach referred to above.

What would a simplified bank balance sheet look like?

Included in this chapter is Exhibit 5.1, which illustrates the typical assets and liabilities on a balance sheet. It also shows how a balance sheet can be used not only a snapshot of the state of a bank's accounts at a particular point in time but also a measure of performance over a period of time, by looking at balance sheet line item averages and by comparing them to interest rates paid on customer deposits held and received on loans and investments. This information is based on the data in the banking book and trading book for a bank's balance sheet.

What is the distinction between a bank's banking book and its trading book?

The banking book records typical core bank activities and transactions, such as loans and deposits and income and costs deriving from them. The trading book records transactions arising from the trading of securities or their derivatives. It is important to understand that on the banking book, transactions follow the centuries-old approach of being recorded and carried at their historical cost. On the trading book, transactions are recorded at their current fair value.

Exhibit 5.1

ILLUSTRATION OF A BANK BALANCE SHEET AND YIELDS AND RATES FOR A YEAR

Dollars in millions

Assets	**Year End**	**Average During the Year**	**Interest Income/Expense**	**Yield/Rate**
Fed Funds Sold and Securities Held	$ 200,000	$ 180,000	$ 2,700	1.5%
Loans				
Mortgages	$ 200,000	$ 180,000	$ 6,300	3.5%
Consumer	$ 100,000	$ 90,000	$ 4,500	5.0%
Commercial	$ 225,000	$ 202,500	$ 10,125	5.0%
Other earning Assets	$ 50,000	$ 45,000	$ 1,800	4.0%
Total Earning Assets	**$ 775,000**	**$ 697,500**	**$ 25,425**	**3.6%**
Cash and Equivalents	$ 25,000			
Allowance for loan losses	$ 80,000			
Fixed Assets	$ 40,000			
Total Assets	**$ 920,000**			
Liabilities				
Interest Bearing Deposits				
Savings accounts	$ 55,000	$ 49,500	$ 371	0.8%
Money Market Accounts	$ 225,000	$ 202,500	$ 4,050	2.0%
CDs	$ 250,000	$ 225,000	$ 2,250	1.0%
Total	**$ 530,000**	**$ 477,000**	**$ 6,671**	**1.4%**
Fed Funds Purchased and Securities Sold	$ 00,000	$ 90,000	$ 1,530	1.7%
Long-Term Debt	$ 110,000	$ 99,000	$ 4,950	5.0%
Total Interest-Bearing Liabilities	**$ 740,000**	**$ 666,000**	**$ 13,151**	**2.0%**
Other liabilities	$ 90,000			
Total Liabilities	**$ 830,000**			
Stockholders' Equity	$ 90,000			
Total Liabilities and Equity	$ 920,000			
Net Interest Income on Earning Assets	**$ 35,000**	**$ 12,274**		**1.8%**

What exactly is fair value and how does it relate to "mark-to-market" value?

Accounting standards in various ways require what is broadly known as "fair value" accounting. The Financial Accounting Standards Board (FASB) has issued guidance in ASC 820 (formerly FAS No. 157). One subset of fair value accounting is called mark-to-market, which uses an actual current market as its determinant of value (not all assets have a market). ASC 820 defines fair value, establishes a framework for measuring fair value in U.S. generally accepted accounting principles ("GAAP"), and requires expanded disclosures about fair value measurements, including mark-to-market measurements.[12] When securities are actively traded, changes in fair value are required to be recognized in the income statement. This is the specific meaning of "mark-to-market" accounting.[13]

What are the most important assets held by a bank, based on their cash value?

Most of the asset side of the bank's balance sheet is made up of securities and loans or leases "in bank credit."

Securities in bank credit are securities held in trading accounts owned by the bank (other than derivative securities). These include securities issued by the U.S. Treasury and federal agencies, including mortgage-backed securities. They are considered held to maturity and available for sale; in other words, they aren't restricted. The accounting for securities in bank credit is complex due to "mark to market" standards that require current valuation rather than historic cost and that offer various options for this accounting.[14]

Loans and leases in bank credit include commercial and industrial loans, real estate loans, and consumer loans and typically constitute from 60 to 70 percent of a bank's assets.

What are the most significant liabilities in a bank, based on their cash value?

Most of the liabilities on the books of commercial banks today are in the form of deposits. Some of these are nontransaction and large time deposits—money market or savings accounts with restrictions on withdrawal. Most, however, are deposits that have no such restrictions, the so-called checkable or transaction deposits. Banks take custody of the money that is in bank accounts, but owners of those accounts can claim it at any time; as such, the deposits are accounted as a liability to a bank. In addition, if the accounts are interest bearing, the bank owes interest on the amounts.

The remainder of a typical bank's liabilities come from borrowing and from trading (including derivative instruments with a negative fair value).

What ratios are the best indicators of profitability?

Some common ratios and performance indicators for profitability are the following, which are tracked by the Federal Deposit Insurance Corporation (FDIC):

- *Return on (average) assets (ROA).* Return on average assets is calculated by dividing annualized net operating income after taxes, including realized gain or loss on investment securities, by average assets.[15] As a rule of thumb, a 1 percent return is desirable and achievable.[16]
- *Return on (average) equity (ROE).* This ratio is computed by dividing annualized net operating income after taxes, including realized gain or loss on investment securities, by average total equity.[17]
- *Net interest margin.* This ratio is calculated by dividing annualized net interest income (interest income on a tax-equivalent basis less interest expense) by average earning assets. In general, a good level for this is above 3 percent. A lower margin would indicate that a bank has a proportionally large volume of low-yielding or nonearning assets.

How do these compare in FDIC-insured commercial banks?

In the first quarter of 2013, for commercial banks, the ratios were the following: average return on assets (1.12), average return on equity (10.06), net interest margin (3.27), and equity to assets (11.22).[18]

What are some ratios that factor out interest income and expense?

Two common ones are noninterest income/average assets and noninterest expense/average assets.

- *Noninterest income/average assets.* The ratio is computed by dividing annual noninterest income by average assets. Noninterest income is derived in part from fee-based bank operations, such as service charges on deposit accounts, consulting and advisory fees, and rental of safe deposit boxes. It also includes income from fiduciary, brokerage, and insurance activities, but it does not include realized gains on securities. Noninterest income supplements interest income, which is the bank's main earnings source. If it weren't for interest income, most banks could not be profitable, since noninterest expenses (overhead) are generally much higher than noninterest income. Currently, this is running at 2 percent,[19] although much lower levels are accepted by some state bank examiners.

- *Noninterest expense/average assets.* The ratio is computed by dividing annual noninterest expenses (also called overhead) by average assets. This is the day-to-day expense associated with bank operations, including the cost of salaries and benefits, any applicable rent or mortgage, cost of fixed assets, and other noninterest expense, but it does not include payments of a purely financial nature, whether or not pertaining to interest payments.[20] The general level for this in a healthy bank should not be much more than 3 percent.[21]

For a more complete list of ratios, see Appendix 5-A.

OTHER ASPECTS OF BANK FINANCIAL STRUCTURE

Moving on from the balance sheet, let's look at the income statement. What are the most important sources of revenue for a bank?

Healthy banks collect a significant amount of net interest income (see Exhibit 5.1), where the interest they earn on their deposits (by investing that money) plus the interest they earn by making loans adds up to a sum higher than the interest they pay on interest-bearing accounts. They also make other kinds of income, such as through fees (so-called noninterest income).

What kinds of fees can a bank charge?

In general, banks also earn fees from the performance of activities that go beyond lending and investing. These activities are valued separately from the other "on-balance-sheet" activities. Typically, if offered by a bank (normally by banks larger than community banks), they include investment advisory services. With these, a bank provides asset management and private banking services. They are usually priced at a percentage of the assets under management (AUM), although sometimes commissions are derived from securities trades (brokerage services) on behalf of customers. The bank is not exposed to the volatility of trades, as the customer assumes that risk. However, the bank does bear the risk of liability as a fiduciary, adding a layer of regulatory expectations and scrutiny.

How are fee-based activities valued?

These activities are typically separately valued from the rest of the bank's activities by identifying and segregating the cost and expenses and capital necessary to support them. After that, standard valuation techniques, as discussed elsewhere in this chapter, are employed.

Is there any ideal balance between interest earned on deposits and interest earned from loans? Can a bank go heavily in one direction or the other?

Between the two, deposits are more central to a bank's mission, but banks need both kinds of business—both deposits (checking and savings), which provide supply of capital, and loans, which respond to a demand for capital.

Deposits don't provide much income, as bank service fees for checking accounts are low, and in the case of savings accounts, it is the bank, not the customer, who is the net payer (even if only 1 percent per year).

Yet having deposits in savings gives banks funds to loan, and depending on the interest rate charged, loans can provide a good source of funds to a bank. Although at any given moment depositors (including savings depositors) may demand their money, a solvent bank can still draw on savings accounts, since the bank can draw on the central bank to make up any shortfall.

Under normal circumstances, the demand for bank loans exceeds the supply of cash on hand, although this situation can reverse itself.[22]

What kinds of expenses are the most common for banks?

Noninterest expenses in the form of operating costs take up a major part of the bank's income statement.[23] These can include, for example, payroll expenses, rent, marketing, and technology costs.

The next most significant expense is the provision a bank must make for loan losses. Since lending is a significant part of a bank's business, it is obviously important to prepare for a contingency reserve or allowance for some loss on loans.

What can professionals conducting preliminary due diligence learn from bank examiners?

When conducting due diligence on a bank, it is important to anticipate what state and federal bank examiners will be looking for. However, there is a role for sound financial analysis that may or may not be reflected in the examination. Some banks believe that the standards used by federal examiners are flawed and inconsistent.[24] The focus of examiners is often a function of the broader economic situation of the time.

BANK RISKS

How are bank risks analyzed from the point of view of the balance sheet?

Banks (and their balance sheets) have various risks: interest rate risks, credit risks, liquidity risks, and trading risks are usually the primary ones encompassed by the balance sheet. Since banks mostly borrow short and lend long, they are exposed to increases in short-term interest rates (interest rate risks), and this would lead to lower net interest margins (NIMs) (see Exhibit 5.1). The credit risk is that too many of those assets will go bad. The liquidity risk also comes from the necessary reliance of banks on their mixes of assets and liability types and terms. Trading risk comes from the daily vicissitudes of trading and owning securities and their derivatives.

What other risks need to be analyzed?

Other risks further described below are operational risks arising from off-balance-sheet sources of revenue and fee income.[25]

How does a bank manage interest rate risks?

Banks, even smaller ones, manage interest rate risk by preparing (in one form or another) an interest rate sensitivity table. This approach to asset and liability management dates back to the various banking crises of the 1970s, when interest rates suddenly began rising rapidly. The bank's balance sheet accounts are first analyzed in terms of the assets and liabilities that are subject to future changes in interest rates and entered into a spreadsheet by future calendar quarters and years appropriate to the particular type of account. The interest rate analysis takes into consideration all assets and liabilities, including off-balance-sheet accounts by maturity dates from an interest rate reset perspective. Each period constitutes a separate time period. A repricing gap results from potential changes in interest rates and this gap is then measured for each period and cumulatively. This facilitates the determination of where the repricing vulnerability or opportunity lies (the repricing gap), on the loan side or the deposit side, and allows management to act accordingly; it also approximates the interest rate risks of the bank being analyzed.

Interest rate sensitivity gap analysis has been greatly improved in recent times by taking into consideration a change in the yield curve.[26] This is the concept of duration analysis whereby an analyst can measure the average duration of a bank's interest-bearing assets and liabilities to see the results of an overall change in interest rates.

How does a bank manage and estimate collection or credit risks?

At its most basic level, commonly known as a default model approach, credit risks are estimated by analyzing the history of loan write-offs as a percentage of loans due, then applying that percentage to the current loan portfolio stratified by different types of loans. The bank's balance sheet is then adjusted through additions or reductions to its allowance for loan losses, which is carried as a reserve on its balance sheet. These additions or reductions can be based on probability theory used increasingly (and with ever greater sophistication) in recent years, especially when analyzing large and complex banks.

With the mark-to-market approach as an analytic tool to estimate the risk inherent in a bank's loan portfolio, the default model approach is enhanced by also taking into consideration downgrades or upgrades of a particular borrower or class of borrowers' credit ratings by independent credit rating services such as Fitch, Moody's, and Standard & Poors.[27] For example, the possibility of a highly rated (AAA) borrower moving into a lower group in the near future (say, a year) is fairly low, whereas the possibility of a lower rated (C) borrower further declining is quite high. Risk distribution in a bank's loan portfolio is very skewed and uneven.[28]

Supervision of the credit risk management function by individual banks should be commensurate with and sufficient for the scope and sophistication of the bank's activities.

This starts with analysis of loans, which are for most banks the biggest part of their business. Indeed, loans are the main reason historically they operate as banks in the first place. It is obvious that credit default risk (also called counterparty risk) has always been the largest source of bank problems and failures. At its root, credit risk can be best described as the potential that a bank borrower will fail to meet its obligations (repayment and other terms) to the bank. The goal of credit risk management therefore is to minimize credit risk exposure. This involves managing not only specific credits (loans) but also the bank's overall loan portfolio.

But credit risk is not just about lending. According to the Basel Committee (discussed in greater detail in Chapter 10), excessive exposure to credit risk is largely due to poor supervision, lax credit standards, and a failure to pay sufficient attention to economic factors—changes in the conditions (microeconomic) and environment (macroeconomic) of both the borrower and the bank.

In its manifesto, *Principles for the Management of Credit Risk,* the Basel Committee has identified the four pillars of managing credit risk:

1. Establishing an appropriate credit risk environment
2. Operating under a sound credit-granting process
3. Maintaining an appropriate credit administration, measurement, and monitoring process
4. Ensuring adequate controls over credit risk[29]

The document declares that these practices should be applied "in conjunction with sound practices related to the assessment of asset quality, the adequacy of provisions and reserves, and the disclosure of credit risk." Furthermore, banks should "identify, measure, monitor and control credit risk as well as ... determine that they hold adequate capital against these risks and that they are adequately compensated for risks incurred."[30]

Underscoring the Basel Committee's general guidance, it is important to note sources of credit risk, including weaknesses in the banking book and in the trading book, both on and off the balance sheet. Banks face credit risk in various financial instruments other than loans, including acceptances, interbank transactions, trade financing, foreign exchange transactions, transaction settlements, financial futures, swaps, bonds, equities, and options, and in the extension of commitments and guarantees. Any of these can "go south" due to bad credit.

What is liquidity risk in a bank?

Liquidity risk—the risk that cash may run short—is inherent in most businesses, but particularly in banking in so far as banks typically borrow (mostly through deposits) for shorter periods of time than their assets (mostly loans) mature. In addition, most banks need to employ (invest or loan) their assets in order to produce income; for this reason, they tend to maintain relatively little amounts of cash on hand. They can always sell assets to obtain cash, but this is best done strategically rather than from a need for cash. A quick assets sale puts the bank at risk of large losses resulting from the lower pricing accepted in such a "fire sale."

Today the management of liquidity risks has risen in importance. Banks are no longer permitted to maintain high debt-to-equity ratios seen before the financial crisis, so they are deleveraging to pass "stress tests." But they operate in a world that is laden with debt—from consumers, to companies, to nations—notably, the United States with its reported public debt of nearly $17 trillion and growing.[31]

Unforeseen events and normal day-to-day operating demands can put huge pressure on a bank's liquidity (or readily available cash position). And unforeseen events do arise both for individual banks and the banking system as a whole. In the 1970s, rising interest rates paid on relatively short-term deposit liabilities of banks created a severe liquidity problems for those financial institutions (many of them savings and loan associations) carrying a disproportionate number of long-term mortgage loans on their books. Again, in 2007 the global liquidity crisis made short-term borrowing very expensive, with credit-adverse lenders in the commercial paper market backing off as subprime loan defaults created a domino effect through the financial world. Those world-shaking events—starting with Paribas PNB's sudden exit from investments in mortgage-backed securities in August 2007—have led to close scrutiny by banks and regulators of liquidity risk for financial institutions worldwide.

Banks have several resources available to them in order to maintain adequate cash to meet day-to-day demands. Among these are

- Their own cash (from daily operations and on hand)
- "Discount window" borrowing from their central banks (in the United States, the "Federal Reserve window")
- The ability to sell or use as collateral directly, or through so-called repurchase ("repo") agreements, certain assets that are relatively liquid themselves, including
  - Sale of securities that are readily marketable and safe, such as short-term U.S. government securities
  - Sale of other assets through securitization, by selling portfolios of on-balance-sheet loans, such as mortgages or credit card debt to outside investors (although it should be noted that decreased interest in asset-backed securities since the global financial crises of 2007–2009 has caused this potential source of funding to become more difficult to obtain)
- Borrowing funds as needed from other banks and financial institutions in the form of commercial paper, longer-term bank borrowing, or bond issuance

How does a bank manage liquidity risks?

Banks operate in an asymmetrical economic system, acting as an intermediary between the short-term needs of some customers and the long-term needs of others and thereby providing degrees of liquidity to both. Therefore, a bank's liquidity management consists in large part of attempts to correlate demand and other short-term deposits (liabilities) with cash commitments on the other side of the balance sheet (loans).

One approach to liquidity management is very similar to interest-risk management (see the interest rate sensitivity gap analysis discussed above) in that spreadsheet-type analyses are done in order to estimate and match likely or known outflows with likely or known inflows, as well as to provide a margin of comfort as a cushion under both normal conditions and a range of stress scenarios.

Other approaches involve establishing and limiting the bank's risk exposures based on a certain level of tolerances. There are several ways to express this risk tolerance, such as expressing this risk boundary as the percentage of debt obligation not fully funded; establishing some early warning indicators to identify the emergence of vulnerabilities, as rapid asset concentrations in particular industry groups or geographical locations; and regular stress testing under various scenarios.[32]

What are trading risks and trading book risks in a bank?

Trading risks come from the daily gains and losses inherent in trading and carrying securities. The trading book reflects these, as it is marked to market (fair value) every day. The gains and losses, except those that result from funds that the bank's asset manager or broker own, are recorded in the bank's income statement as increasing or decreasing a bank's net income accordingly. Securities may include such items as shares of stock ("equities") and derivatives. Derivatives are financial instruments whose value is based on other assets (hence the word *derivative*); their value changes in response to the value of the underlying assets. As instruments, derivatives may take the form of equities, futures, options, forward agreements, and so forth. The assets underlying these instruments are similarly diverse, including all of the above types of instruments, as well as currencies, interest rates, and commodities.

How does a bank manage trading risks?

Trading risk is also known as value at risk (VAR) in the trading book. As mentioned earlier, banks, at least sophisticated larger ones, typically use stress testing approaches along with probability theory and similar modeling to test scenarios that give them an idea of the probability of losses occurring in a given period in excess of a stated amount. Reports are developed and circulated among appropriate management, especially traders reflecting current risk by sector based on the bank's portfolio. At a microlevel, banks may in some instances manage risk by hedging. Hedging simply means off-setting an investment by a matched investment that will move the opposite direction.

What is operational risk in a bank?

The Basel Committee defines operational risk as the risk of loss resulting from inadequate or failed internal processes, people, and systems or from external events. It may also include other classes of risk, such as fraud, legal risks, and physical or environmental risks. Operational risks may be understood as those risks incurred involuntarily in the course of operating a business, as opposed to risks voluntarily incurred in order to generate income, such as interest rate, credit, and similar risks intrinsic to balance sheet activities.

How is operational risk managed by a bank?

Banks generally use an approach called the advanced measurement approach. In this approach, analysts try to measure operational risk (including the risks inherent in off-balance-sheet, fee-based activities or fiduciary risk). To do so, they aggregate statistical data and use sophisticated modeling based on the number of negative incidents occurring in the past and the magnitude of losses associated with those occurrences. Probability theory is then applied, and estimates of future risk are derived.

A problem with this are so-called black swan events—game-changing events with high impact that do not appear in historical data and are not susceptible to estimation. The term *black swan*, previously used only in mathematical circles, was applied to economics and popularized by Nassim Nicholas Taleb in his influential 2007 book *The Black Swan: The Impact of the Highly Improbable*.[33]

Another challenge is strategic and reputational risks, which are not considered to be operational under Basel standards, yet they can have an enormous impact.

Strategic risks relate to decisions. Consider poor expansion decisions, changes in business activity focus, encroachment of competition, and similar risks. In assessing strategic risks, an acquirer needs to ask, this: how does this bank stand in relation to its competition? What are its competitive strengths and weaknesses?

Reputational risks can be ongoing (e.g., when a bank has a bad reputation for customer service), or they can be single-incident driven (such as an incident of fraud). Reputational risks can be more difficult to predict and contain. The question here is how the public views the target.

How can banks manage risk, according to Basel standards?

Basel standards (as discussed in Chapter 10) recommend that banks use any one of three approaches:

- The basic indicator approach, which establishes the banks required allocation of capital to operational risk capital as a percentage of its annual gross revenue. For example, according to Basel standards, operational capital reserved for operational risks should be about 12 percent of regulatory capital.
- The standardized approach, which divides the activities of a bank into eight business lines, then applies a fixed percentage of risk capital to each. These range from 12 to 18 percent, depending on the business line. The business lines are corporate finance, payment and settlement, agency services, asset management, commercial banking, retail banking, trading and sales, and retail brokerage.
- The advanced measurement approach, discussed above

Aside from the ratios and modeling discussed previously and from compliance with Basel standards, what is the role of bank managers in managing risks overall?

Although all the standards mentioned earlier are important, management and management policies are where it all begins. Modeling and stress testing should be viewed as situation analysis—important but insufficient. By contrast, close management and management policies are the ongoing life blood of risk management. These need to be reviewed carefully in due diligence, at times in the preliminary stage to derive an overall impression and at other times in the final stage to confirm and verify.

How can an acquirer assess a bank's risk management in general? According to the FDIC, common risk elements observed at troubled or failed de novo institutions during their first seven years of operation include

- Rapid growth
- Overreliance on volatile funding sources
- Concentrations without compensating controls
- Significant deviations from approved business plans
- Noncompliance with the order approving deposit insurance
- Weak risk management practices
- Unseasoned loan portfolios
- Significant consumer protection problems
- Problematic third-party relationships

STRESS TESTING

When conducting preliminary due diligence on a bank, how important is "stress testing"?

Stress testing is a good idea for banks today whether required by regulators or not. The practice of stress testing emerged in the wake of the 2007–2009 financial crisis. During that period, U.S. banking regulators issued extensive guidance on this process.[34] Stress testing is a series of exercises (including baseline scenario, adverse scenario, and severely adverse scenario) used to assess the potential impact of various possible future adverse events and scenarios on a banking organization. For example, the stress test undergone by Bank of America in September 2013 ran the bank holding company through a hypothetical scenario that saw real GDP falling 4 percent over six quarters and the unemployment rate rising to 11.7 percent, increasing four full percentage points over eight quarters.

In addition, the scenario assumed house prices would decline 21 percent from first quarter 2013 levels without any appreciable recovery. The international component of the severely adverse scenario included a 5 percent decline in Eurozone real GDP, an almost 11 percent decline in Japan's real GDP, a severe slowdown in China, and a surge in Canadian unemployment of over 5 percentage points. The scenario also assumed high equity market volatility and an equity market decline of almost 60 percent.[35] Such stress testing makes sense as a process to be used by any potential acquirer making a bank acquisition.

As a required practice, stress testing is relatively new. In 2011 stress testing became required for all large banks overseen by the FDIC, the Federal Reserve (Fed), and the Office of the Comptroller of the Currency (OCC)—the three main bank regulators. Their joint guidance on stress testing is applicable to all institutions supervised by the agencies with more than $10 billion in total consolidated assets.

- With respect to the FDIC, these banking organizations include state nonmember banks, state savings associations, and insured branches of foreign banks.
- For the Fed, these banking organizations include state member banks, bank holding companies, savings and loan holding companies, and all other institutions for which the Federal Reserve is the primary federal supervisor.
- For the OCC, these banking organizations include national banking associations, federal savings associations, and federal branches and agencies.

Are there any limitations to stress testing as a way of assessing risk?

Absolutely. Stress testing merely studies the quality of the bank's assets and the pressures of its liabilities. It does not pretend to pass judgment on a bank's internal controls. Sometimes, despite a healthy balance of assets and liabilities, a bank can experience financial challenges as a consequence of weak internal controls. This is why the Federal Reserve devotes extensive coverage to internal controls in its *Commercial Bank Examination Manual.*[36] Many of the standard ratios used for financial analysis apply to banks. For a comprehensive list of relevant ratios, see Appendix 5-A.[37]

What is an example of a bank that had good results on a stress test but then experienced a crisis? How did that affect its rating?

In March 2012, the Fed released the results of stress testing for the $10 billion-plus banks it oversees. Fifteen out of 19 banks passed the test—in results challenged by some of the losing banks.[38] One of the banks to pass was JPMorgan Chase.

In May of that year, however, a $2 billion trading loss tarnished the bank's reputation, leading to a decline in share price that amounted to $20 billion by at one peak-to-trough point. By May of the following year, the loss was being reported as a $6 billion hit. The bank's CEO himself said that the trades were "flawed, complex, poorly reviewed, poorly executed, and poorly monitored."[39] In reports issued in January 2013, JPMorgan management and the board analyzed what had gone wrong, making recommendations on how to avoid such calamities in the future.[40] Also, in a separate development that came to light in early 2013, a unit of JPMorgan was accused of rigging electricity rates. The bank settled with the Federal Energy Regulatory Commission for $410 million in July 2013.

Despite these developments, JPMorgan passed its March 2013 stress test. One reason was that it had been preparing for a rise in interest rates and yield (and thus a drop in bond prices), one of the scenarios tested.

Yet only time will tell the ultimate impact of JPMorgan's negative events on future stress test results. Judging from stock market trends, which have been positive for the bank, it does not appear that these negative events have put a major financial strain on the bank, at least not in the eyes of Wall Street: the JPMorgan stock price rose gradually and steadily throughout this crisis.

CONCLUDING COMMENTS

When it comes to bank M&A, valuation and due diligence are inseparable. To develop even the most general idea of bank value, a close look at the record is required. Approaches to valuation vary, but for banks, the balance sheet is a key component. However, revenue and income are also vitally important to understand when it comes to the financial structure of banks. The astute acquirer will look at these elements but also be aware of risks and stresses—the subject of much testing in this postcrisis era. The next chapter will show how to delve deeper into all of these issues.

APPENDIX 5-A

Summary Ratios from the Federal Financial Institutions Examination Council's Uniform Bank Performance Report User's Guide[41]

1 **Interest Income on a Tax Equivalent (TE) Basis?**

Interest Income (TE) as a percent of Average Assets

All income from earning assets plus the tax benefit on tax-exempt loans, leases, and municipal securities, divided by average assets.

2 **Interest Expense**

Interest Expense as a percent of Average Assets

Total interest expense divided by average assets.

3 **Net Interest Income (TE)**

Net Interest Income (TE) as a percent of Average Assets

Total interest income, plus the tax benefit on tax-exempt income, less total interest expense, divided by average assets.

4 **Noninterest Income**

Noninterest Income as a percent of Average Assets

Income derived from bank services and sources other than interest-bearing assets, divided by average assets.

5 **Noninterest Expense**

Noninterest Expense as a percent of Average Assets

Salaries and employee benefits, expenses of premises and fixed assets and other Noninterest expense divided by average assets.

6 **Provision: Loan & Lease Losses**

Provision for Loan & Lease Losses as a percent of Average Assets

Provision for loan and lease receivables losses divided by average assets.

7 **Pretax Operating Income (TE)**

Pretax Operating Income (TE) as a percent of Average Assets

Net interest income on a tax-equivalent basis plus Noninterest income, less noninterest expenses, the provision for loan and lease-financing receivables losses and the provision for allocated transfer risk, divided by average assets.

8 **Realized Gains/Losses Sec**

Realized Gains(Losses) on the sale of Securities as a percent of Average Assets

Pretax net gains or losses from the sale, exchange, retirement, or redemption of securities not held in trading accounts divided by average assets. After December 31, 1993, includes available-for-sale and held-to-maturity transactions.

9 **Pretax Net Operating Income (TE)**

Pretax Net Operating Income (TE) as a percent of Average Assets

Pretax operating income, plus securities gains or losses divided by average assets.

10 **Net Operating Income**

Net Operating Income as a percent of Average Assets

After tax net operating income, including securities gains or losses (which does not include extraordinary gains or losses), divided by average assets.

11 **Adjusted Net Operating Income**

Adjusted Net Operating Income as a percent of Average Assets

Net operating income after taxes and securities gains or losses, plus the provision for possible loan and lease losses, less net loan and lease losses, divided by average assets.

12 Net Income Attributed to Minority Interests

Net Income Attributed to Minority Interests as a percent of Average Assets

Net income attributed to minority interests divided by average assets. A minority interest is the portion of equity in a bank's subsidiary not attributable, directly or indirectly, to the parent bank. If the amount reported in this item is a net loss, enclose it in parentheses.

13 Net Income Adjusted Sub S

Net Income Adjusted for Subchapter S Status as a percent of Average Assets

Net income after securities gains or losses, extraordinary gains or losses, and applicable taxes, adjusted for Subchapter S status divided by average assets. Estimated income taxes is substituted for any reported applicable income taxes for banks that indicate Subchapter S status. Estimated income taxes: Federal income tax rates are applied to net income before extraordinary items and taxes plus nondeductible interest expense to carry tax-exempt securities less tax-exempt income from securities issued by states and political subdivisions, less tax-exempt income from leases, less tax-exempt income from other obligations of states and political subdivisions. This ratio will only be displayed for banks that elect Subchapter S status.

14 Net Income

Net Income as a percent of Average Assets

Net income after securities gains or losses, extraordinary gains or losses, and applicable taxes divided by average assets.

15 Average Earning Assets to Average Assets

Average Earning Assets as a percent of Average Assets

Year-to-date average of average total loans (net of unearned income) in domestic and foreign offices, lease-financing receivables, U.S. Treasury, agency and corporation obligations, mortgage backed securities, other securities, assets held in trading accounts, interest-bearing balances due from depository institutions, and federal funds sold and securities purchased under agreements to resell, plus a five-period average of interest-only strips (mortgage loans and other) and equity securities divided by average assets.

16 Average Interest-Bearing Funds to Average Assets

Average Interest-Bearing Funds as a percent of Average Assets

Average interest-bearing domestic and foreign office deposits, federal funds purchased and securities sold under agreements to repurchase, other borrowed money, and notes and debentures subordinated to deposits, divided by average assets.

17 Interest Income (TE) to Average Earning Assets

Interest Income (TE) as a percent of Average Earning Assets

Total interest income on a tax-equivalent basis divided by the average of the respective asset accounts involved in generating that income.

18 Interest Expense to Average Earning Assets

Interest Expense to Average Earning Assets

Total interest expense divided by the average of the respective asset accounts involved in generating interest income.

19 Net Interest Income (TE) to Average Earning Assets

Net Interest Income (TE) as a percent of Average Earning Assets

Total interest income on a tax-equivalent basis, less total interest expense, divided by the average of the respective asset accounts involved in generating interest income.

20 Net Loss to Average Total LN&LS

Net Loss as a percent of Average Total Loans and Leases

Gross loan and lease charge-off, less gross recoveries (includes allocated transfer risk reserve charge-off and recoveries), divided by average total loans and leases.

21 Earnings Coverage of Net Losses (X)

Earnings Coverage of Net Losses (X)

Net operating income before taxes, securities gains or losses, and extraordinary items, plus the provision for possible loan and lease losses divided by net loan and lease losses. If gross recoveries exceed gross losses, NA, for not applicable, is shown.

22 LN&LS Allowance to LN&LS Not HFS

Ending balance of the allowance for possible loan and lease losses divided by total loans and lease-financing receivables not held for sale.

23 LN&LS Allowance to Net Losses (X)

Loan and Lease Allowance to Net Loss (times)

Ending balance of the allowance for possible loan and lease-financing receivable losses divided by net loan and lease losses. If gross recoveries exceed gross losses, NA is shown.

24 LN&LS Allowance to Total LN&LS

Loan and Lease Allowance to Total Loans and Leases

Ending balance of the allowance for possible loan and lease losses divided by total loans and lease-financing receivables.

25 Total LN&LS-90+ Days Past Due

Total Loans and Leases 90+ Days Past Due to Gross Loans and Leases

The sum of loans and lease financing receivables past due at least 90 days, and still in accrual status, divided by gross loans and lease-financing receivables outstanding.

26 Total LN&LS-Nonaccrual/Nonaccrual

Total LN&LS/Nonaccrual

Total loans and leases on nonaccrual status divided by total loans and leases.

27 Noncurrent Loans and Leases to Gross Loans and Leases

Noncurrent Loans and Leases to Gross Loans and Leases

The sum of loans and lease financing receivables past due at least 90 days, plus those in nonaccrual status, divided by gross loans and lease-financing receivables outstanding.

28 Net Non-Core Fund Dep New $250M

Net Non Core Funding Dependence $250M

Noncore liabilities less short-term investments divided by long-term assets. Noncore liabilities defined using deposit insurance limits [$250,000] for time deposits.

29 Net Loans & Leases to Assets

Net Loans and Leases to Total Assets

Loans and lease-financing receivables net of unearned income and the allowance for possible loans and lease financing receivable losses divided by total assets.

30 Tier One Leverage Capital

Tier One Leverage Capital

Tier One Leverage Ratio.

31 Cash Dividends to Net Income

Cash Dividends to Net Income

Total of all cash dividends declared year-to-date divided by net income year-to-date. If net income is less than or equal to zero, NA is shown.

32 Retained Earnings to Average Total Equity

Retained Earnings to Average Total Equity

Net income, less cash dividends declared, divided by average equity capital.

33 Restructured Loans + Nonaccrual Loans + Real Estate Acquired to Equity Capital + Loan and Lease Allowance

The sum of loans and leases which are on nonaccrual, restructured but 30–89 days past due, restructured but over 90 days past due, restructured and in compliance with modified terms and non-investment other real estate owned divided by the sum of total equity capital plus the allowance for possible loan and lease losses.

34 Total Assets

The annual change in total liabilities and capital. The annual change is the percent change from the prior year comparable quarter to the current quarter.

35 Tier One Capital

Tier One Capital 12-month growth rate. The percentage is determined by subtracting the account balance as of the corresponding reporting period in the previous year from the current period account balance and dividing the result by the previous year balance.

36 Net Loans & Leases

Net Loans and Leases 12-month growth rate. The percentage is determined by subtracting the account balance as of the corresponding reporting period in the previous year from the current period account balance and dividing the result by the previous year balance.

37 Short-Term Investments

Short-Term Investments 12-month growth rate.

The percentage is determined by subtracting the account balance as of the corresponding reporting period in the previous year from the current period account balance and dividing the result by the previous year balance. Short-term investments equals the sum of interest-bearing bank balances + federal funds sold + securities purchased under agreements to resell + debt securities with a remaining maturity of one year or less.

38 Short-Term Non-Core Funding

Short Term Non-Core Funding 12-month growth rate.

The percentage is determined by subtracting the account balance as of the corresponding reporting period in the previous year from the current period account balance and dividing the result by the previous year balance.

CHAPTER 6

Confirmatory Bank Due Diligence

Trust but verify.

—*Ronald Reagan*

Confirmatory due diligence of a bank acquisition target is a time for digging deeper. Once a potential acquirer has conducted a preliminary study or preliminary due diligence of a target bank to estimate its value, risks, and a ballpark price, then it is time for a closer look at the bank in light of a future combination. In Chapter 6, we described the main factors of a bank's typical balance sheet and income statement, which can be used to analyze (as well as manage) various bank risks, and reported commonly used ratios. We also discussed the related topics of stress testing. In this chapter, we will take a closer look at bank solvency through an in-depth review of finances, management, legal compliance, and deal documentation. This extensive process is known as formal or confirmatory due diligence.

CONFIRMATORY DUE DILIGENCE

What does confirmatory due diligence for bank acquisition entail?

The basic function of due diligence in any bank merger or acquisition (or any merger, for that matter) is to assess (usually at the preliminary due diligence stage, as described in Chapter 5) and verify (usually at the confirmatory due diligence stage) the potential risks of a proposed transaction by inquiring more deeply into, and verifying independently, all relevant aspects of the past, present, and predictable future of the bank to be purchased. The concept of due diligence is also used in securities law to describe the duty of care and review to be exercised by officers, directors, underwriters, and others in connection with public offerings of securities.

Although the term *due diligence* is applied in securities law—statutory law set by legislatures—the term itself originated in so-called common law (also known as *case* law), the law that develops through decisions of judges in settling actual disputes. In this type of law, as opposed to law passed by legislatures, judges use the precedents of previous case decisions in order to render their own decisions. Much of U.S. common law has been codified in the statutes of individual states and in a broadly used document called the Uniform Commercial Code—not to be confused with the U.S. Code, which sets forth statutory laws enacted by Congress, or the Code of Federal Regulations (C.F.R.), listing regulations based on those laws.

The due diligence effort in a bank merger transaction should include basic activities to meet diligence standards of common law and best practices. If a bank is ensured by the Federal Deposit Insurance Corporation (FDIC), the acquirer can use the FDIC's bank examination outline to conduct due diligence (see Appendix 6-A).

What are the basic steps of confirmatory due diligence for a bank acquisition?

In a sense, confirmatory due diligence is "déjà vu all over again" because it goes over the same ground covered in the preliminary valuation process. In the confirmatory stage, managers and professionals review initial findings (or hunches) in greater depth.

Confirmatory due diligence activities for a bank merger include the following:

- *Further financial statements review:* to actually confirm the existence and accuracy of assets, liabilities, and equity in the balance sheet, which in turn will further verify the results of financial operations of the bank based on the income statement.

The income statement and balance sheet are closely related in so far as balance sheet errors and misstatements feed directly into and out of the income statement. An income statement is an operating statement, while a balance sheet is a statement of financial condition; obviously, financial condition depends in part on operations. During this review of financial statements, internal or external auditors review and verify the results of the earlier review during the valuation phase.

- *Management and operations review:* to determine the quality and reliability of financial statements, systems, and procedures and to gain a further sense of contingencies that might be beyond the obvious ones disclosed in the financial statements
- *Legal compliance review:* to check for the bank's ongoing compliance with the myriad of banking laws that apply to it
- *Document and transaction review:* to ensure that the paperwork of the deal is in order and that the structure of the transaction is appropriate

If the acquirer is buying a bank that is being divested due to an antitrust challenge, it may be the subject of a due diligence review itself. The Department of Justice (DOJ) will want to see evidence that the purchase has the managerial, operational, technical, and financial capability to compete effectively in the market over the long term.[1]

FINANCIAL REVIEW

What does the financial statement review of a bank entail?

In Chapter 5, we reviewed the nature of a bank's balance sheet and income statement, along with risks in connection with pricing and preliminary due diligence, and gave an overview of stress testing for the largest banks.

As a check against the findings in initial due diligence, it can be helpful to use a bank's main financial disclosure requirements.

One type of checklist is the list of disclosures that bank holding companies must make annually to the Securities and Exchange

Commission (SEC) under the Securities Exchange Act of 1934. Banks must disclose

- Distribution of assets, liabilities, and stockholders' equity
- Interest rates and interest differentials
- Investment portfolios
- Types of amounts of loans
- Summary of loan-loss experience
- Deposits
- Return on equity and assets
- Short-term borrowings

For a more detailed outline, see Appendix 6-B. These disclosures may be incorporated by reference in registration statements made on Form S-4.

What is Form S-4?

Form S-4 is used to register securities in connection with publicy held business combinations and exchange offers. It is required for merging banks as in other industries.[2]

However, the transaction will be automatically effective in 20 days if the transaction meets certain conditions.[3] The bank must publish an annual report compliant with generally accepted accounting principles and cannot have plans to issue more stock in relation to the transaction. Also, there cannot be a material adverse change in the financial condition of the company being acquired since the latest fiscal year.[4]

How can global standards help in the conduct of confirmatory financial due diligence?

In addition to this basic financial analysis (along with verification of the data), a potential acquirer can analyze a potential bank acquisition using global standards. The dominant standards come from the Group of 10 countries that have a mutual borrowing agreement,[5] but this agreement now applies to a larger number of countries (to date, 28) that have formed the Basel Committee. The latest such set of standards is known as Basel III. These standards are discussed in Chapter 10.

What exactly is Basel III, and why does it matter to a bank acquirer?

Basel III, according to the Bank for International Settlements, is the third and latest version of an ongoing series of reform measures developed by the Basel Committee on Banking Supervision to strengthen banks. In recent years, several countries, including the United States with the Dodd–Frank law in 2010, have enacted their own capital standards similar but not identical to Basel III, as described in Chapter 10. The Federal Reserve sets requirements that would apply tougher capital rules for the commercial banks insured by the FDIC.[6]

How does the FDIC review capital adequacy?

According to the FDIC examination manual, the capital adequacy of an institution is rated based on, but not limited to, an assessment of the following evaluation factors:

- The level and quality of capital and the overall financial condition of the institution
- The ability of management to address emerging needs for additional capital
- The nature, trend, and volume of problem assets, and the adequacy of the allowance for loan and lease losses and other valuation reserves
- Balance sheet composition, including the nature and amount of intangible assets, market risk, concentration risk, and risks associated with nontraditional activities
- Risk exposure represented by off-balance-sheet activities
- The quality and strength of earnings and the reasonableness of dividends

- Prospects and plans for growth, as well as past experience in managing growth
- Access to capital markets and other sources of capital, including support provided by a parent holding company

In reviewing the financial health of a bank, regulators will study the status of the bank's basic finances, along the lines of disclosures in any bank prospectus (see Exhibit 6.1).

MANAGEMENT AND OPERATIONS REVIEW

What issues should be considered in the management and operations review?

Perhaps the largest category, and the one that is the most challenging, is human capital—the people a bank employs. Human resources (HR) professionals will have the best insights on this subject. They have professional expertise (and in some cases follow professionally recognized standards) in all aspects of HR.[7]

HR management has multiple parts that can be grouped in many different ways. One recognized way to group them during confirmatory due diligence is as follows:

- Recruitment, retention, and retirement: patterns for these trends at the target bank, including any employment agreements that must be honored
- Performance management and rewards (compensation): identifying any change of control "golden parachute" agreements that the transaction may set in motion
- Career development, succession planning, and education/training
- Leadership structure (reporting relationships): planning leadership and reporting lines in the new entity
- HR systems and initiatives: how the acquired bank has achieved labor law compliance, effective communications with employees, workplace diversity, and so forth[8]

Exhibit 6.1

	As of or for the Year Ended December 31,			2012 Change from 2011	
	2012	2011	2010	Amount	Percent
	(Dollars in thousands, except per share data)				
Summary financial data:					
Total assets	$2,073,129	$1,833,450	$1,659,752	$239,679	13.1%
Total loans	1,641,628	1,406,995	1,283,745	234,633	16.7%
Total deposits	1,823,379	1,637,126	1,470,600	186,253	11.4%
Total revenue	62,445	49,966	46,497	12,479	25.0%
Pre-tax, pre-provision net revenue	24,580	15,972	12,905	8,608	53.9%
Net income (loss) available (attributable) to common shareholders	9,147	5,700	13,410	3,447	60.5%
Diluted earnings (loss) per share	$ 0.47	$ 0.33	$ 0.83	$ 0.14	42.4%
Summary asset quality data:					
Net charge-offs to average loans	0.43%	0.46%	0.31%		
Nonperforming assets to total assets	1.10%	0.90%	0.92%		
Key ratios:					
Net interest margin	3.00%	2.72%	2.66%		
Efficiency ratio	60.64%	68.03%	72.25%		
Return on average equity	5.24%	3.97%	9.68%		
Tier 1 leverage capital ratio	10.35%	10.18%	9.85%		
Tier 1 risk-based capital ratio	10.95%	10.63%	11.48%		
Total risk-based capital ratio	11.88%	11.60%	12.59%		

Aside from human capital, what other factors need to be considered in a management and operations review?

The two main issues for a due diligence management and operations review in any bank merger should be

- IT aka back office technology /bank information systems
- Branch operations

What are the key issues for information technology?

Information technology (IT) is a huge expense for banks in the information age. It exceeds all other noninterest expense categories except salaries. Opportunities may be abundant to cut duplicate IT costs through mergers, but different IT solutions and platforms used by the merger parties can also be a serious negative factor in accomplishing a merger. They can lead to internal strife between the IT groups of the merger parties. These two polarities need to be examined thoroughly in due diligence as they may create integration opportunities or integration nightmares.

Among other IT factors that need to be considered are

- Consistency with the acquiring bank's business goals and/or merger purpose
- Reliability and efficacy of acquirer and target legacy IT systems
- Fit or lack of fit between these systems
- Expenses of integration of two or more separate systems
- Payroll layoffs in one or both IT staffs

What should an acquirer look for when it comes to branch operations?

Banks with a high concentration of consumer or retail business, such as checking accounts, rely on branches not only to administer that business but also to drive it. Types of branches are full-service brick-and-mortar, full-service retail (in-store), and limited service. As a practical matter, ATM machines constitute mini-branches.

Perhaps the most obvious integration opportunity will be to combine close or proximate branch locations. But this is not the only item on the branch consolidator's list. There is also a need for creating or integrating a common presentation, style (how welcoming is a branch?), and branch banking rules and check cashing policies, hours, days of operation, local authority, and IT integration. The exploration and consideration of this aspect of a merger will be of serious concern both at the due diligence phase and at the integration phase.

Closely related to branches in this context are limited service offices, such as loan production offices (see activities list below).

What other activities should an acquirer study?

Other relevant activities are

- Broker/dealer activity
- Insurance
- Internal controls/internal audit function
- Investments
- Marketing/reputation
- Risk management
- Service center operations (e.g., loan production offices)
- Trust activities
- Wire transfer services (domestic and international)

LEGAL AND REGULATORY COMPLIANCE REVIEW

What occurs in a legal compliance review?

A legal compliance reviewer will check to learn of any pending or potential future litigation against the bank to be acquired. This requires general familiarity with both business law and banking law.

What general business laws should be considered when conducting confirmatory due diligence on a bank?

A quick overview of all the main legal areas can be beneficial. Business laws fall into several basic categories. A good corporate law firm will have a litigation department with specialists in all the legal areas that attract the most exposure lawsuits and will be able to tailor due diligence to the bank being studied. In general, law firms divide their litigation practices into the following categories:

- Antitrust
- Bankruptcy
- Employment/labor/pensions
- Environmental
- Intellectual property
- International trade
- Product liability/consumer rights
- Securities litigation
- Tax
- White-collar crime

It is not necessary to go looking for problems in all these areas, but when studying a potential bank, it is good to know what lawsuits it might have had in the past and what programs it now has in place to avoid such problems. In addition, specific banking laws will come into play. In some cases, a law firm will have an entire department focusing on financial services.[9]

What banking laws will come into play in a merger, and how can a due diligence team check for any exposures to liability in these areas?

The skilled due diligence team will be generally familiar with banking law, as described earlier in Chapter 2 (see Appendix 2-A).

There are several general principles of banking that have been expressed in law and that are also areas of challenge for bank operations. They are fair disclosure to customers, respect for customer privacy, fair lending (especially locally), and various protections against fraud and money laundering. When law firms have a financial services practice area, they will typically be expert in these specific areas.[10]

What are some common banking laws in these areas?

In order of passage, key consumer-focused laws include

- Truth in Lending Act (1968), Pub. L. 90-321. This law has been amended 28 times since enactment, most recently via the Dodd–Frank Act of 2010.
- Fair Credit Reporting Act of 1970, Pub. L. 91-508
- Equal Credit Opportunity Act (1974), Title VII of the Consumer Credit Protection Act, Pub. L. 90-321, 82 Stat. 146
- Real Estate Settlement Procedures Act (1974), Pub. L. 93-533
- Community Reinvestment Act (1977), Pub. L. 95-128, Title VIII of the Housing and Community Development Act of 1977

In addition to these federal laws, banks need to attend to state usury and installment sale statutes.

In general, the newer the law, the more likely it is that the bank has not yet fully integrated or institutionalized compliance into its operations. Therefore, an effective compliance review starts with the most recent laws—namely, Dodd–Frank and related rules and regulations, as discussed in Chapter 2.

DOCUMENT AND TRANSACTION REVIEW

When it comes to approval of an actual merger, what laws come into play?

As for merger approval, counsel should be familiar with antitrust and securities laws.

What are some key points to know about antitrust laws when it comes to bank mergers?

As noted in Chapter 2, antitrust regulators rarely reject bank mergers, but they often require divestitures. When antitrust regulators examine mergers, they ask, among other things, if the merger causes horizontal and/or vertical integration (structure) and if it enables collusion and/or exclusion (conduct). Any given transaction could raise issues in any of the four quadrants (see Exhibit 6.2). Horizontal integration occurs when two competitors merge. Vertical integration occurs when a customer and supplier merge. Most bank mergers involve horizontal structures.

What are the main U.S. antitrust laws?

The three main U.S. antitrust laws are the Sherman Act and the Clayton Act, which outlaw monopolies, and the Hart–Scott–Rodino Antitrust Improvements Act, which requires the parties to a proposed acquisition transaction to furnish certain information about themselves and the deal to the Antitrust Division of the DOJ and to the Federal Trade Commission (FTC).

Exhibit 6.2 An Antitrust Quadrant for M&A Due Diligences

	Structure	Conduct
Vertical		
Horizontal		

Antitrust regulators ask if mergers cause vertical and/or horizontal integration and if it enables collusion and/or exclusion (conduct). Any given transaction could raise issues in any of the four quadrants.

What should bank acquirers know about the Sherman Act?

The Sherman Act has 20 sections. For the purpose of due diligence for M&A, the most important ones to know are

- Section 1, outlawing restraint of trade or commerce
- Second 2, outlawing monopoly
- Section 18, outlawing the purchase of stock with the intention to monopolize.

A key question—and one that pertains to bank M&A—is whether regulators consider parents and subsidiaries to be separate companies or one company when it comes to accusing companies of restraining trade or commerce, or trying to monopolize. Fortunately, the general consensus is that parents and subsidiaries are considered to be one company, so they cannot be accused of colluding. However, when one company owns only a minority share in another company, the courts may find antitrust violations.

What exactly does the Clayton Act say?

The two key sections of the Clayton Act are Sections 7 and 8.

Section 7 of the Clayton Act, which is enforced by the FTC and the DOJ, prohibits a corporation from acquiring the stock or assets of another corporation if the acquisition might "substantially lessen competition or tend to create a monopoly" in any line of commerce in any section of the country. A violation of Section 7 may give rise to a court-ordered injunction against the acquisition, an order compelling divestiture of the property or other interests, or other remedies.

Section 8 of the Clayton Act disallows any person from serving as a director or officer of two companies that are competing in the same industry or market, if the companies have a certain market value and/or sales level, with thresholds set annually based on the change in gross national product. As of 2013, no person can serve as a director or officer of two competing organizations if each competitor has capital, surplus, and undivided profits aggregating more than $28,883,000, except that neither corporation is covered if the competitive sales of either corporation are less than $2,888,300.

The DOJ's Antitrust Division has published the *Policy Guide to Merger Remedies* in which it spells out what acquirers can do to satisfy antitrust concerns.[11] It classifies these remedies as follows:

- Structural remedies
  - Divestiture of all assets necessary for the purchaser to be an effective, long-term competitor
  - Divestiture of an existing business entity
  - Divesting rights to critical intangible assets
- Conduct remedies
  - Firewall provisions: preventing improper dissemination of information within a firm
  - Nondiscrimination provisions: requiring acquirer to offer equal terms to the acquired firm's competitors
  - Mandatory licensing provisions: when an acquirer would license technology or other assets on fair and reasonable terms that would prevent harm to competition
  - Transparency provisions: requiring the merged companies to make disclosures to regulators beyond the normal scope
  - Antiretaliation provisions: preventing the acquirer from retaliating based on competition by competitors or complaints by customers
  - Prohibitions on restrictive or exclusive contracts with customers

There can also be "hybrid remedies" that combine both structural and conduct elements.

How do the three main banking regulators—the Fed, the FDIC, and the Office of the Comptroller of the Currency (OCC)—play a role here?

The DOJ guide states that whenever the Antitrust Division is considering a remedy for a merger in a regulated industry, it will collaborate with the appropriate regulatory agency.

Mergers of companies with foreign operations or subsidiaries sometimes require review and approval by foreign governments. In addition, some foreign countries (most notably Canada) have their own premerger notification programs that require compliance. See Chapter 10.

What does the Hart–Scott–Rodino Act say?

The Hart–Scott–Rodino Antitrust Improvements Act of 1976 (the HSR Act), as mentioned in Chapter 2, requires the parties to a proposed acquisition transaction to furnish certain information about themselves and the deal to the FTC and the Antitrust Division of the DOJ before the merger is allowed to go forward. The information supplied is used by these government agencies to determine whether the proposed transaction would have any anticompetitive effects after completion. If so, in general, these effects must be cured prior to the transaction's closing. A mandatory waiting period follows the agencies' receipt of the HSR filings.

What mergers or acquisitions require premerger notification under the HSR Act?

Generally, all mergers and acquisitions that meet three size criteria must be reported under the HSR Act and the related premerger notification rules. Size criteria are adjusted annually.

The following sizes now trigger review, effective February 2013:

- As a result of the transaction, the acquiring firm will hold an aggregate total amount of voting securities, assets, and/or interests in noncorporate entities of the acquired firm valued in excess of $70.9 million. (Transactions larger than $283.6 million are reportable, regardless of this size of person test.)
- One of the firms has annual net sales or total assets of $141.8 million or more, and the other has annual net sales or total assets of $14.2 million or more.
- One of the persons involved is engaged in U.S. commerce or in an activity affecting U.S. commerce.[12]

The "persons" in the transaction include not only the corporations that are directly involved, but also any other corporation that is under common control. "Control," for purposes of the HSR Act, is defined as ownership of 50 percent or more of a company's voting securities or having the contractual power to designate a majority of a company's board of directors. Special control rules apply to partnerships and other unincorporated entities. The HSR Act has additional thresholds for occasions when an acquirer who previously bought only part of a company buys additional shares.

About how many HSR notifications do the FTC and DOJ receive every year, and what percentage are for bank mergers?

Over the past 10 years the number of reports has varied from 1,000 to more than 2,000 per year. In fiscal 2012, the agencies received reports on 1,429 transactions, of which 1.6 percent were banks (as sources of credit intermediation).[13] In fiscal year 2012, the DOJ's Antitrust Division investigated First Niagara's proposed acquisition of HSBC Bank USA involving acquisition of 195 HSBC branches in New York and Connecticut and required divestiture of 26 branches with approximately $1.6 billion in deposits in Erie, Niagara, and Orleans Counties, New York. The division approved the transaction contingent to the divestitures, and pending approval by the OCC, which gave final approval in April 2012.[14]

What information is required to be included in the HSR premerger notification form?

The HSR Notification and Report form requires a description of the parties and the proposed merger or acquisition, certain current financial information about the parties, and a breakdown of the revenues of the parties according to industry. The FTC and DOJ use this breakdown of revenues to determine whether the proposed combination of the businesses would result in anticompetitive effects. The information filed is exempt from disclosure under the Freedom of Information Act, and no such information may be made public except pursuant to administrative or judicial proceedings.

After the premerger notification form has been filed, how long must the parties wait before the merger or acquisition can be consummated?

When the acquisition is being made by a cash tender offer, the parties must wait 15 days before the purchaser may accept shares for payment. In all other cases, the parties must wait 30 days before the transaction can be completed. If the acquisition raises antitrust concerns, the government may extend the waiting period by requesting additional information from the parties. In that case, the waiting period is extended for 30 more days (10 more days in the case of a cash tender offer) past the time when the additional information is provided. The parties may request early termination of the waiting period. If the acquisition raises no antitrust concerns, the government may grant the request at its discretion.

Are certain mergers and acquisitions exempt from giving notice under the HSR Act?

Yes. Acquisitions made through newly formed corporate acquisition vehicles are frequently exempt from the reporting requirements of the HSR Act because the vehicle does not meet the "size of person" test.

Special rules are also used to determine the size of a newly formed corporation, and care must be taken to avoid making contractual commitments for additional capital contributions or for guarantees of the new corporation's obligations until after the formation has been completed. In general, the assets of a newly formed acquisition vehicle do not include funds contributed to the vehicle or borrowed by the vehicle at the closing to complete the acquisition. The HSR Act and FTC rules also provide numerous exemptions for special situations.

Just because a transaction is exempt from HSR does not mean that it will be approved by regulators, however. Regulators are perpetually concerned about market concentration caused by horizontal mergers and have issued additional guidelines concerning such mergers.

What about securities laws?

The federal securities laws require that the issuers of securities make certain disclosures at certain times. These disclosure rules ensure that anyone who buys or sells securities has the basic information necessary to determine their value. The laws also ensure that all shareholders have equal access to such material information, as those who have access to material nonpublic information *are restricted from trading*.

All these laws are enforced by the SEC, which was established under the Securities Act of 1933 and the Securities Exchange Act of 1934 as an independent, nonpartisan, quasi-judicial regulatory agency charged with administering federal securities laws.

The SEC also regulates firms engaged in the purchase or sale of securities, people who provide investment advice, and investment companies, such as mutual funds.

What are the primary federal securities laws?

The primary securities laws that may apply to banks are as follows:

- *Securities Act of 1933.* This law requires that investors receive financial and other information concerning securities that are being offered for public sale. It has led to the promulgation of hundreds of rules and regulations related to the registration of securities and the publication of information related to registration. As mentioned earlier under Financial Review, under this act, there is a detailed guide for the statistical disclosures that must be made by bank holding companies in any prospectus offering securities for sale.[15]
- *Securities Exchange Act of 1934.* This law requires that investors have access to current financial and other information regarding the securities of publicly held corporations, particularly those that trade on the national exchanges or over the counter. The 1934 act has led to the promulgation of hundreds of rules and regulations concerning the operation of the markets and the actions of participants,

including proxy solicitations by companies and shareholders, tender offers, and buying securities on credit (so-called margin purchases).

- *Investment Company Act of 1940.* This law governs the activities of companies, including mutual funds, that are engaged primarily in investing, reinvesting, and trading in securities, and that offer their own securities to the investing public. Under this law, investment companies are subject to certain statutory prohibitions and to regulation by the SEC. Public offerings of investment company securities must be registered under the Securities Act of 1933.
- *Investment Advisers Act of 1940.* This law contains provisions similar to those in the Securities Exchange Act of 1934 governing the conduct of securities brokers and dealers. It requires that persons or firms who are compensated for advising others about securities investment must register with the SEC and conform to statutory standards designed to protect investors.
- *Trust Indenture Act of 1939.* This law applies to debt securities, including debentures and notes, that are offered for public sale. Even though such securities may be registered under the Securities Act of 1933, they may not be offered for sale to the public unless a formal agreement between the issuer of the bonds and the bondholder, known as a trust indenture, conforms to the statutory standards of this law. This law was revised substantially in 2009, following the global financial crisis of the preceding three years.

This is clearly a broad array of laws for the SEC to enforce, especially given the commission's relatively small size. To extend its reach, the commission relies on what it calls a "public-private partnership." That is, the commission sets standards for the issuance and trading of securities, but much of the direct, day-to-day regulation of the securities market participants is done under SEC oversight by the so-called self-regulatory organizations—stock exchanges.

Federal securities laws give the SEC and/or the stock exchanges enforcement powers. In addition, the investing public itself has the remedy of "private ordering" and/or "private action."

- *Private ordering* refers to mechanisms that enable shareholders and others to propose and adopt changes that are suited to their situations, rather than conforming to a law that sets a single standard.
- *Private right of action* refers to the right to sue in court based on the language or implications of a law.

What is the role of state securities laws?

State securities laws, commonly known as blue sky laws, set forth registration requirements for brokers and dealers, registration requirements for securities to be sold within the state, and prohibitions against fraud in the sale of securities.

A majority of states, with the notable exception of New York and California, have adopted the Uniform Securities Act (USA) of 1956, which is frequently updated.

In addition, there are state corporate statutes governing corporate existence, charters, and bylaws. These establish the rights of the holders of securities. Corporate statutes vary from state to state, but there is some uniformity, thanks to the influence of Delaware corporate law (which is often used as a prototype for state corporate statutes) and the Model Business Corporation Act, which was first created in 1946 and is regularly updated under the auspices of a committee of the Business Law Section of the American Bar Association (ABA).

FEDERAL SECURITIES LAW PERTAINING TO PUBLIC COMPANIES

What are the most important federal laws to consider when conducting due diligence on an acquisition involving a public company?

At the federal level, securities laws are encompassed in two of the laws mentioned earlier: the Securities Act of 1933 (commonly referred to as the

Securities Act), which sets forth registration requirements for companies seeking to sell securities to the public, and the more extensive Securities Exchange Act of 1934 (commonly called the Exchange Act), which sets the disclosure and filing requirements.

In general, Securities Act rules are numbered from 100 on up, based on when they were approved, while Exchange Act rules are numbered from 01 on up, after sections. Thus, for example, under Section 10(b), there are rules from 10b–1 on up. Regulations and forms are also named in accordance with sections.

The basic text of these laws has been amended and expanded over time and now includes hundreds of related rules. Rules of the Securities Act and the Securities Exchange Act have undergone many amendments and additions.

Could you give an overview of all the Securities Act and Exchange Act rules pertaining to mergers or acquisitions?

M&A transactions are complex and situation-specific, so any given transaction could require knowledge of one or more of hundreds of securities laws. In any transaction involving a public company, it will be important to engage the services of an experienced securities lawyer, whether as inside or outside counsel or both.

That said, here is a brief list of the Securities Act and Exchange Act rules that are most relevant to M&A.

Key Securities Act rules for M&A include the following:

- Rule 144 provides an exemption from registering with the SEC for certain securities sales where there are a small number of buyers who meet certain requirements.
- Rule 145 rescinds a previous exemption by including reclassification of securities, mergers, consolidations, and acquisitions of assets as events requiring registration with the SEC.

Key Exchange Act rules for M&A include the following:

- 10b-1 to 10b-21 ban “manipulative and deceptive devices and contrivances.”

- 13d-1 to 13f-1 under Regulation 13(d) require disclosure (on Schedule 13D or 13G) of beneficial ownership of 5 percent or more within 10 days.
- 14a-1 to 14b-2 under Regulation 14(a) cover the solicitation of proxies (used to achieve a change of control by getting shareholders to cast proxy votes for a dissident slate).
- 14d-1 to 14d-11 under Regulation 14(d) pertain to tender offers (used to achieve a change of control by getting shareholders to sell or "tender" their shares to the entity making the tender offer).
- 14e-1 to 14e-8 under Regulation 14(e) deal with unlawful tender offer practices, such as short tendering.
- 16b-1 through 16b-8 deal with the timing of sales (curbing illegal insider trading by banning "short-swing" trades by insiders within six months of obtaining shares); Rule 16b-7 exempts mergers, consolidations, and recapitalizations from this rule.

Beyond these rules, there are more than a dozen additional regulations with their own numbering systems and in some cases related forms. Some of these are very general, such as Regulation S-K, which provides additional rules pertaining to securities registration, and Regulation S-X, which gives additional guidance on financial statements. The regulation pertaining specifically to M&A is called Regulation M-A, and it requires the filing of a Schedule TO for tender offers.

Regulation M-A added Items 1000 to 1016 under the Securities Act and the Securities Exchange Act, effective January 24, 2000. This regulation (created entirely by the SEC, not by Congress) is applicable to takeover transactions, including tender offers, mergers, acquisitions, and similar extraordinary transactions. The revised rules permit increased communication with security holders and the markets. The amendments aimed to

- Balance the treatment of cash versus stock tender offers
- Simplify and centralize disclosure requirements
- Eliminate inconsistencies in the treatment of tender offers versus mergers

What exactly is a tender offer?

A tender offer is a public invitation to a corporation's shareholders to purchase their stock for a specified consideration. A short, somewhat tautological definition of a tender offer appears in Exchange Act Rule 13e–4(a)(2). In that rule, the term *issuer tender offer* is defined as "a tender offer for, or a request or invitation for tenders of, any class of equity security, made by the issuer of such class of equity security or by an affiliate of such an issuer."

Most tender offers involve a general, publicized bid by an individual or group to buy the shares of a publicly owned company at a price above or at a premium to the current market price. During a tender offer, the offeror may not directly or indirectly purchase or arrange to purchase, other than pursuant to the tender offer, securities that are the subject of that offer until the end of the offer (Rule 10b–13). This prohibition also includes privately negotiated purchases. Some purchases made before a public announcement may be permissible, even if the purchaser has made the decision to make the tender offer, but purchase agreements that are scheduled to close during the offering period are illegal no matter when they were or are made.

What does Regulation M-A require of companies engaged in tender offers and mergers?

Under Regulation M-A, acquiring companies (referred to as "filing persons") must provide security holders with a summary term sheet, written in plain English, that describes in bullet points the most material terms of the proposed transaction. The summary term sheet must provide security holders with sufficient information to understand the essential features and significance of the proposed transaction. The bullet points must cross-reference more detailed disclosures found in Schedule TO, the disclosure document disseminated to security holders.

Items in the term sheet include

- *Subject company information.* This includes name and address, securities now trading, trading market and place, dividends, prior public offerings, and prior stock purchases. This is basic information about the company whose securities may be acquired.

- *Identity and background of the filing person.* This includes name and address, business background of entities, business background of natural persons, tender offer and class of securities to which the offer relates, and Internet contact, if any.
- *Terms of the transaction.* This includes material terms, purchases from insiders, differing terms for shareholders, appraisal rights, provisions for unaffiliated security holders, and eligibility for listing or trading.
- *Past contacts, transactions, negotiations, and agreements.* This includes details on past transactions between the subject company and the filing person; significant corporate events involving the two, such as a merger, consolidation, acquisition, tender offer, election of a director to the board of the subject company, or sale or transfer of a material amount of assets of the subject company; name of the person who initiated contacts or negotiations; conflicts of interest; and agreements involving the subject company's securities.
- *Purpose of the transaction and plans or proposals.* This includes purposes, use of securities, and subject company negotiations.
- *Source and amount of funds or other consideration.* This includes the source of funds, conditions, and expenses. The filer may request confidentiality regarding the source of borrowed funds.
- *Interest in the securities of the subject company.* This includes securities ownership and securities transactions.
- *Persons and/or assets retained, employed, compensated, or used.* This includes solicitations or recommendations, employees, and/or corporate assets.
- *Financial statements.* This includes financial information, pro forma information, and summary information.
- *Reports, opinions, appraisals, or negotiations.* This includes a description of the report and its preparer.

Regulation M-A also has a section on going-private transactions. Prior to Regulation M-A, individuals who were interested in understanding a transaction had to go to many different reports to get information. The Regulation M-A term sheet provided a way for anyone to see "at a glance" all the material aspects of a merger or acquisition transaction.

Are all securities lawsuits brought under the Securities Act and Exchange Act or related regulations?

No. Other laws may be applied in securities cases. For example, RICO has been applied.

What is RICO, and how could it pertain to bank M&A?

The Racketeer Influenced and Corrupt Organizations Act, or RICO, was passed in 1970 as part of broad anticrime legislation. RICO sets steep penalties, which include asset freezes, treble damages, and up to 20 years in jail, for organizations that engage in a "pattern" of crime. It was first applied in securities fraud cases in the late 1980s in the Southern District of New York under then-U.S. Attorney Rudolph Giuliani. Since that time, the U.S. Supreme Court has clarified some aspects of the law.

Since the 1980s, application of RICO in securities matters has been rare, in part because of judicial interpretations narrowing the application of the statute. In *Holmes v. Securities Corp.* (1992), the high court ruled that RICO plaintiffs must prove that the alleged wrongdoing did direct harm to the plaintiffs. In *Boyle v. United States* (2009), the court affirmed that to be charged under RICO, an entity must have a "structure," defining that to mean, at the very least, "a purpose, relationships among the associates, and longevity sufficient to permit the associates to pursue the enterprise's purpose." These conditions have made it more difficult for the government to accuse merger planners of any kind of racketeering.

However, in the aftermath of the 2007–2009 financial crisis, there was lingering talk of using RICO against banks for alleged conspiracies against customers. Still, before acquiring a bank, merger planners should make sure that there is no pending RICO litigation, as the penalties are severe.

CONCLUDING COMMENTS

Multiple teams consisting of professionals with different expertise conduct due diligence. Depending on the size of the target when examining the more or less pure financial aspects of the target, different auditing samples will be decided upon and applied. Various techniques may also be employed and tested by the professionals, including, so-called "gap analysis" for interest rate sensitivity and stress testing for various scenarios using various techniques for simulation, including the well-known Monte Carlo approach, which estimates the probability of various outcomes by running simulations (trial runs) many times over, using randomly chosen variables.[16]

As a cautionary note, due diligence is not a strictly "by the numbers" game, and no book can address all of the possibilities of postmerger risks and losses. Due diligence is about imagination and sleuthing: talking to management, lending, HR, internal audit, and IT officers at various levels, anticipating integration issues well before they take place. Paying attention to both the adequacy of systems of checks and balances, including credit analysis and credit approval systems, and the degree of actual and consistent compliance with them is important. Like all businesses, banks are ultimately run by people and represent their individual and collective decisions. The people aspect of due diligence should not be given short shrift. Accordingly, the next section of this book begins with a close look at the integration of resources—financial, physical, and—importantly—human.

APPENDIX 6-A

FDIC Bank Examinations: Outline of Areas Examined[17]

Supervisory Issues

- Supervisory Insights
- Composite Ratings Definition List

Safety & Soundness

- FDIC Enforcement Decisions & Orders
- Merger Decisions: Annual Report to Congress
- Risk Management Manual of Examination Policies
- Bank Secrecy Act/Anti-Money Laundering Manual
- Bank Secrecy Act and Anti-Money Laundering
- Guide to the Interagency Country Exposure Review Committee Process
- Guidelines for Payday Lending
- Credit Card Activities Manual
- Credit Card Securitization Manual

Trust

- Trust Examination Overview
- Trust Examination Manual

Information Technology

- FFIEC Information Technology Examination Handbook
- Information Technology Examination Officer's Questionnaire

- Financial Institution Letters (FILs) Addressing Information Technology Issues
- Technology Regulations and Publications for Financial Institutions
- Interagency Guidelines Establishing Information Security Standards Small Entity Compliance Guide (Federal Reserve)

Community Reinvestment Act (CRA)

- CRA Statute & Tools
- CRA Sunshine Requirements
- What is a Performance Evaluation?
- CRA Examination Schedule
- Monthly List of Banks Examined for CRA Compliance
- CRA Ratings & Performance Evaluations
- Applications Subject to CRA & Public Comments
- FDIC CRA Regional Office Contacts
- Community Reinvestment Act (CRA) Interagency Joint Public Hearing

Compliance

- Offshore Outsourcing of Data Services by Insured Institutions and Associated Consumer Privacy Risks
- Offshore Outsourcing of Data Services by Insured Institutions and Associated Consumer Privacy Risks
- Compliance Examination Manual
- Compliance & CRA Examination Guidance
- Mortgage Loan Prequalifications
- Side by Side: A Guide to Fair Lending
- Financial Privacy

APPENDIX 6-B

Statistical Disclosure by Bank Holding Companies (Guide 3: Outline Only)[18]

The SEC has published this guide for description of business portions of bank holding company registration statements for which financial statements are required. The following outline presents the main elements of an extremely detailed set of guidance.

I. *Distribution of Assets, Liabilities and Stockholders' Equity; Interest Rates and Interest Differential*
   - Average balance sheets.
   - Net interest earnings.
   - Dollar amount of change in interest income and the dollar amount of change in interest expense.

II. *Investment Portfolio*
   - Book value of investments in obligations of equity and debt securities.
   - Amount of each investment category listed above which is due for various time periods, with weighted average yield for each range of maturities.
   - Name of any issuer, and the aggregate book value and aggregate market value of the securities of such issuer, when the aggregate book value of such securities exceeds ten percent of stock-holders' equity.

III. *Loan Portfolio*

   Amount of loans in each category listed below (as well as related loan totals):

   Domestic:
   - Commercial, financial and agricultural;
   - Real estate-construction;

- Real estate-mortgage;
- Installment loans to individuals;
- Lease financing.

Foreign:

- Governments and official institutions;
- Banks and other financial institutions;
- Commercial and industrial;
- Other loans.

B. *Maturities and Sensitivities of Loans to Changes in Interest Rates*

C. *Risk Elements*

- Nonaccrual, Past Due and Restructured Loans—provided separately for domestic and for foreign loans for each reported period. (See Appendix 10A for details on "Foreign Outstandings.")

IV. *Summary of Loan Loss Experience*

- Analysis of the Allowance for Loan Losses
- Allocation of the Allowance for Loan Losses

V. *Deposits*

- Amount of and average rate paid on each of the following deposit categories that are in excess of 10 percent of average total deposits (domestic and foreign).
- Categories other than those specified.
- Deposits by foreign depositors in domestic offices (aggregate amount).
- Time certificates of deposit in amounts of $100,000 or more and other time deposits of $100,000 or more (amount outstanding)—both domestic and foreign.

VI. *Return on Equity and Assets* For each reported period, present the following:

- Return on assets (net income divided by average total assets).
- Return on equity (net income divided by average equity).

- Divided payout ratio (dividends declared per share divided by net income per share).
- Equity to assets ratio (average equity divided by average total assets).

VII. Short-Term Borrowings

- The amounts outstanding at the end of the reported period, the weighted average interest rate thereon, and the general terms thereof;
- The maximum amount of borrowings in each category outstanding at any month-end during each reported period;
- The approximate average amounts outstanding during each reported period and the approximate weighted average interest rate thereon.

SECTION 3

SYNERGIES

The first two sections of this book explained the regulatory framework surrounding bank mergers and the strategies and standards that should inform them. This section addresses the equally important topic of synergies, defined as the incremental value created through combination. **Chapter 7, Postmerger Integration for Banks,** explains why and how banks combine their resources, processes, and responsibilities through mergers. **Chapter 8, Bank M&A: Case in Point,** provides a brief but instructive example of success. **Chapter 9, Banking on the Future,** concludes this section by providing a look at the future of banking.

CHAPTER 7

Postmerger Integration for Banks

It has to be a big crescendo. It all has to come together at the same time.

—*Patricia Haxby, Chief Information Officer, Pacific Continental Bank*[1]

Bank mergers often look good on paper, but the true test of their value comes when two or more banks actually merge. No matter what purpose brings them together—be it a need to survive in a changing marketplace, an ambition to achieve rapid growth in assets, the creation of a unique new competitive advantage, or all of these goals combined—merging banks need to consider certain core questions common to every bank merger. How can we retain both acquired and legacy customers? How will the conjoined information technology systems (often referred to as a bank's "back office") function? What previous policies will continue to apply, and which will change? These are some of the practical questions that can arise in any bank merger.

Answers, of course, will vary by institution. Although the combination of two similarly sized banks is called a "merger of equals," in fact no two banks are alike. Each bank contains a unique set of resources, processes, and responsibilities—all of which are in flux at any given time. For this reason, successful postmerger management will involve, as early as possible in the merger process and then throughout the process, an ongoing review of all key resources, processes, and responsibilities, as well as a plan for managing them in the future. This plan may involve combining elements, leaving them separate, or, in some cases, divesting or discontinuing them.[2] While it is beyond the scope of this book to provide guidance on all bank elements to be merged, this chapter will touch on some of the most important ones.

OVERVIEW OF RESOURCES, PROCESSES, AND RESPONSIBILITIES

What is synergy in the M&A context, and how can integration bring it about?

Synergy is a buzzword used to put a positive light on merger transactions. It may or may not apply to any given transaction. Indeed, a well-respected corporate director known for his astute skepticism once said (in a closed meeting): "When I hear the word *synergy*, I stop listening." Yet the concept of synergy is sound. Derived from the root words *syn*, meaning "together," and *ergon*, meaning "work," in the M&A context it means that the value of two companies combined may be greater than the two companies operating separately. Certainly, this concept can apply to bank mergers, if acquirers make a concerted effort to integrate them in the degree and manner that preserves and enhances the economic value of their resources, processes, and responsibilities.

INTEGRATING RESOURCES

Merging bank "resources" is a very broad concept. Where can managers begin?

High priority resources to integrate include financial resources, such as customer accounts and financial reports; physical resources, such as bank branch real estate, whether owned or leased; and human resources, such as branch employees.

Merging Financial Resources

What usually happens to customer accounts in merging banks after a merger?

First, let's recall a few key terms from the opening chapters of this book. A merger is the combination of two or more separate institutions into a single institution, whether via a statutory merger, a consolidation, an acquisition, or the purchase of assets and assumption of liabilities.[3] The single institution that is formed is called the merged institution or the survivor. The bank that is merged into the survivor is called the nonsurvivor.

Beginning with the so-called maintenance period in which the merger took place, the survivor of a merger must maintain its reserve balance requirement and the nonsurvivor's reserve balance requirement in a single master account at the Fed.[4] In most cases, the nonsurvivor's master account will be closed or converted to a subaccount at the time of the merger. For banks that are not operationally prepared to do this closing or conversion at the time of the merger, the Federal Reserve offers a transitional arrangement involving multiple accounts intended to support restructuring after a merger.

The multiple-accounts arrangement, which may last no longer than one year past the effective date of the merger, requires certain steps:

- The surviving entity has to file a single, consolidated FR 2900 form.[5] The combined institution will receive one exemption amount (the amount of an institution's reservable liabilities subject to a 0 percent reserve requirement)[6] and one "low reserve" tranche. (For more on tranches, see Chapter 2.)[7]
- The reserve balance requirement for the merged institution will be calculated from the deposit data provided on the consolidated FR 2900 form.
- For the maintenance period in which the merger took place, the balances in the survivor's master account and the balances in the nonsurvivor's former master account are combined to satisfy the merged institution's reserve balance requirement. After this period, only the surviving entity's master account balances can satisfy this requirement; the balances in the transitional account cannot be used for this purpose.
- Also, only the surviving entity's master account may hold respondent pass-through balances maintained to satisfy reserve balance requirements.

What requirements do bank regulators impose on postmerger financial statements?

The three bank regulators—the Federal Reserve (Fed), the Office of the Comptroller of the Currency (OCC), and the Federal Deposit Insurance Corporation (FDIC)—have a joint standard for financial statement integration, namely, the Uniform Bank Performance Report (UBPR). This report was developed by the Federal Financial Institutions Examination Council (FFIEC) for bank supervisory, examination, and management purposes. Bankers and examiners alike use these reports to assess banks' financial condition.

If the bank has gone through a merger, the UBPR report notes this (on page 1) and may make adjustments to the financial report accordingly. In general, the UBPR does not try to make any historical adjustments to restate information prior to the date of a merger.[8] However, after a significant merger—defined as one that causes assets to grow more than 25 percent—the UBPR does attempt to minimize the effects of the merger on year-to-date profitability, yield, and rate calculations by adjusting them to include only average assets and liabilities reported after the merger; premerger asset data are ignored in the year of the merger. (Income and expense data are used as reported without adjustment, except for some aspects of the reporting under push-down accounting, as described below.)

The UBPR adjusts one quarter annualized earnings ratios when push-down accounting is indicated. The adjustment applies only to income and expense data. Average asset and liability data are not adjusted because they apply only to one quarter. When push-down accounting is indicated for an individual bank, the UBPR does not subtract prior from current income or expense items to develop data for one quarter. Instead, the income or expense item is annualized as reported.

What exactly is push-down accounting, and how does it affect general financial results (not just the UBPR report) in a merger?

Push-down accounting refers to the establishment of a new accounting and reporting basis in an acquired bank's separate financial statements, following the purchase and substantial change of ownership of its outstanding voting equity securities. The acquirer's purchase price is "pushed down" to the acquired bank and is then used to restate the carrying value of that bank's assets and liabilities. Push-down accounting is accepted under U.S. generally accepted accounting principles (GAAP) but not under International Financial Reporting Standards (IFRS).[9]

For example, if an acquirer buys all of a target's voting equity securities, it would then restate those assets and liabilities using fair market values, so that the entire excess of the restated amounts of the assets over the restated amounts of the liabilities exactly equals the buyer's purchase price.

If a bank is acquired by another institution during the reporting fiscal year, and the acquirer uses push-down accounting in its financial statements, the acquired bank should not include income or expense for the period of the calendar year prior to the acquisition date for comparative purposes in its future self-examinations. (This would be like comparing apples and oranges, since the two accounting methods are different.)

The UBPR uses an annualization algorithm to reflect the actual number of days that have elapsed since a push-down transaction was reported. The algorithm divides the number of days in the year by the number of days since a push-down transaction was reported. For affected banks, the revised annualization factor will replace the standard annualization factor in the relevant year.

In what circumstances should push-down accounting be applied?

The Securities and Exchange Commission (SEC) requires the use of push-down accounting by public enterprises with respect to target corporations that are substantially or wholly owned. The SEC stated that when the form of ownership is within the control of the buyer, the basis of accounting for purchased assets and liabilities should be the same regardless of whether the entity continues to exist or is merged into the buyer. The SEC recognized, however, that the existence of outstanding public debt, preferred stock, or a significant minority interest in a subsidiary might affect the buyer's ability to control the form of ownership. As a result, the SEC, although encouraging push down, generally does not insist on it in these circumstances. Push-down accounting is optional for the separate financial statements of a nonpublic target.

If a bank uses push-down accounting for financial statement purposes, no income or expense for the period of the calendar year prior to the acquisition date should be included in the result.

Merging Physical Resources: Real Estate

Moving from financial resources to physical real estate, what are some considerations regarding bank branches? Can acquirers do whatever they want with the real estate and leases they acquire?

Acquirers have a great deal of freedom with respect to branch real estate, but regulatory boundaries do apply. That is, the retention of bank branches after a merger, like the opening of branches under normal circumstances, does receive regulatory attention. Indeed, there is an entire section of federal law devoted to branches for state and national banks, including guidance on merger scenarios.[10]

Federal law (Section 29 under Title 12 of the U.S. Code) provides that a national bank may purchase, hold, and convey real estate if it is "necessary for its accommodation in the transaction of its business," with certain exceptions in situations where the real estate was used as collateral.[11] The reason for these restrictive conditions was well expressed in the U.S. Supreme Court case of *Union National Bank v. Matthews* (1878), which stated that the real estate limits under national banking law were intended "to keep the capital of the banks flowing in the daily channel of commerce; to deter them from embarking in hazardous real estate speculations; and to prevent the accumulation of large masses of such property in their hands."[12] (For this and other Supreme Court cases, see Appendix in the back of this book.) The *Union National Bank* case also made it clear, however, that Section 29 does not prohibit a national bank from owning or leasing premises simply because they are larger than its current needs.

What happens if a bank winds up with excess real estate as a result of a merger? What can it do?

Divestiture is the normal tactic, but subleasing may be permitted. In one recent case, a national bank wound up with too much real estate and asked the OCC for permission to sublease it. Specifically, the bank proposed to invest in a "bank premises corporation" and enter into a long-term ground lease with it. The premises corporation planned to demolish the existing branch building and construct the new bank complex. The bank complex would consist of two buildings, ground-level covered parking, and an underground parking facility shared by the two buildings. Upon completion of the construction, the bank would lease space in the new complex from the premises corporation for its branch and other bank operations. The survivor bank knew it would take up only about 22 percent of the total space (including parking) in the complex. The question before the OCC was, could the bank sublease the remainder? The OCC approved the plan, citing *Union National Bank v. Matthews*.

How common is it for a bank acquirer to divest or close branches following a merger?

It is increasingly common. Although the total number of bank branches in the United States grew in the first decade of this century, it has been declining since then.[13] Experts such as the consulting firm Celent are now predicting a long-term trend toward branch closings—up to 40 percent of all branches operating now to close by 2020. Mergers are very much a part of the reason.

Acquirers may sell or close branches in order to comply with antitrust regulators concerned about market concentration;[14] however, it is more common for them to sell, close, or consolidate branches to achieve cost savings. For a discussion of bank sales and closings due to antitrust concerns, see Chapter 6.

What is an example of a branch sale, closing, or consolidation for cost savings?

Research indicates that anticipated costs savings are a primary motivator for mergers.[15] Part of the cost savings from mergers involve shuttering physical branches. This is particularly the case in mergers of equals—banks of similar size in similar markets. The following examples illustrate the point:

- When Wells Fargo bought Wachovia in 2008, it closed more than 300 branches.[16]
- When PacWest acquired First California Bank in 2013, it closed nine branches—seven from the nonsurvivor (which were closed completely) and two from the survivor (which were integrated into other branches).[17]

What regulations govern branch closings?

The Federal Deposit Insurance Corporation Improvement Act of 1991 requires banks to give notice before closing branches—meaning brick-and-mortar establishments. The law requires an insured depository institution to submit a notice of any proposed branch closing to the appropriate federal banking agency no later than 90 days prior to the date of the proposed branch closing.[18] The required notice must include a detailed statement of the reasons for the decision to close the branch and statistical or other information in support of such reasons.

The law also requires an insured depository institution to notify its customers of the proposed closing.[19] The institution must mail the notice to the customers of the branch proposed to be closed at least 90 days prior to the proposed closing. The institution also must post a notice to customers in a conspicuous manner on the premises of the branch proposed to be closed at least 30 days prior to the proposed closing.

For an interstate bank (defined as a bank that maintains branches in more than one state) proposing to close a branch located in a low- or moderate-income area, additional disclosures and actions are required, as described below under Integrating Responsibilities. Finally, the law requires each institution to adopt policies regarding branch closings[20] (see Exhibit 7.1).

How does the law apply to branch closings after bank mergers?

An institution must file a branch closing notice whenever it closes a branch, including when the closing occurs in the context of a merger,

Exhibit 7.1 Sample Branch Closing Policy: Enterprise Banking

BRANCH OPENING, CLOSING, RELOCATION, AND REDUCTION IN SERVICE POLICY

It is and shall be the policy of Enterprise Bank (the "Bank") that each of its branches be profitable at all times except for a start-up period determined as part of the process by which the proposed branch is approved by the Board of Directors (the "Board") and for such other circumstances as the Board or Senior Management may specify in writing. For any period during which a branch is not profitable, purchase premium expense excluded, other than the start-up phase usually the first three (3) years, Senior Management shall report to the Board the reasons for such lack of profit, the amount of any loss incurred in the current period and cumulatively, if appropriate, and what plan management has implemented to bring the branch to profitability. Such report shall be given to the Board on each non-profitable branch on a semi-annual or more frequent basis until the branch becomes profitable.

In determining whether a branch is profitable, management may make good faith use of any reasonable method provided that the same method is applied to all branches of the Bank with such reasonable exceptions for limited service branches, automated teller machines, and similar exceptional branches as the Board may approve from time to time. In particular, any form of "support" for branches from the main office or any other area of the Bank shall be allocated based purely on business considerations and not on the racial or ethnic makeup of a branch's surrounding community.

Because of the regulatory sensitivity of such closings, any proposed closing of a branch shall be referred to the Board for final decision. The economic reasons for closing such a branch shall be part of the materials presented to the Board, together with information addressing the following points:

1. Actions taken to attempt to return the branch to profitability.
2. The presence in the branch's neighborhood of other financial institutions and the accessibility and services of such institutions.
3. Proposed actions to advise the branch's local community of the planned closing including meetings with key leaders in the community.
4. Planned actions to minimize the impact of the branch's closing on its neighborhood.

(Continued on page 172)

BRANCHES OPENED, CLOSED, AND RELOCATED DURING THE CURRENT AND PAST TWO YEARS:

Opened

Hudson, New Hampshire: February 2011

Pelham, New Hampshire: February 2012

Tyngsboro, Massachusetts: November 2012

Lawrence, Massachusetts: April 2013

Relocated/ Closed

None

Source: Enterprise Bank. https://www.enterprisebanking.com/branch-relocation-reduction-service-policy.html. This notice is contained in the bank's Community Reinvestment Act Public file, which Enterprise Bank is required to maintain and, upon request, make available for the public inspection. The bank has posted this policy on its website for more convenient public access.

consolidation, or other form of acquisition. Branch closings that occur in the context of transactions subject to the Bank Merger Act (12 U.S.C. § 1828) require a branch closing notice, even if the transaction received expedited treatment under that act.

The responsibility for filing the notice lies with the acquiring or resulting institution, but either party to such a transaction may give the notice. Thus, for example, the purchaser may give the notice prior to consummation of the transaction when the purchaser intends to close a branch following consummation, or the seller may give the notice because it intends to close a branch at or prior to consummation. In the latter example, if the transaction were to close ahead of schedule, the purchaser, if authorized by the appropriate federal banking agency, could operate the branch to complete compliance with the 90-day requirement without the need for an additional notice.

What about relocations and consolidations?

The law does not apply when a branch is relocated or consolidated with one or more other branches if the relocation or consolidation occurs within the immediate neighborhood and does not substantially affect the nature of the business or customers served.

Generally, relocations will be found to have occurred only when short distances are involved, for example, moves across the street, around the corner, or a block or two away.[21] Moves of less than 1,000 feet will generally be considered to be relocations. In less densely populated areas or where neighborhoods extend farther, and a long move would not significantly affect the nature of the business or the customers served by the branch, a relocation may occur over substantially longer distances.

Consolidations of branches are considered relocations for purposes of this policy statement if the branches are located within the same neighborhood, and the nature of the business or customers served is not affected. Thus, for example, a consolidation of two branches on the same block following a merger would not constitute a branch closing.

The same guidelines apply to consolidations as to relocations.

Changes of services at a branch, even a temporary closing due to an event beyond the branch's control, are not considered a branch closing. A change from a brick-and-mortar to an ATM would be considered a branch closing.

Suppose a bank has made a commitment to provide services to underserved communities. Do regulators give a break here?

Yes. OCC guidelines state that a national bank may establish branches for the sole purpose of serving an underserved community and may acquire a noncontrolling investment company that specializes in providing these services.[22] Also, a national bank's operating subsidiary may acquire a company engaged in providing government "welfare to work" counseling. The acquired company counsels welfare-to-work program beneficiaries on work skills and program benefits, connects them with potential employers, and handles payments from the sponsoring government agency to employers and employees participating in the program.[23]

Merging Human Resources

What do merging banks need to know about merging human resources?

Bank mergers, like all mergers, are really about change management—times two. While principles of change management apply, the best advice comes from bankers and consultants who have been involved in mergers. One worthwhile list comes from Deloitte Touche Tohmatsu Ltd., which offers five guidelines:

- Start with the end in mind—think strategically.
- Think roles, not people.
- Hang on to key talent.
- Prepare for emotion.
- Get a handle on employee data.[24]

With all this in mind, how do banks integrate staff positions?

Branches tend to operate autonomously. When two banks merge, there are three possibilities for each branch:

- Remain staffed as is
- Consolidate with another branch
- Close

The three positions involved are typically the branch manager, the personal bankers, and tellers.

It is common to downsize the workforce after a merger. When should managers let people know about layoffs, and how should they be told?

One good example of a message appears in a brochure explaining the merger between Nicolet Bank and Mid-Wisconsin, a stock-for-stock transaction that resulted in a newly combined bank with 350 employees and $1.1 billion in assets in April 2013.[25] In speaking of employees, the brochure states:

> Talented, hard-working people drive success. Nicolet Bank expects people to understand the mission of the organization and what it takes to succeed together. We understand that mergers create real anxiety. There will be some consolidation because efficiency of size matters. This will result in the loss of jobs that overlap. What we can't answer right now is what jobs and who will be affected. We need time to evaluate people and positions. We can assure you that we really need experienced bankers who understand the values and culture and who are connected to their community. We will be counting on many of you to help us move forward with a successful model of community banking.[26] ...

The brochure also states:

> All current benefit programs will remain in effect until further notice. Prior to the expected closing in the second quarter of 2013, we will be providing you with comprehensive information regarding employee benefits.[27]

Regarding management and board positions, there is an assurance of continuity and its rationale:

> Nicolet Bank's Management Team has many decades of successful experience in community banking and will remain intact after the merger. We expect that new management talent will be found to support the work we will be doing. The Nicolet Board is comprised of a diverse group of current and former business owner-operators who understand the mission of a community bank. They maintain a substantial investment in the bank. Approximately 40% of Nicolet Bank stock is held by current and former Board members and other insiders. We are very pleased to have two members of Mid-Wisconsin Bank joining the Nicolet Board following the merger.[28]

INTEGRATING PROCESSES

The Horizontal Merger Guidelines of the Department of Justice and Federal Trade Commission, as revised in 2010, identify two broad motivations for merging: capturing cost efficiencies and obtaining market power.[29] Recent research on bank mergers suggest that they are primarily motivated by the desire to increase efficiencies or reduce costs, rather than to expand market power.[30] As such, the integration of systems—particularly information technology (IT)—is relevant to bank mergers.

Information Technology

What are some of the IT aspects of banks that may have to be merged?

Some of the key systems include the card and merchant management systems and the ATM/POS switch, notes BPC Group, a consultancy in banking technologies.[31] Typical postmerger IT changes from the customer's point of view may be

- The number and type of credit and/or debit cards issued
- The number of delivery channels such as ATMs and point of sale (POS) transaction processing systems (credit card processors)
- The types of delivery channels, such as Internet, mobile, and 3D secure

Regarding integration of card systems, what advice would you give?

Appropriate guidance is based on the types of systems that the participants currently have, as well as the resultant size and aims of the surviving bank. Here are some common scenarios involving one or more third-party provider, as described by BPC Group and Smart Vista, a third party provider.[32]

- *Both organizations outsourced to same TPP.* In this case, the initial transition period is simplified, and it gives the final entity time to do a proper evaluation of the business case for moving the processing in-house or remaining with the current vendor, especially as the increased volumes could result in better terms and conditions with the revised contract.

- *Both organizations outsourced to different TPP.* Although there is the higher cost of keeping two systems running in parallel, there is no urgency on moving the systems; this situation gives the surviving bank time to do a proper evaluation of the business case for moving the processing in-house or which of the current vendors to remain with. This requires rapid evaluation of which TPP, if any, can provide all the necessary features to support both sets of products and the new products required in the future.
- *One outsourced and one in-house.* In this situation, although it is costly to keep two systems running in parallel, it may not be advisable to bring everything in-house immediately. The merged entity should evaluate if the current internal system can cope with the new business parameters before migrating to the legacy system.
- *Both organizations doing in-house processing with same vendor.* This scenario gives the final surviving bank time to evaluate the business case for keeping the current vendor's system, especially as the increased volumes could stress the system. Some data migration is required, and both systems will have to be brought to the same level before migration to ensure smooth operation.
- *Both organizations doing in-house processing with different vendors.* This requires an immediate review of both systems, focusing on their ability to cope with higher capacities and processing levels. A full migration is required of at least one system.

Does consolidation of IT systems in merging banks save costs?

It can, but the savings are hardly automatic. Merging IT systems is one of the most challenging aspects of bank mergers. Indeed, it has been called the "moment of truth."[33]

IT consolidation has potentially large savings potential in a merger because the fixed costs of hardware and software far exceed the costs that vary based on transaction volumes.[34] IT costs are somewhat less transparent than branch and purchasing costs, but given the frequent movement of IT professionals between banks and the heavy use of (often the same) TPPs, reasonable estimates can be made. The additional problem associated with merger savings in IT is that achieving the savings is difficult, costly, and takes years of effort. Estimates of IT savings in mergers are invariably high and contribute to the tendency to overpay, as noted earlier, and estimates of the cost and time to achieve the savings are invariably low.

INTEGRATING RESPONSIBILTIES

What stakeholders may banks need to accommodate as they merge?

Like all companies, banks serve multiple stakeholders, including not only shareholders, but also customers and local communities. This section looks at these latter key stakeholders in the merger context.

Postmerger Customer Relations

How can banks deal with customer dissatisfaction following a merger?

Many bank mergers do cause a decline in customer satisfaction[35] and attrition. In one fairly recent survey of bank customers by the Deloitte Center for Banking Solutions, affiliated with Deloitte Touche Tohmatsu, 17 percent said they had changed banks due to a merger, and another 14 percent were considering it.[36] Of those who had switched, the customers had an average of six products and that bank, while those who stayed had only four—compounding the loss.

When customers change banks, they often do so for emotional reasons. In the survey from Deloitte Center for Banking Solutions cited above, more than one in three customers who switched banks following a merger said they changed because they had lost trust and confidence in their new bank, had concerns about the security of accounts, felt that their new bank did not value them or look out for their best interests as their old bank had, and lost a personal relationship with bank employees. Competitive offers was given as a distant second (17 percent) reason, followed by account serving, fees, convenience, and other factors, reported by no more than 1 in 10. Most customers leave their bank within the first month of a merger, so time is of the essence.[37] In response, most banks have set up Frequently Asked Question (FAQ) pages on their websites to answer customer concerns.

What happens when two banks merge if a customer has accounts in both banks that exceed the insurable limit of $250,000?

First, the customer has a six-month grace period to restructure accounts if necessary. Under FDIC rules, for at least six months after the merger, any transferred deposits will be separately insured from any previous accounts the customer already had at the surviving bank. This grace period gives a depositor the opportunity to restructure his or her accounts, if necessary.[38]

The basic FDIC insurance amount is $250,000 for each depositor at each bank. So if the customer has money in two banks that merge into one, as long as the combined total (including accrued interest) is $250,000 or less, all the money is fully protected.

But even if the merger results in the customer's having more than $250,000 in the combined banks, he or she may still be fully insured. Deposits held at a bank have different "ownership categories"—such as joint, single, and retirement accounts—and each is separately insured to at least $250,000.

What happens to a customer's loan when banks merge?

The loans a customer has at an old bank generally will not be affected. That's because a loan is a binding contract between the customer and the lender. The customer is obligated to make payments according to the loan agreement. Also, a fixed rate on a car loan or mortgage will remain the same.

What about credit card terms? Are banks responsible for keeping these terms the same?

Following a merger, there may be changes for existing deposit accounts and credit cards. Financial institutions have the right to change the interest rate or certain other terms of deposit accounts and credit cards if they provide advance notice to customers, and the account contract permits the change.

How can merging banks fulfill their responsibilities toward communities?

Banks originate in communities and expand to communities; they draw from communities for their customer base both for deposits and loans.

First and foremost banks can serve communities simply by operating in them. Banks help communities by their very function—receiving deposits (that are in turn insured by the FDIC) and making loans to local businesses and individuals. This function is enhanced when banks make a special effort to serve lower income areas.

Therefore, the first and most fundamental problem facing any community when a bank merges is the risk of having branches close—especially in a low-income neighborhood where only a few banks operate. (Note that from mid–2008 to mid–2013, banks closed 1,826 branches, and 93 percent of those were in postal codes where the household income is below the $52,762 national median.[39])

How do federal laws address branch closings—especially in low or moderate income neighborhoods where branches are less common?

If an interstate bank proposes to close any branch in a low- or moderate-income area, it must provide customers with the mailing address of the appropriate federal banking agency and tell them that they can send comments on the proposed closing there.

If the agency gets a comment that claims credibly there will be an adverse effect, the agency will consult with community leaders in the affected area and convene a meeting of representatives of the agency and other interested depository institution regulatory agencies and others as appropriate to explore the feasibility of obtaining adequate alternative facilities and services for the affected area, including the establishment of a new branch by another depository institution, the chartering of a new depository institution, or the establishment of a community development credit union, following the closing of the branch.

Regarding community lending, as mentioned in Chapter 2, the Community Reinvestment Act (CRA) requires that all banks insured by the FDIC must be evaluated by federal banking agencies to determine if the banks and savings and loans offer credit in all communities in which they are chartered to do business and in which they take deposits.

What about programs to benefit local charities?

Many bank managements make a strategic decision to support community organizations. Bank mergers can have an adverse affect on these programs and on the local communities they serve. This is why the Interagency Bank Merger Application Form,[40] a disclosure required for bank mergers overseen by the main bank regulators, contains questions about community programs, namely

- "If any of the combining institutions have entered into commitments with community organizations, civic associations, or similar entities concerning providing banking services to the community, describe the commitment."
- "If the Resultant Institution will not assume the obligations entered into by the Target Institution, explain the reasons and describe the impact on the communities to be affected."

(For the actual form, see Appendix 7-A.)

CONCLUDING COMMENTS

No two bank mergers are alike, so integrating them can be challenging. By identifying key resources, processes, and responsibilities, bank managers can advance their goals in their "new world" after a merger. Chapter 8 will provide an example of success in this regard.

APPENDIX 7-A

Expiration Date: 05/31/2015

INTERAGENCY BANK MERGER ACT APPLICATION[41]

This application is used to effect a transaction under section 18(c) of the Federal Deposit Insurance Act (FDIA), as amended (12 U.S.C. 1828(c)), and for national banks, 12 U.S.C. 215, 215a. This application is used for a merger, consolidation, or other combining transaction between nonaffiliated parties as well as to effect a corporate reorganization between affiliated parties (affiliate transaction). An affiliate transaction refers to a merger, consolidation, other combination, or transfer of any deposit liabilities, between depository institutions that are controlled by the same holding company. It includes a business combination between a depository institution and an affiliated interim institution. Applicants proposing affiliate transactions are not required to complete questions 12 through 14 of this form.

INTERAGENCY BANK MERGER ACT APPLICATION

Check all that apply:

Type of Filing

Affiliate/Corporate Reorganization
Combination with Interim
Depository Institution
Nonaffiliate Combination
Other

Form of Transaction

Merger
Consolidation

Purchase and Assumption

Branch Purchase and Assumption

Other

Filed Pursuant To

12 U.S.C. 1828(c)

12 U.S.C. 1815(d)(2)

12 U.S.C. 1815(d)(3)

12 U.S.C. 215, 215a

12 U.S.C. 1815(a)

Other

Applicant Depository Institution

Name Charter/Docket Number

City State ZIP Code

Target Institution

Name Charter/Docket Number

Street

City State ZIP Code

Resultant Institution (if different than Applicant)

Name Charter/Docket Number

Street

City State ZIP Code

Contact Person

Name Title/Employer

City State ZIP Code

Telephone Number Fax Number

INTERAGENCY BANK MERGER ACT APPLICATION

1. Describe the transaction's purpose, structure, significant terms and conditions, and financing arrangements, including any plan to raise additional equity or incur debt.[42]
2. Provide a copy of (a) the executed merger or transaction agreement, including any amendments, (b) any board of directors' resolutions related to the transaction, and (c) interim charter, names of organizers, and related documents, if applicable.
3. Describe any issues regarding the permissibility of the proposal with regard to applicable state or Federal laws or regulations (for example, nonbank activities, branching, qualified thrift lender's test).
4. Describe any nonconforming or impermissible assets or activities that Applicant or Resultant Institution may not be permitted to retain under relevant law or regulation, including the method of and anticipated time period for divestiture or disposal.
5. Provide the indicated financial information and describe the assumptions used to prepare the projected statements, including those about the effect of the merger transaction. Material changes between the date of the financial. statements and the date of the application should be disclosed. If there are no material changes, a statement to that effect should be made.
   a. Pro Forma Balance Sheet, as of the end of the most recent quarter and for the first year of operation after the transaction. Indicate separately for the Applicant and Target Institution each principal group of assets, liabilities, and capital accounts; debit and credit adjustments (explained by footnotes) reflecting the proposed acquisition; and the resulting pro forma combined balance sheet. Goodwill and all other intangible assets should be listed separately on the balance sheet. Indicate the amortization period and method used for any intangible asset and the accretion period of any purchase discount on the balance sheet.

b. Projected Combined Statement of Income for the first year of operation following consummation.
c. Pro Forma and Projected Regulatory Capital Schedule, as of the end of the most recent quarter and for the first year of operation, indicating:
    - Each component item for Tier 1 (Core) and Tier 2 (Supplementary) Capital, Subtotal for Tier 1 and Tier 2 Capital (less any investment in unconsolidated or nonincludable subsidiaries), Total Capital (*include Tier 3 if applicable*).
    - Total risk-weighted assets.
    - Capital Ratios: (1) Tier 1 capital to total risk-weighted assets; (2) Total capital to total risk-weighted assets; and (3) Tier 1 capital to average total consolidated assets (leverage ratio).

6. List the directors and senior executive officers of the Resultant Institution and provide the name, address, position with and shares held in Resultant Institution or holding company, and principal occupation (if a director).[43]
7. Describe how the proposal will meet the convenience and needs of the community. For the combining institutions, list any significant anticipated changes in services or products that will result from the consummation of the transaction. If any services or products will be discontinued, describe and explain the reasons.
8. Discuss the programs, products, and activities of the Applicant or the Resultant Institution that will meet the existing or anticipated needs of its community(ies) under the applicable criteria of the Community Reinvestment Act (CRA) regulation, including the needs of low and moderate-income geographies and individuals. For an Applicant or Target Institution that has received a CRA composite rating of "needs to improve" or "substantial noncompliance" institution-wide or, where applicable, in a state or a multi-state MSA, or has received an evaluation of less than satisfactory performance in an MSA or in the non-MSA portion

of a state in which the applicant is expanding as a result of the combination, describe the specific actions, if any, that have been taken to address the deficiencies in the institution's CRA performance record since the rating.

9. The Riegle-Neal Interstate Banking and Branching Efficiency Act of 1994 imposes additional considerations for certain interstate mergers between insured banks. Savings associations are not subject to 12 U.S.C. 1831u. If subject to these provisions, discuss authority; compliance with state age limits and host state(s) filing requirements; and applicability of nationwide and statewide concentration limits. In addition, discuss any other restrictions that the states seek to apply (including state antitrust restrictions).
10. List all offices that (a) will be established or retained as branches, including the main office, of the Target Institution, (b) are approved but unopened branch(es) of the Target Institution, including the date the current federal and state agencies granted approval(s), and (c) are existing branches that will be closed as a result of the proposal to the extent the information is available and indicate the effect on the branch customers served. For each branch, list the popular name, street address, city, county, state, and ZIP code.
11. As a result of this transaction, if the Applicant will be or will become affiliated with a company engaged in insurance activities that is subject to supervision by a state insurance regulator, provide:
    a. The name of company.
    b. A description of the insurance activity that the company is engaged in and has plans to conduct.
    c. A list of each state and the lines of business in that state in which the company holds, or will hold, an insurance license. Indicate the state where the company holds a resident license or charter, as applicable.
12. Discuss the effects of the proposed transaction on existing competition in the relevant geographic market(s) where

Applicant and Target Institution operate. Applicant should contact the appropriate regulatory agency for specific instructions to complete the competitive analysis.

13. If the proposed transaction involves a branch sale or any other divestiture of all or any portion of the bank, savings association or nonbank company (in the case of a merger under 12 U.S.C. 1828(c)(1)) to mitigate competitive effects, discuss the timing, purchaser, and other specific information.
14. Describe any management interlocking relationships (12 U.S.C. 3201–3208) that currently exist or would exist following consummation. Include a discussion of the permissibility of the interlock with regard to relevant laws and regulations.

CERTIFICATION

We hereby certify that our board of directors, by resolution, has authorized the filing of this application, and that to the best of our knowledge, it contains no misrepresentations or omissions of material facts. In addition, we agree to notify the agency if the facts described in the filing materially change prior to receiving a decision or prior to consummation. Any misrepresentation or omission of a material fact constitutes fraud in the inducement and may subject us to legal sanctions provided by 18 U.S.C. 1001 and 1007.

We acknowledge that approval of this application is in the discretion of the appropriate federal banking agency. Actions or communications, whether oral, written, or electronic, by an agency or its employees in connection with this filing, including approval of the application if granted, do not constitute a contract, either express or implied, or any other obligation binding upon the agency, other federal banking agencies, the United States, any other agency or entity of the United States, or any officer or employee of the United States. Such actions or communications will not affect the ability of any federal banking agency to exercise its supervisory, regulatory, or examination powers under applicable law and regulations. We further acknowledge that the foregoing may not be waived or modified by any employee or agent of a federal banking agency or of the United States.

Signed this day of ___, ___.

by

(Applicant) (Signature of Authorized Officer)

(Typed Name)

(Title)

by

(Target Institution) (Signature of Authorized Officer)*

(Typed Name)

(Title)

*In multiple-step combinations, applicants should ensure that authorized officers of the combining institutions sign.

COMPTROLLER OF THE CURRENCY

OFFICE OF THRIFT SUPERVISION

SUPPLEMENT TO INTERAGENCY BANK MERGER ACT APPLICATION

All OCC and OTS Applicants should provide the following supplemental information with their application:

15. If any of the combining institutions have entered into commitments with community organizations, civic associations, or similar entities concerning providing banking services to the community, describe the commitment.
16. If the Resultant Institution will not assume the obligations entered into by the Target Institution, explain the reasons and describe the impact on the communities to be affected.

If filing with the OCC:

17. Identify and state the activity of each subsidiary to be acquired. If acquiring a non-national bank subsidiary, provide the information and analysis of the subsidiary's activities that would be required if it were established pursuant to 12 C.F.R. 5.34 or 5.39.

If filing with the OTS:

18. Provide the information to satisfy the requirements of 12 C.F.R. 563.22(d)(1)(vi).

FEDERAL RESERVE SYSTEM

SUPPLEMENT TO INTERAGENCY BANK MERGER ACT APPLICATION

All FRB Applicants should provide the following supplemental information with their application:

15. If the pro forma consolidated assets of Applicant's parent holding company are less than $150 million and parent company long-term debt will exceed 30 percent of parent company equity capital accounts on a pro forma basis, provide cash flow projections for the parent company which clearly demonstrate the ability to reduce the long-term debt-to-equity ratio to 30 percent or less within 12 years of consummation.

FEDERAL DEPOSIT INSURANCE CORPORATION

SUPPLEMENT TO INTERAGENCY BANK MERGER ACT APPLICATION

All FDIC Applicants should provide the following supplemental information with their application:

15. This section supplements question 12 of the Interagency Bank Merger Act Application for transactions between nonaffiliated parties. Additional guidance relating to the FDIC's consideration of the competitive factors in a proposed merger transaction is contained in the FDIC's Rules and Regulations (12 C.F.R. 303 Subpart D) and Statement of Policy on Bank Merger Transactions (2 FDIC Law, Regulations, and Related Acts (FDIC) 5145).

I. Delineation of the relevant geographic market(s).

The relevant geographic market includes the areas in which the offices to be acquired are located and from which those offices derive the predominant portion of their loans, deposits, or other business. The relevant geographic market also includes the areas where existing and potential customers impacted by the proposed merger may practically turn for alternative sources of banking services.

(a) Prepare schedules for the Applicant Institution and Target Institution showing the total number of accounts and total dollar volume of deposits for each municipality or census tract, where applicable, according to the recorded address of the depositor (do not submit supporting data). Small amounts may be aggregated and identified as "other." *If the Applicant Institution is a multi-office institution, Applicant Institution deposit information should be provided only for those offices within or proximate to the area(s) described below under paragraph (b).*

(b) Identify those areas where existing and potential customers of the offices to be acquired may practically turn for alternative sources of banking services. If consideration of the availability of such alternative banking services results in a market area considerably different from that indicated by the sources of deposits, discuss and provide necessary supporting information.

(c) Using the information collected in paragraphs (a) and (b), provide a narrative description of the delineated relevant geographic market(s).

(d) Provide any additional information necessary to support the delineated relevant geographic market(s). Supporting information may include relevant demographic information, locations of major employers, retail trade statistics, and/or information on traffic patterns. *Applicants may consult with the applicable FDIC Regional Office in determining whether additional information is necessary.*

II. Competition in the relevant geographic market(s).

(a) Prepare a schedule of participating and competing banking institutions' offices, divided into three sections:

(i) Applicant Institution offices within or proximate to the relevant geographic market(s);

(ii) Target Institution offices within or proximate to the relevant geographic market(s); and

(iii) Competitor banking offices located or competing within the delineated relevant geographic market(s).

To the extent known, also include banking offices approved but not yet open. The following presentation format is suggested:

Distance and Direction

From Nearest Office

Name and Location of Banking

Office

Total

Deposits

Applicant

Institution

Target

Institution

(b) For each office listed in paragraph (a), provide the street address; total deposits as reported in the most recent *FDIC Summary of Deposits Data Book* (www.fdic.gov/databank); and distance and general direction from the nearest office of Applicant and Target Institution. *In cases where the delineated relevant geographic market includes a significant portion of a larger metropolitan area, provide only a listing of financial institutions and the aggregate total deposits of all offices operated by each within the delineated relevant geographic market(s).*

(c) Discuss the extent and intensity of competition in the delineated relevant geographic market(s) provided by nonbank institutions, such as other depository institutions (for example, credit unions) and non-depository institutions (for example, industrial loan companies, finance companies, and/or government agencies). For those institutions regarded as competing in the delineated relevant geographic market(s), provide name, address, and services supplied.

CHAPTER 8

Bank M&A: Case in Point

Nothing is more contagious than example.

—François Duc de la Rochefoucauld

When it comes to reputation, bankers know all too well M&A's downside. Merger news stories do not always laud banking success. Instead, accounts may cite community protests over bank closings; customer complaints about postmerger operations or opportunities, especially with respect to lending; shareholder lawsuits over loss of share value; or regulatory concerns about market concentration or megabank impunity—"too big to fail" and "too big to jail."

These accounts are not without merit. Bank closings may result in abandoned buildings and the proliferation of inferior credit offerings in a community.[1] Business borrowers may indeed suffer in the aftermath of megamergers.[2] Mergers can fail to deliver improved results to shareholders,[3] and the most recent financial crisis provides ample proof that national economies can suffer when large financial institutions fail.

But these accounts and catchphrases tell only part of the story. The rest of the truth is that bank M&A success is possible. Just as there are "deals from hell," to cite Dean Robert Bruner, so there are deals that "made in heaven." That is the focus and hope of this chapter, which features questions and answers designed to show the positive side of a recent bank consolidation involving a community bank—Trustmark's 2013 acquisition of BancTrust Financial Group in early 2013.

THE TRUSTMARK ACQUISITION OF BANKTRUST

Trustmark National Bank (Trustmark), founded in 1889 and headquartered in Jackson, Mississippi, is a subsidiary of Trustmark Corporation, a bank holding company offering banking, wealth management, and insurance solutions through subsidiaries in Florida, Mississippi, Tennessee, Texas, and, most recently, Alabama.[4] The parent corporation also owns Somerville Bank in Tennessee.

In 2012 Trustmark acquired BayBank, an established bank in Florida. Then, in 2013, Trustmark merged with the BancTrust Financial Group holding company, based in Mobile Alabama, for $55.4 million. As a result, it became the owner of the holding company's depository instituion, BankTrust, making it the 102nd largest depository organization in the United States. Trustmark's 2012 annual report noted the geographic and financial impact of the transaction:

> With 49 offices, BancTrust provides entry to more than 15 attractive Alabama markets, including Mobile, Montgomery and Selma, as well as enhances our franchise in the Florida Panhandle. These transactions illustrate our commitment to increase shareholder value through disciplined mergers and acquisitions.[5]

Today, following as a result of the merger, Trustmark has some $8 billion in deposits and just over $10 billion in assets—putting it on the high end of community banks in the country.[6]

While it is risky for any author to laud a success, especially in a book meant to last for several years, it does seem that Trustmark provides a positive example of a bank merger. As one scholar noted in an article on bank mergers written nearly two decades ago, "[A]verages obscure the fact that *many good mergers occur,* which add efficiency gains, and that can be explained on a case by case basis."[7] This is such a case, we believe.

Why did Trustmark buy BancTrust?

Most bank-to-bank acquisitions are motivated by a desire to grow in size, but in this case, growth in service was another motivation. Setting a positive tone for life after the acquisition, Gerald Host, Trustmark CEO, told *Alabama Business News*: "We don't go in with this preconceived idea that since we're the buyer, we know more than they do," he said. "It's not just about cost saves, it's about bringing more to the customer than [BancTrust] might have been able to bring together as a stand-alone."[8]

Did this merger receive regulatory review?

Yes—by both the Office of the Comptroller of the Currency (OCC) and the Federal Reserve (Fed). By January 2013, the merger had received approval from both the OCC and the Board of Governors of the Fed.[9]

What were some of the issues explored by the OCC?

The OCC reviewed this transaction in order to approve a charter, studying the typical array of elements (market demand, customer base, competitive and economic conditions, and service risks), and found the transaction to be acceptable.

When the transaction was still pending, the OCC asked Trustmark to decribe its "community outreach efforts."[10] Trustmark responded that it had received an "outstanding" rating from the OCC for its Community Reinvestment Act (CRA) performance (a rating received by only 5 percent of banks audited).[11] The CRA requires the federal financial supervisory agencies (including the OCC and Fed) to encourage insured depository institutions to help meet the credit needs of the local communities in which they operate, consistent with their safe and sound operation, and requires the appropriate federal financial supervisory agency to take into account a relevant depository institution's record of meeting the credit needs of its entire community, including low- and moderate-income neighborhoods, in evaluating bank expansionary proposals.

Regarding loan origination policies, the acquirer stated,

> Each Trustmark originator is expected to reach out to all areas of the community, making every effort to generate new mortgage applications from low to moderate income borrowers. All originators are required to make 6 business development calls each year to minority agents and/or agents who work with minority homebuyers on a regular basis. Each originator is required to host and/or teach at least one Homebuyer Education workshop each year. [12]

A coordinator is available to help non-profits in each market that partner with Trustmark on these initiatives."

What were the issues studied by the Fed?

The Fed's review focused on market concentration, but considered other factors as well, financial condition, managerial resources, community resources and needs, and impact on the nation's financial stability.

What did the Fed say about this transaction's market concentration?

As mentioned in Chapter 3 on bank holding companies, the Bank Holding Company Act requires the Fed to consider local and national market concentration. In this case, the Fed noted that the two banks competed in Florida (Fort Walton and Panama City), but it determined that the benefits of the merger outweighed this increase in local market concentration. It also determined that the transaction would not exceed the 10 percent national market concentration set by the law. (The Federal Reserve will not approve an application by a bank holding company to acquire an insured depository institution outside its state if the holding company controls or would control more than 10 percent of deposits of insured depository institutions in the nation as a whole.)

What about the acquirer's financial condition? What did the Fed say about that?

The Fed reviews the financial condition of the organizations involved on both a parent-only and consolidated basis, as well as the financial condition of the subsidiary depository institutions and the organizations' significant nonbanking operations. In evaluating financial factors in "expansionary proposals" by banking organizations, the Fed considers a variety of information, including capital adequacy (deemed "especially important"), asset quality, and earnings performance. It evaluates the financial condition of the combined organization, including its capital position, asset quality, and earnings prospects, and the impact of the proposed funding on the transaction. In addition, it considers the ability of the organization to absorb the costs of the proposal and the proposed integration of the operations of the institutions.

The Fed found that Trustmark and its banks (Trustmark Bank and Somerville Bank), as acquirers, were well capitalized and would remain so on consummation of the proposed transaction—a bank holding company merger structured as an exchange of shares. The Fed noted that Trustmark would issue new shares of common stock to complete the transaction and stated that Trustmark was in "stable financial condition." Furthermore, the Fed found that the asset quality and earnings of both Trustmark Bank and Somerville Bank were "consistent with approval." On a pro forma basis, the Fed determined that the acquisition of BancTrust would not adversely impact Trustmark's operations financially. "Based on its review of the record, the Board finds that the organization has sufficient financial resources to effect the proposal," said the Fed's report.[13]

What about the managerial resources of the acquirer?

The Fed reviewed the examination records of the acquirer (merging banks Trustmark, Trustmark Bank, and Somerville Bank), including assessments of their management, risk management systems, and operations, and found that they were all "considered to be well managed, and their boards of directors and senior management are considered experienced and capable." The Fed's report noted that, after the merger, BancTrust, the holding company, and BankTrust, the bank, would be integrated into Trustmark's operations and governed by Trustmark's risk management, corporate governance, and compliance policies and procedures. "Trustmark's existing risk management program and its directorate and senior management are considered to be satisfactory," said the Fed report,[14] noting that the directors and senior management of Trustmark, Trustmark Bank, and Somerville Bank, and the risk management program of Trustmark, would not change as a result of the proposal. In addition, the Fed considered its supervisory experiences and those of other relevant banking supervisory agencies with the organizations and their records of compliance with applicable banking law, including antimoney-laundering laws.

Based on all the facts of record, the Fed concluded that the acquirer's financial and managerial resources and future prospects were consistent with approval.

Turning to "convenience and needs," what were the Fed's findings with respect to the banks involved?

Like the OCC, the Fed took into account records under the CRA—but went beyond the CRA to other aspects. The Fed looked at records for Trustmark and Somerville as the acquirers and BankTrust as the bank to be acquired. To assess the acquirer's broader record in the community, the Fed considered not only CRA reports but also all the facts of record, including the bank's own reports, data reported by the bank under the Home Mortgage Disclosure Act (HMDA), confidential supervisory information, and one public comment received on the proposal. The commenter objected to the proposal on the basis of Trustmark Bank's record of mortgage lending to African American and Hispanic applicants. Upon investigation, the Fed did confirm that the bank's rate of denial for loans was higher than its competitors, but it also found that it was originating more loans, which could help explain the denial rate (considering a broader pool of applicants). In general, the report found a good record of serving the credit needs of the most economically disadvantaged assessment areas, low-income individuals, and very small businesses consistent with safe and sound business practices.

The Fed also found many strong points in this regard, including high origination rates and a general pattern of community support.[15] The report noted that Trustmark Bank had an excellent record of lending inside its assessment areas by number and dollar amount of loans and that its community development lending performance was excellent. In particular, examiners stated that Trustmark Bank used flexible and innovative loan products. The bank received a "high satisfactory" rating on the lending test and "outstanding" ratings on both the investment and service tests. Examiners concluded that Somerville Bank exhibited a reasonable penetration of lending among individuals of different income levels and had an excellent record of small business lending.

Highlights from Trustmark's record include the following:

- Qualified investments, grants, and donations totaling $36.3 million in the bank's full-scope assessment areas in Mississippi. Most of those investments provided for the construction, repair, and expansion of schools serving primarily low- to moderate-income

(LMI) students; funding home ownership and rental housing for LMI households; and a project to revitalize and stabilize a low-income area.

- Some 14,000 HMDA, small business, and small farm loans totaling approximately $2 billion for 2011
- Fifty community development loans totaling $65 million during 2010 and 35 community development loans totaling $59 million in 2011
- Some $54 million in qualified community development investments from July 10, 2010, through July 2012, including investments in Ginnie Mae and Fannie Mae mortgage-backed securities, low-income-housing tax credits, new market tax credit projects, and contributions to nonprofit organizations serving LMI individuals

The Fed also considered information about Trustmark Bank's compliance and risk management systems and the steps it has taken to ensure compliance with fair lending laws. Trustmark Bank has instituted policies and procedures to help ensure compliance with all fair lending and other consumer protection laws and regulations. Contrary to the impression left by the public comment about the bank's alleged discriminatory lending, Trustmark Bank has a second review committee, which reviews all home mortgage loan applications initially recommended for denial or for approval based on a policy exception. Moreover, the bank completes quarterly reviews of compliance with Trustmark Bank's fair lending policies.

The Fed report noted that Trustmark's risk management systems, as well as its "policies and procedures for assuring compliance with fair lending laws," would be implemented at the combined organization. On the plus side, the Fed report noted that the merger would provide access to a larger ATM network to current customers of Trustmark Bank and BankTrust, and would provide BankTrust customers access to Trustmark Bank's expertise as a Small Business Administration Preferred Lender.

Considering all the elements above, the Fed found that Trustmark met requirements for community service, but noted that it "encourages Trustmark Bank to continue to seek opportunities to assist in meeting the credit needs of the communities it serves."[16]

What did the Fed say about the impact of the transaction on the nation's financial system?

As stated in Chapter 2, the Dodd–Frank Act requires the Fed to consider the extent to which a proposed bank M&A transaction would result in greater or more concentrated risk to the stability of the U.S. banking or financial system.

To assess the likely effect of this transaction (as other transactions), the Fed considered the future systemic "footprints" of the banks involved, including the size of the resulting firm; the availability of substitute providers for any critical products and services offered by the resulting firm; and the interconnectedness of the resulting firm with the banking or financial system. As a result of these considerations, it approved the transaction.

So what was the overall conclusion of the Fed's report on this merger?

The Fed's report noted that the transaction would not result in more concentrated risks to the stability of the U.S. banking or financial system. After studying bank reports, from bank supervisors, and comments from the public, the Fed was able to approve the transaction based in part on

- Financial and managerial resources (including "competence, experience, and integrity of officers, directors, and principal shareholders")
- Future prospects of the company and banks concerned
- Effectiveness of the company in combating money laundering
- Convenience and needs of the community to be served
- No negative impact on national financial stability

TRUSTMARK'S POSTMERGER PERFORMANCE

How has Trustmark performed since the acquisition?

Highlights for the second quarter mentioned by Trustmark's director of investor relations in the earning call with analysts included net income of $31.1 million or $0.46 per share, which produced a return on average tangible common equity of 14.09 percent and a return on average asset of 1.06 percent. Trustmark's spokesperson recalled that the company had completed its merger with BancTrust in February, and in March completed the operational conversion. The second quarter, he said, was the first full quarter that included the financial results of the merger; he was "pleased to report net income attributable to BancTrust totaled $6.1 million in the second quarter, which included $2 million after tax from recoveries on payoffs on acquired loans."[17]

Also, the board declared a quarterly cash dividend of $0.23 per share payable September 15 to shareholders of record on September 1.

In July 2013, Trustmark announced that it had fulfilled its branch purchase and assumption agreement with SouthBank, FSB, thus acquiring two branches serving the Oxford, Mississippi, market. Trustmark assumed selected deposit accounts of approximately $11.8 million, as well as physical branch offices.

CONCLUDING COMMENTS

Whenever banks expand through merger, they put their reputations on the line and under a spotlight. Any problems before, during, or after the transaction are likely to be magnified through media attention. This Trustmark case so far has stood up to scrutiny as a positive example of bank consolidation.

CHAPTER 9

Banking on the Future

> The public can learn to respect and trust bankers again—but this will only happen through our actions, through helping businesses grow, and thereby participating in the economic recovery. But growth in itself is dependent on a strong banking sector. You don't make the economy stronger by making the banks weaker.
>
> *—Ana Botin*
> *CEO, Santander*[1]

To perform profitably and sustainably, banks need leaders who can foresee the future beyond banking—through key trends in economics, demographics, and technology. Forecasting can inform any industry, but it is particularly critical in commercial banking. To store deposits, make loans, and provide other financial services effectively, banks must maintain constant awareness of what is happening to the economy, to people, and to technology.

Therefore, this chapter will depart from the formulas of the previous eight to explore the overall topic of the future, reporting on the major changes that forward-looking economists, demographers, and technologists anticipate, along with our best prediction of how this will affect the future of commercial banking.

ECONOMY

Banks' decisions to buy or merge into other banks revolve around their sense of what tomorrow will bring. The service charges banks impose on deposits, as well as the interest they pay on loans, must be set according to the bankers' prediction of what the cost of capital will be in the future—both near and long term. The cost of capital is affected by the economic measures described below and other factors, such as tax rates.

What are some aspects of the economy and economic policy that bankers need to predict, and what are the tools for predicting them?

Since the economy is a broad concept, there are, not surprisingly, a great number of indicators. A mid-2013 survey of forecasters from the Federal Reserve Bank of Philadelphia reported on 23 economic indicators for the nation, ranging from gross domestic product (GDP) to personal consumption expenditure (PCE) measured through a "chain" price index, less food and energy.[2] Chain, also called chain-type or chained, means that the index is linked to other measures. When it comes to PCE, the other measures are the cost of substitute products. This measure was introduced a decade ago by the U.S. Department of Labor and is in wide use today.[3]

Economic and policy trends of greatest interest to bankers are inflation rates, interest rates, the rate of economic growth, and the rate of taxation.

Inflation Rates

As discussed in Chapter 4, inflation is an important indicator for banks. The banks that belong to the Federal Reserve system (state-chartered banks) are likely to look to the Fed for their inflation rate forecasts. Banks that are chartered by the Office of the Comptroller of Currency (OCC) (national banks) may look to that agency for their forecasts.

Both Fed and OCC policymakers monitor several price indexes to gain their sense of inflation rates, including indexes from the U.S. Department of Commerce and the U.S. Department of Labor.

On its website, the Fed notes the following about its inflation predictions:

- Because inflation numbers can vary erratically from month to month, policymakers generally consider average inflation over longer periods of time, ranging from a few months to a year or longer.
- Furthermore, policymakers routinely examine the subcategories that make up a broad price index to help determine if a rise in inflation can be attributed to price changes that are likely to be

temporary or unique events. Since the Fed's policy decisions occur well in advance of their economic impact (the so called fiscal policy "time lag"),[4] it must make policy based on its best forecast of inflation. Therefore, the Fed must try to determine if an inflation development is likely to persist or not.

- Policymakers consider a variety of core inflation measures aimed at predicting longer-term trends in prices. The most common type of core inflation measures exclude items with prices that tend to be volatile, such as food and energy items.

The Fed uses its inflation projections to inform its decisions about interest rates. In July 2013, in announcing its decision to keep downward pressure on interest rates, the Fed stated that this was depending on a scenario that included inflation in 2013–2014 at no more than a half percentage point above the committee's 2 percent longer-run goal.[5] It should be noted that the forecast of inflation, like any science, is still evolving. As Federal Reserve Chairman Ben Bernanke noted early in his tenure, there are several outstanding issues, including inflation's link to commodity prices, the role of labor costs in the price-setting process, the need to make policy decisions in real time under conditions of uncertainty, and the determinants and effects of changes in inflation expectations.[6]

This last item brings to mind the theory of economic reflexivity advanced by successful investor George Soros in his classic work *The Alchemy of Finance.*[7]

As Soros stated in an early lecture, "Reflexivity is, in effect, a two-way feedback mechanism in which reality helps shape the participants thinking and the participants' thinking helps shape reality in an unending process in which thinking and reality may come to approach each other but can never become identical."[8] Thus bankers' predictions can influence what they are predicting, both for inflation and for other indicators.

Interest Rates

The Fed does not merely predict interest rates for banks; it effectively sets them through its Open Market Committee (OMC). As mentioned in Chapter 2, the OMC is the Federal Reserve's principal means for implementing monetary policy. The committee buys and sells U.S. Treasury bonds and other federal securities; these transactions largely determine the interest rate at which depository institutions lend balances at the Fed to other depository institutions overnight, which in turn affects monetary and financial conditions, including general interest rates charged or paid by financial institutions. In a July 2013 statement, the OMC announced steps it had taken to "maintain downward pressure on longer-term interest rates."[9]

As for the OCC, this agency does not engage in predicting interest rates, but it does analyze the impact of predictions by others. In a mid–2013 report, it stated that the current low interest rate environment increases the vulnerability of banks that "reach for yield," defined as acquiring interest income with decreasing regard for interest rate or credit risk. This historically low interest rate environment, says the OCC report, increases the risk that banks will become too concentrated in longer-term assets and build significant extension or credit risk. When interest rates increase, notes the report, banks that reached for yield could face significant earnings pressure, possibly to the point of capital erosion.[10]

Rate of Economic Growth Indicated by the Bond Yield Curve

A primary tool for predicting the rate of economic growth—or at least whether or not an economic slowdown is looming—is the slope of the bond yield curve—the difference between the current yields on short- and long-term maturity bonds.[11] Interestingly, banks are on the cutting edge of this prediction. As one banker has written, "In its simplest form, the business of banking entails yield curve arbitrage; that is, banks borrow at the short end of the yield curve and lend at the long end."[12] For a bond, the current yield is the bond interest rate (the rate promised by the bond) as a percentage of the current price of the bond. The rule of thumb is that an inverted yield curve (short-term rates being higher than long-term rates) indicates a recession in about a year. Although there have been false-positives (times when inverted yield curves have not predicted recession), it is also true that yield curve inversions have preceded each of the last seven recessions. Yield curves hold predictive power for one year ahead but not for longer periods.[13]

Prediction of Changes in Gross Domestic Product

A number of authorities predict growth rate in the GDP, measured annually as percentage change from year to year. For example, the World Bank publishes annual GDP growth rate numbers for 214 economies, including the United States. (This is one of more than 2,000 economic indicators the World Bank tracks.) Looking at growth rates across the globe, it is easy to realize that GDP growth rate by itself does not indicate economic strength. Indeed, larger economies tend to have lower growth rates.[14]

The Bureau of Economic Analysis (BEA), a common source for actual GDP measurement, continually refines its methods and recently revised them based on new data, including census data.[15] As of mid-2013, the Organization of Economic Cooperation and Development (OECD) was predicting a GDP growth rate of 2.8 percent for the United States for the year 2014.[16] A similar forecast came from a mid-2013 survey of securities professionals who forecast a GDP growth rate of 2.6 percent for the year.[17]

Corporate Profits and Tax Rates

Whereas it is difficult to predict what tax policy will be, it is possible to predict tax rates (corporate tax receipts as a percentage of domestic economic profits) by predicting how existing policy will play out, given known economic trends.[18] Effective tax rates are based on the amount of profits; rates are higher when profits are high and lower when profits are low. In general, it is anticipated that in the near term in the United States, the corporate tax rate will rise to 27 percent in 2014 and then plateau, with corporate profits increasing at 9.4 percent per year from 2014 to 2017. While this rate will be higher than the effective rates paid during the financial crisis (due to low profits), it is lower than the rates effectively charged in past decades.[19]

"Game Changers"

Another way bankers can predict the future for the economy is to identify catalysts for economic change. In mid-2013, the prominent consulting firm McKinsey & Company identified five such forces. To make the top five list, each development had to be a catalyst with the ability to drive substantial growth in GDP, productivity, or jobs. It had to be poised to achieve scale now and capable of producing tangible impact by 2020. It also had to have the potential to accelerate growth across multiple sectors of the economy. McKinsey looked for areas in which new technologies, discoveries, or other factors have been operating.[20]

According to McKinsey, each of the following could raise U.S. GDP substantially by 2020.

- *Energy:* Capturing the opportunity represented by shale oil and gas as a source of power could raise GDP by 3.7 percent.
- *Trade:* Increasing U.S. competitiveness in knowledge-intensive industries could raise GDP by 3.1 percent.
- *Big data:* Harnessing digital information to raise productivity could raise GDP by 1.7 percent. (For more on big data, see the section on Technology below.)
- *Infrastructure:* Building a foundation for long-term growth could boost GDP by 1.7 percent.
- *Talent:* Investing in America's human capital (including results from K–12 education reform, workforce skills, and immigration) could boost GDP by 1.4 percent.

A useful tool in this regard is the OCC report on national bank lending patterns by industry sector. A recent report showed an upward spike in loans for energy, suggesting that bankers have a good instinct for this game changer.[21]

What future involvement might banks have in the sustainability movement?

In recent years, like leaders in other industries, bankers have become more aware of how dependent their operations can be on broader environmental and social trends, and this awareness is likely to continue progressing. According to the International Institute for Sustainable Development, banks are operating more sustainably in two main respects:

- *Operational.* They are undertaking environmental initiatives (e.g., recycling programs or improvements in energy efficiency) and socially responsible initiatives (e.g., support for cultural events, improved human resources practices, and charitable donations).

- *Strategic.* They are putting environmental and social considerations into product design, mission, and policy. For example, bankers are developing new products that provide easier access to capital for environmental initiatives or for social groups the bank wishes to help (community lending). Also, they are considering environmental and/or social criteria in lending and investment strategy.[22]

What about unforeseeable events, such as the legendary "black swan" mentioned in the risk literature?

Bankers would do well to include crisis planning in their scenarios. This is an immensely complex and challenging topic, which we cannot address adequately here. Bankers need to remain alert to materials about risk management, bearing in mind the wise words of one risk expert who stated: "Only a messy, qualitative, judgmental and somewhat unsatisfying process of grappling institutionally with potential crisis scenarios and their impact can set the stage for prompt action when low-probability, high-impact events take place. Anything that discourages this arduous process should be avoided at all cost."[23]

DEMOGRAPHICS

What are some key demographic trends in the United States that could be relevant to banks?

Very broadly, when it comes to investment, population growth is considered positive. Although it is not a sine qua non for bank value,[24] in combination with other factors it tends to be associated with growth in assets. Since most population growth over the past three decades has occurred in metropolitan areas, bank branches located in these areas are considered desirable acquisitions; indeed, banks headquartered in metro areas have seen more growth than their nonmetro peers.[25]

Of course, population growth alone does not drive bank futures—real customers and real employees do. Who will they be? The most recent census data, taken in 2010 and released in subsequent years, has given rise to some new predictions about the future of population trends. One source of these is the Weldon Cooper Center for Public Service.[26] Key projections from this think tank include the following:

- *The graying of America.* Around the country, one in five individuals (18.4 percent) are projected to be 65 or older by 2030, with higher percentages in parts of New England—Maine (27 percent), Vermont (25 percent), and New Hampshire (24 percent). Utah, on the other hand, is projected to experience substantially less population aging than other states, with only 12 percent of residents 65 or older by 2030. Considering an even longer term, more than one in every five individuals in the United States will be over the age of 65 by 2060, up from one in seven (15 percent) in 2015. Moreover the number of people age 85 and older is expected nearly to triple to 18 million over the same period.
- *A rise in racial diversity.* In the future, racial categories may become less distinct, while cultural categories may become more important. The proportion of the population that is white is expected to continue to decline, while the category "other race" (including races other than white alone, black alone, and Asian alone) is projected to grow substantially, primarily reflecting "increases in multiracial identification and interracial marriage and childbearing," reports the Weldon Cooper Center, as well as growing Hispanic populations. In some states, including Illinois and New York, the "other race" category is projected to surpass black or African American as the largest minority racial category by 2040. Continued growth among the Hispanic population is projected over the coming decades, with California, Texas, and New Mexico all projected to be majority Hispanic in the coming decades.

What implications does the aging population have for banking?

Banks located in communities with aging populations can make a special effort to offer financial services for this specific group. Based on an extensive report from the Fed's Division of Consumer and Community Affairs,[27] representing views of nearly 1,500 older adults using banking services, it appears that their confidence and sense of independence are relatively high even into advanced age, and they experience relatively low levels of stress compared to middle aged respondents. However, one in three do report experiencing major financial stress within the past three years. Financial issues facing this age group include cash flow, expectations for retirement, and planning for incapacity, death, or illness of a spouse, according to the survey report. Four in five say they have made no preparations for possible incapacitation. All of these survey findings could represent opportunities to expand services to this group.

What implications does increasing racial diversity in the general population have for banking?

Race by itself means very little, but diversity of race in groups may be associated with outcomes superior to single-race decisions.[28] There is a lesson here for banks. A major goal of commercial banks of any size is to provide profitable services to consumers and businesses. The more positive a consumer's experience is with a bank, the more likely the customer is to continue patronizing it. As the general population becomes more diverse, banks can stay ahead of the trend by continuing to be diversity-minded in recruiting and assigning individuals, from teller ranks to the boardroom. Bank of America partners with 40 organizations that are devoted to increasing diversity in corporate America, including many focused on racial diversity.[29]

TECHNOLOGY

What are some technology trends for banks?

Trends of greatest importance include migration to the cloud, use of mobile devices, virtual currency, and the possible future conversion from open source to micropayments.

What is the cloud, and why is it relevant to banking?

The term *cloud* is commonly attributed to Eric Schmidt, then chairman and CEO of Google, who spoke at an industry conference in 2006 about an "emergent new model" that "starts with the premise that data services and architecture should be on servers."[30] Yet internal use of the term dates back to 1996 at Compaq and a now-defunct company called NetCentric, which had applied unsuccessfully to trademark the term in 1997.[31] Some would see the origins as even earlier: "The cloud is a metaphor for the Internet. It's a rebranding of the Internet," notes Reuven Cohen, a technology educator cited in *MIT Technology Review*.[32]

The National Institute of Standards and Technology (NIST), noting that cloud computing is an "evolving paradigm," defines it as "a model for enabling ubiquitous, convenient, on-demand network access to a shared pool of configurable computing resources (e.g., networks, servers, storage, applications, and services) that can be rapidly provisioned and released with minimal management effort or service provider interaction."[33]

NIST notes that this cloud model is composed of five essential characteristics, three service models, and four deployment models.

- The essential characteristics are on-demand self-service, broad network access, resource pooling, rapid elasticity, and measured service.
- The service models are software-as-service, platform-as-service, and infrastructure-as-service. (In all cases, the infrastructure is managed and controlled by a third party, not the user.)
- The deployment models are private (user only), community (shared by multiple users), public (open to all), or hybrid, with features of more than one approach.

What does cloud infrastructure involve?

A cloud infrastructure is the collection of hardware and software that enables the five essential characteristics of cloud computing described above. As noted by the NIST, the cloud infrastructure has both a physical layer and an abstraction layer.[34] The physical layer consists of the hardware resources that are necessary to support the cloud services being provided, which typically include server, storage, and network components. The abstraction layer consists of the software deployed across the physical layer, which manifests the essential cloud characteristics.

What relation does cloud computing have to so-called big data?

Cloud computing is essentially about where advanced computing will be done; big data is basically about what data will be analyzed there. And as suggested by the word *big*, it is bigger, better, and faster. The technology consulting firm Gartner Inc. defines these data as "high-volume, -velocity, and -variety information assets that demand cost-effective, innovative forms of information processing for enhanced insight and decision making."[35] In the view of this experienced technology consulting firm, big data is one of the top 10 trends impacting information infrastructure today.

How will cloud technology change the future of banking?

A relatively recent study by the consulting firm Accenture identifies three main trends: [28]

- Cloud-based services will leverage social and mobile media to transform the banking experience and relationships for customers.
- Private clouds will come to dominate core banking.
- The public cloud will dominate noncore and nondifferentiated banking activities.

What long-term impact will mobile devices have on banking?

Simple observation of people today in work, educational, or social settings makes it clear that much of the world has "gone mobile," with individuals carrying most of what they need in a single portable devide. The impact on banking will continue to grow. Gartner has predicted global mobile transaction volume and value to average 35 percent annual growth between 2012 and 2017, and we are forecasting a market worth $721 billion with more than 450 million users by 2017; the current market (annual total predicted for 2013) is already at some $235 billion.[36] To the extent that banks adapt to this technology they will retain and grow their customer base. Alternatively, the technology does increase the ability to bypass certain aspects of traditional bank services such as physical checks and credit cards, as well as the use of brick and mortar branches.

What is virtual currency?

This is an attempt to create currency without any reliance on a nation and its treasury or banking system. The prominent example is Bitcoin, a "consensus network" that enables a new payment system and money that is entirely digital. This system is still small and relatively risky (with reportedly volatile inflation rates) but it is generating payments—with reportedly some $1.5 billion worth of coins in circulation now.[37] The money that is circulating through Bitcoin is not circulating through banks, so this represents a potential future loss, however tiny or fleeting it may appear at present, of customer base for banks.

What are micropayments and how might they affect the future of banking?

Micropayments are simply payments in very small amounts enabled by technology. Blue chip companies that have been involved in this trend peripherally include IBM and Visa; the most prominent enabler of micropayments is PayPal. To date, micropayments have been a source of transactional activity for banks, because they generally require access to bank accounts to facilitate payments and credits. The challenge for institutions involved with processing micropayments is that the cost of processing transactions can exceed the value of any service fee received for facilitating the transaction.[38]

In his book *Who Owns the Future?*, technologist Jaron Lanier advocates for a new way of treating the vast amount of intellectual property currently gathered and mined by large networked computers, which he calls "siren servers." He advocates a shift from an open source approach for this information to a micropayment approach in which the owners of the intellectual property receive royalty payments, however small, every time the information is used. This scenario may unfold through banks and complementary organizations such as PayPal or Visa. If so, banks will want to ensure that their transaction costs remain lower than their service fees—a matter largely determined by technology.

What is the near-term outlook for information technology (IT) spending by banks?

Certainly spending on cybersecurity will continue for banks, as they adapt to new technologies. Every IT innovation brings a new gateway for potential cybercrime, and new ways to combat it. Fortunately, awareness of cybersecurity risks issues is high among national and international policymakers, so banks will have support for their efforts to manage these risks.[39]

According to a recent study by the consulting firm Cap Gemini, growth in IT spending by the banking sector is predicted to reach $184.7 billion by 2014, with most of this growth coming from Asia-Pacific banks.[40] The retail banking sector dominates IT spending, which is expected to reach $99.2 billion, with a compound annual growth rate of 3.6 percent through 2014. Corporate banking is the second most important segment, with IT spending expected to reach $49.9 billion by 2014. The highest growth is expected in North America.

In addition to ongoing banking platform migration, Cap Gemini sees the following key trends driving increased investments in technology:

- Banks are restructuring their balance sheets, making adjustments to business models, and examining their product mix to enhance capital adequacy.[41]
- Financial services institutions are increasingly adopting and adapting to social media.

- Convergence of mobile and online banking technology is driving digital channel transformation.
- Big data collection and improving analytics (both of business and customer trends) will be driving desired improvements in client service and profitability.

CONCLUDING COMMENTS

The futures of banking and the economy are interdependent. Strong banks can help build a stronger economy; conversely, a strong economy can support stronger banks. This chapter has reviewed trends in economics, demographics, and technology expected in the days and years ahead for banking and bank M&A.

SECTION 4

SPECIAL SITUATIONS

Up to now this book has covered material useful for most banks or bank holding companies engaged in merger transactions. This section, by contrast, focuses on special situations. **Chapter 10, Cross-Border M&A**, presents trends and issues in transactions that involve banks from two or more countries. **Chapter 11, Distressed and Failed Banks**, takes the reader through the difficult journey of bank insolvency. **Chapter 12, Investing in Bank Stocks,** ends on a more positive note by broadening the horizons of this book. This final chapter offers guidance for all investors, both institutional and individual, interested in aligning a part of their investment portfolios—and thus an important aspect of their own economic future—with commercial banks domestic or foreign, solvent or distressed, as they face their ever-evolving economic destiny.

CHAPTER 10

Cross-Border Bank M&A

Banks live globally but die locally.

Sir Mervyn King, chairman, International Integrated Reporting Council[1]

Generally speaking, U.S. financial institutions have been much more heavily regulated ... than have their foreign counterparts.

Scott Besley and Eugene F. Brigham, Principles of Finance *(2012)*[2]

Cross-border bank M&A transcends the mere buying and selling of banks across national boundaries. It forms an integral part of a vast and complex global financial system epitomizing the best and worst of free enterprise today. On the positive side, global banking networks can raise large amounts of capital for worthy transactions with near-lightning speed. At the same time, this very power to do global business quickly can also serve as a conduit for high-risk transactions, such as large trades of complex global derivatives.

M&A plays a leading part in the global banking story. Without large-scale crossborder changes of control among banks, and without deal financing from third-party banks, transnational finance would not be as widespread and powerful as it is today. And the larger banks are, the more difficult it is for their leaders to oversee the banks' activities, so their exposure to financial risk grows.

The correlation between large size and financial risk is not lost on regulators. As explained in earlier chapters, the Dodd–Frank law has designated large global banks as systemically important financial institutions (SIFIs)—having a significant impact on the economy. For this reason, and for antitrust reasons, modern global banks must conform to a variety of regulations when buying or selling bank ownership or control across borders.

To explore these various aspects of global bank M&A, this chapter will be organized into three main parts. We begin with a look at global banking—defining it, exploring current issues of change and controversy, and reporting on transaction tallies. In closing we will summarize the regulation of crossborder bank M&A transactions both inbound (into the United States) and outbound (when U.S. banks acquire overseas).

THE GLOBAL BANKING SYSTEM

What kind of financial needs do global banks meet, and how do they meet them?

Global banking today facilitates a broad spectrum of financial clients. At an individual level, these may be small multicurrency checking accounts for individual expatriates or loans to individuals outside national boundaries—so-called foreign consumer loans. At the other end of the spectrum, the services of a global bank may include large multinational syndicated loans for corporations. In addition to deposits and loans, the traditional areas for banks, there is a crossover into other industries at the global level, such as insurance, creating a one-stop financial shop called "bancassurance" in Europe.

Global financial institutions meet all these evolving needs by providing worldwide systems. As noted by a leading financial attorney involved with the unwinding of failed financial institutions, global financial institutions generally operate as a single enterprise, typically with consolidated management, an integrated technology base, and—most significantly—a common capital and liquidity pool, but they typically consist of thousands of legal entities incorporated in multiple jurisdictions.[3] For example, Lehman comprised some 8,000 legal entities in 40 countries.[4]

What are some of the main differences in banking in different countries around the globe?

Perhaps the most significant difference is the level of involvement and ownership by government. In the United States and many other developed countries, a national bank is not owned by the federal government; it is merely regulated by it. By contrast, in developing countries, the government owns each national bank.

Is there a global banking system, and if so, who runs it?

There is no single, unified system of banking, much less a leader of it. However, there are many international organizations that help banks coordinate policies and activities. Many of these are interrelated. Some leading players are

- *Bank for International Settlements (BIS),* established in 1930, is the world's oldest central financial organization. It provides central banks with a wide range of financial services, including reserve management and fiduciary services. BIS acts as a prime counterparty to the financial transactions of central banks and serves as an agent or trustee for their international financial operations. Its staff provides a secretariat for the Basel Committee on Banking Supervision (see below). BIS has a Committee on the Global Financial System (CGFS), which attempts to identify potential sources of stress in worldwide financial markets and to offset those risks by promoting improvements to the functioning and stability of these markets. The CGFS oversees the collection of the BIS international banking and financial statistics. BIS also has a Committee on Payment and Settlement Systems (CPSS), a global standard-setting body for payment and securities settlement systems. It serves as a forum for central banks to monitor and analyze trends in cross-border and multicurrency settlement, as well as payment, settlement, and clearing systems within national boundaries.
- *Basel Committee on Banking Supervision* (Basel) is the primary global standard setter for the prudential regulation of banks and provides a forum for cooperation on banking supervisory matters.[5] Its mandate, as stated in its charter, is to strengthen the regulation, supervision, and practices of banks worldwide with the purpose of enhancing financial stability. With a secretariat provided by the Bank for International Settlements, Basel provides a forum for regular cooperation among central banks of the 28 member countries on banking supervisory matters.[6] When

needed, the Basel committee's members develop guidelines and standards for central banks. Such guidelines include global standards on capital adequacy, known as the Basel accords. So far, there are three—known as Basil I, II, and III.

- *Group of 8 (G8)* is a forum for the leaders of the world's largest national economies—today considered to be, Canada, France, Germany, Italy, Japan, Russia, the United Kingdom, and the United States. It launched in 1975 as a Group of 6, but over time added Canada (becoming G7, a group that still convenes) and Russia.
- *Group of 10 (G 10)* is a group of countries that agreed to participate in the General Arrangements to Borrow (GAB).
- *Group of 20 (G20)* is a forum for the world's 20 largest economies, including the European Commission. Its participants are finance ministers and central bank governors.[7]
- *International Monetary Fund (IMF)* fosters international cooperation in macroeconomic and monetary issues. With its 185 member countries, it aims to ensure the stability of the international monetary system.
- *Organization for Economic Cooperation and Development (OECD).* Originally founded in 1947 as a European group (and with that in its name), this group grew to include what are now 34 nations dedicated to mutual cooperation.
- *World Bank Group (World Bank).* This economic development icon consists of five organizations, all of them dedicated to reducing poverty. The members of the World Bank are the International Bank for Reconstruction and Development (IBRD), which lends to governments of middle-income and creditworthy low-income countries; the International Development Association, which provides interest-free loans (credits) and grants to governments of poor countries; the International Finance Corporation (IFC), a development finance channel working with some 750 banks in developing countries to make investments in or provide loans to businesses in developing countries; the Multilateral Investment Guarantee

Agency (MIGA), which offers political risk insurance to investors in developing nations; and the International Centre for Settlement of Investment Disputes (ICSID), for conciliation and arbitration of crossborder investment disputes.

What exactly is Basel III, and why does it matter to a bank acquirer?

Basel III, according to the BIS, is the third and latest version of an ongoing series of reform measures developed by the Basel Committee on Banking Supervision to strengthen banks. They can improve a bank's ability to absorb shocks from financial or economic stress, strengthen risk management and governance, and improve bank disclosures. They also can lower bank profitability by limiting bank flexibility.

The Basel standards have led to greater uniformity in bank capital around the world, even though implementation remains voluntary and varies from country to country.

Among other things, the Basel standards define the kind of capital banks should have, setting minimums for high-quality versus inferior capital.

Under Basel III, Tier I capital must be in the form of common shares and retained earnings, which must be at least half of the bank's capital. Tier II capital—certain types of reserves and debt—is acceptable, but total value cannot exceed Tier I. More structured forms of capital, such as credit default swaps and special investment vehicles, formerly known as Tier III, will not count as meeting capital requirements.

Another important aspect of Basel III is a new concept of financial risk. It will replace the concept of value-at-risk with expected shortfall, an approach some have criticized.[8] Both concepts measure bank assets under risky conditions, but for one approach (value-at- risk), the proverbial cup is half full; for the other (expected shortfall), the cup is half empty.

In recent years, several countries, including the United States with the Dodd–Frank law in 2010, have enacted their own capital standards similar but not identical to Basel III. For example, Dodd–Frank has capital standards.[9] Nonetheless, these same countries may adopt Basel standards anyway. For example, Basel III standards may soon be a de facto regulatory requirement in the United States, despite the Dodd–Frank standards.

In September 2013 the Federal Reserve published interim final rules that would apply tougher capital rules for the nearly 7,000 banks insured by the Federal Deposit Insurance Corporation (FDIC).[10]

Banks involved in crossborder M&A may wind up holding significant assets and/or liabilities in a foreign currency. What is the impact of this holding?

Even with volatile exchange rates, the holding of foreign currency poses no particular challenges for banks, except for one particular scenario. Analysts have identified a problem called "foreign currency assets and liabilities mismatch," in which there are unequal amounts of assets versus liabilities in the foreign currency. When depreciation (or appreciation) of the domestic currency causes an increase (or decrease) in the value of the foreign currency, this changes the value of equity shown on the balance sheet. (There is no impact if the foreign currency is held in equal amounts on the asset and liabilities side.) This balance sheet mismatch is more common in developing countries, which are more likely to hold foreign currency.

What exactly is global liquidity, and why does it matter to banks involved in crossborder M&A?

Global liquidity has been defined as the ease of financing at the global financial level. Official liquidity is a macroeconomic condition set by central banks through monetary policy; this policy both responds to and influences credit supply and credit demand at the macroeconomic level. Private liquidity is how banks respond to this environment; in this realm, the tighter credit is, the fewer risks banks will take.[11]

With respect to global banking, what is international risk sharing?

Risk increases when a nation is consuming more than it is producing. Availability of credit across borders can compensate for this discrepancy. To see the extent to which a particular country is sharing risk across borders, consider the ratio of gross foreign assets relative to the country's gross domestic product. When this is high, risk is being offloaded. The problem is that, eventually, the piper must be paid; eventually, production must equal or surpass consumption.

When a U.S. bank loans to foreign customers, are there any special reporting requirements?

Yes. Banks must disclose the foreign location of their outstandings, defined as significant loans, acceptances, interest-bearing deposits with other banks, other interest-bearing investments, and any other monetary assets that are denominated in dollars or other nonlocal currency.[12] To be significant, they must exceed 1 percent of the bank's total assets. Guidance for this disclosure appears in the *Industry Guide for the Securities and Exchange Commission.*[13] Banks must disclose the name of the country and the amount of the outstandings.

To the extent that material local currency outstandings are not hedged or are not funded by local borrowings, these amounts should be included in cross-border outstandings.

For purposes of determining the amount of outstandings to be reported, loans made to, or deposits placed with, a branch of a foreign bank located outside the foreign bank's home country should be considered as loans to, or deposits with, the foreign bank.

CROSS-BORDER M&A

What kinds of returns do shareholders receive from cross-border M&A?

Recent research shows that, globally, the percentage of banking revenues from developing markets has been rising along with performance, compared to developed nations.[14]

A recent Accenture study of postmerger returns from 89 cross-border bank transactions announced during the first decade of this century found generally positive returns.[15] The Accenture research indicated that cross-border deals where 50 percent or more of the target bank is acquired tended to boost financial returns. Also, majority-stake deals largely outperformed minority-stake deals over time, although minority-stake deals can be successful in terms of revenue generation.

A majority of the cross-border deals, the Accenture study found, have resulted in both short- and long-term success for the foreign acquirer—especially those involving emerging-market partners.

- Sixty-nine percent of cross-border bank deals realized positive equity returns.
- Forty-two percent of majority-stake deals realized profitability improvements in the first year, while 53 percent resulted in an improved efficiency ratio.
- Minority deals resulted in an average 19.5 percent compound annual growth rate and made up four of the six best-performing deals.
- Emerging-market deals have generated a higher level of annual revenue expansion (18.7 percent compound annual growth rate) than those completed in developed markets (14.6 percent compound annual growth rate).
- Of the 15 best-performing deals overall in terms of revenue generation, 12 were done in emerging markets.

The study found that when a bank acquires another bank in an emerging market, the deal tends to outperform those in which the target firm was located in a developed market. In Accenture's opinion, reasons for this trend could include

- Emerging markets present a greater opportunity because of low banking penetration.
- They present global markets with the opportunity to acquire operations with long-term growth prospects at low prices.
- Emerging markets can offer a lower cost platform for global banks.
- Governments in emerging markets are often receptive to foreign investments.
- Growing payment flows between emerging and developed markets offer further opportunities for global banks with interests in emerging market.

A separate study showed that global bank M&A in emerging markets falls prey to the same patterns seen across industries and regions: selling shareholders tend to do better than the shareholders of the acquiring institutions, at least in the short term.[16] Yet another paper looks at the downside of capital inflows to emerging economies. Because the flows can be volatile, putting pressure on central banks, countries have taxed short-term borrowing from foreign sources. They have also put limits on banks' exposure to foreign exchange derivatives, seeking to reduce the short-term external debt that banks might use to hedge these derivatives.[17]

Can an acquirer use investments in developing countries to make an inroad into a more mature economy?

Yes. A case in point are two global banks based in Spain—BBVA and Santander—which started acquiring in Latin America and then focused their attention on expansion in the U.S. market.[18]

What kind of growth rates have banks had in emerging versus developed economies—and what is the outlook for the long-term future?

During the recent financial crisis, U.S. bank performance declined more dramatically during the crisis years but is now recovering. According to a series of reports by McKinsey & Company, in the United States, banking revenues (after provisions for loan losses) declined 11.8 percent from 2007 to 2010. By contrast, banks in emerging economies grew over the same period—revenues increased by 19.8 percent in India, 17.6 percent in Brazil, and 13.7 percent in China during the same period.[19] The following year, however, China's growth declined by 3.7 percent (bringing it to 10 percent), according to McKinsey, while the United States showed "moderate but sustainable" growth.[20]

Some experts have predicted growth for the banking sector in emerging economies within the so-called E7 (emerging economies of China, India, Brazil, Mexico, Russia, Indonesia, and Turkey) versus the G7 (developed economies of the United States, Japan, Germany, the United Kingdom,

France, Italy, and Canada) by 2050, according to the accountancy firm PricewaterhouseCoopers.[21]

- China could overtake the United States in terms of the size of its domestic banking sectors by around 2023.
- By 2050 the leading E7 emerging economies could have domestic banking assets and profits that exceed those in the G7 by around 50 percent.
- India has particularly strong long-term growth potential, and projections suggest it could become the third-largest domestic banking sector by 2050 after China and the United States, but ahead of Japan, the United Kingdom, and Germany.
- Brazil could also rise in importanceover this period.[22]

An Accenture analysis of 2011–2014 business plans for a group of 30 global banks estimated a 6.5 percent average growth, with 4 percent Europe/North America average) following negative (−0.5) percent retail revenue growth for 2008–2011.[23]

Are there international restrictions on insider trading in global mergers?

Most jurisdictions outlaw the practice, at least in principle. More than 85 percent of the world's securities and commodities market regulators have rules against insider trading. This is in part because they are members of the International Organization of Securities Commissions (IOSCO) and have signed on to the Core Principles listed in IOSCO's "Objectives and Principles of Securities Regulation," published in 1998 and updated in 2003.[24] It states that one of the primary objectives of good securities market regulation is investor protection. The principles say: "Investors should be protected from misleading, manipulative or fraudulent practices, including insider trading, front running ahead of customers and the misuse of client assets." Note also that the World Bank and the IMF use the IOSCO Core Principles in assessing the financial risk of countries.

INBOUND BANK ACQUISITIONS

What U.S. banking laws address foreign acquirers of U.S. banks?

The Edge Act, a law passed after World War I to facilitate cross-border business by American banks, limits foreign ownership of corporations chartered by the Federal Reserve Board to engage in international banking and finance.[25] Furthermore, under the Edge Act, the U.S. federal government has jurisdiction over all lawsuits "to which any corporation organized under the laws of the United States shall be a party, arising out of transactions involving international or foreign banking, or banking in a dependency or insular possession of the United States."[26] As interpreted by courts in the Southern District, the Edge Act creates federal jurisdiction when "(1) the case is civil in nature, (2) one of the parties is a corporation organized under the laws of the United States (i.e., a national bank), and (3) the suit arises out of transactions involving international banking or international financial operations (including territorial banking)." [27]

More generally, when a foreign bank seeks to acquire a U.S. bank, the Federal Reserve must consider the quality of supervision that bank receives in its home jurisdiction and will generally place restrictions on the activities of the acquirer.

The regulatory structure for foreign banks in the United States is vast and complex. In fact, there is an extensive tome, *Regulation of Foreign Banks and Affiliates in the United States,* now in its sixth edition.[28]

What special disclosures are required of U.S. banks that sell to foreign acquirers?

Under the International Investment and Trade in Services Survey Act of 1976, all businesses must report ownership by a foreign investor that owns 10 percent or more directly or indirectly. The Bureau of Economic Analysis has a right to request such a report of any U.S. person (individual, partnership, corporation, estate, trust, not-for-profit, etc.) that had a foreign affiliate at the end of its fiscal year.[29]

More generally, the Securities and Exchange Commission (SEC) requires disclosure of "foreign activities."[30] Foreign corporations registering securities in the United States may have to fill out one or more of a series of forms called "Foreign Forms," including Form 4, which pertains to mergers. In general, these forms require U.S. standards of disclosure with some leeway for other systems.

What does the SEC require U.S. banks that are publicly traded to disclose about their foreign activities?

SEC rules require separate disclosure of foreign activities when they reach a certain financial level. Foreign activities include loans and other revenues producing assets and transactions in which the debtor or customer, whether an affiliated or unaffiliated person, is domiciled outside the United States.

Reports must be made for any period in which assets, revenue, or income (loss) before income tax expense, or net income (loss), each as associated with foreign activities, exceeded 10 percent of the corresponding amount in the related financial statements. Public companies reaching or exceeding the limit must

- Disclose total identifiable assets (net of valuation allowances) associated with foreign activities
- State the amount of revenue, income (loss) before taxes, and net income (loss) associated with foreign activities
- Disclose significant estimates and assumptions (including those related to the cost of capital) used in allocating revenue and expenses to foreign activities
- Describe the nature and effects of any changes in such estimates and assumptions that have a significant impact on comparability between reporting periods

The SEC requires this information to be presented separately for each significant geographic area[31] and in the aggregate for all other geographic areas not deemed significant.

What major rules apply to foreign acquirers of U.S. banks?

In December 2012, the Federal Reserve Board proposed rules requiring foreign banking organizations with a significant U.S. presence to create an internal layer of supervision in the form of an intermediate holding company (IHC) to oversee their U.S. subsidiaries. Under the proposed rule, which was still pending as this book went to press, foreign banks would also be required to maintain stronger capital and liquidity positions in the United States. IHCs with $50 billion or more in consolidated assets also would be subject to the Federal Reserve's capital plan rule, as well as enhanced liquidity risk management standards, and would be required to conduct liquidity stress tests and hold a 30-day buffer of highly liquid assets. The proposal includes measures regarding capital stress tests, single-counterparty credit limits, overall risk management, and early remediation. Foreign banking organizations with global consolidated assets of $50 billion or more on July 1, 2014, would be required to meet the new standards on July 1, 2015.[32]

Is it permissible for a foreign bank to underwrite securities in the United States?

Yes, if it establishes a separate U.S. broker-dealer affiliate. The U.S. government regulates not only the domestic securities activities of domestic banks but also the U.S. branches and agencies of foreign banks. So if a non-U.S. bank wants to engage in securities underwriting or similar activities in the United States (or involving U.S. companies or investors), it generally will need to set up a separate U.S. broker-dealer affiliate to do this. This is a common practice. In fact, one-third all U.S. dollar-denominated securities underwriting is done by U.S. broker-dealer subsidiaries of foreign banks.[33]

Are foreign banks subject to the "living wills" requirement described in Chapter 2?

Yes. For the past few years, the resolutions have been cascading in, starting with the largest banks in 2012 (foreign banks with $250 billion or more), then moving to smaller banks the following year (foreign banks with $50 billion or more in global assets, and at least one branch or agency located in the United States). Resolution plans of foreign banks with between $100 billion and $250 billion in U.S. nonbank assets were submitted by July 2013.

Resolution plans of foreign banks with less than $100 billion in U.S. nonbank assets were due by year-end 2013.[34]

Are deposits in foreign branches of U.S. banks insured by the FDIC?

No. In September 2013, the Fed approved a final rule clarifying that deposits in foreign branches of U.S. banks do not receive FDIC insurance protection.[35]

OUTBOUND BANK ACQUISITIONS

What are some of the principal issues a U.S. company should know about in connection with the acquisition of a non-U.S. business or a U.S. business with significant foreign assets?

Some of the key areas to focus on are as follows:

- Differences in rights accorded to employees
- Sources of overseas financing
- The ability to use foreign assets to support financing from lenders
- Regulatory requirements and limitations with respect to the acquisition itself and postacquisition operations

Suppose a U.S. bank wants to buy a European bank. How does the European Union (EU) merger review process work?

The European Commission has 25 working days after a deal is filed for a first-stage review. It may extend that by 10 working days to 35 working days, to consider either a company's proposed remedies or an EU member state's request to handle the case.

Most mergers win approval, but occasionally the commission opens a detailed second-stage investigation for up to 90 additional working days, which it may extend to 105 working days.

Under the simplified procedure, the commission announces the clearance of uncontroversial first-stage mergers without giving any reason for its decision. Cases may be reclassified as nonsimplified—that is, ordinary first-stage reviews—until they are approved. In January 2013, this fast track was granted to Elavon Financial Services Ltd., a subsidiary of U.S. bank Bancorp, and Spanish bank Banco Santander to set up a (premerger) joint venture.

What about taxes? What are the regulations here?

The taxation of banks with outbound or inbound deals surpasses the scope of this chapter, but a brief highlight is worth mentioning.

U.S. investors owning 5 percent or more of any foreign company stock must file a Form 5471 with the Internal Revenue Service. Conversely, every domestic or foreign company that is "engaged in a trade or business in the U.S." and "controlled" by a "foreign person" must file an information return to the Internal Revenue Service on Form 5472.

"Control" for the purposes of this reporting requirement is deemed to occur in a tax year if at any time in the year a foreign person owns at least 25 percent of the value or voting power of a corporation's stock.[36]

CONCLUDING COMMENTS

All banks operate in a global economy, but few banks venture beyond their national borders to establish operations abroad. As this overview has shown, the challenges are many and complex. With proper professional guidance, however, bank holding companies that wish to expand globally can do so successfully.

CHAPTER 11

Distressed and Failed Banks

> That is why it is possible for banks to fall apart when people don't pay their mortgages back. Banks sell assets that are partially made of the future intents of borrowers. When borrowers do something other than promised, those assets no longer exist.
>
> —*Jaron Lanier, Author,* Who Owns the Future[1]

Operating any business means risking failure, and bankers from the nation's 6,000-plus banks know this from experience. In any given year, 1 bank in 10 is likely to be suffering losses, and 1 in 20 has a probability of failing within three years, according a recent Federal Reserve analysis.[2] Tellingly, since October 1, 2000, the Federal Deposit Insurance Corporation (FDIC) has taken more than 500 banks into receivership.[3]

As financial institutions, banks are especially vulnerable to monetary and economic risks, such as volatility of interest rates, steep changes in the rate of inflation, and economic panics. And because the money that commercial banks store and process belongs to other people, banks more than other businesses may be exposed to heavy-handed and even "fatalistic" regulation. Banking authorities can declare a bank dead—"failed"—even if the bank itself possesses the assets and talents to live on and succeed.

Yet the distressed banks' story has a bright side. The three-year, 1-in-20 failure rate of banks is very low compared to the business population in general, where the chance of failure is close to one in five within the first year.[4] Also, distressed banks often live on through M&A. All but 40 of the FDIC-insured banks that the FDIC took into receivership were absorbed into other banks.[5] This is only the tip of the iceberg when it comes to distressed bank M&A, because not every bank that undergoes financial stress lets it go far enough to go into receivership. Many a merger occurs when the bank is still in the safe zone. No one may ever know the extent of troubles these banks have seen, except for their acquirers.

To explore how distressed banks and their acquirers arrive at optimal unions, this chapter will provide an overview of distressed bank M&A and explain the central role of the FDIC.

DISTRESSED BANKS: THE SCORE

You mentioned that at any given time, 1 in 10 banks may be experiencing losses. How does that vary based on timing, size, and location?

The pattern of bank losses varies over time and by bank size. At the height of the financial crisis of 2007–2009, approximately half of all large banks in the United States were experiencing losses, compared to 40 percent for midsize banks and 30 percent for the smallest banks.

Since then larger banks appear to have mostly recovered, but some smaller banks are still experiencing loses. As of June 2013, no $50 billion-plus bank reported losses, while 2 percent of midsized banks did, and 7.82 percent of the smallest banks did.[6]

Bank profitability varies by location. In 2009, toward the end of the most recent financial crisis, banks in the West and Southeast showed a lower level of profitability than other banks around the country—a general "heat map" of financial distress that has held steady since then even as average profitability has increased in all states.[7]

What is the long-term survival rate of community banks versus noncommunity banks, and how do their failure rates compare?

Banking regulators have three decades of data on this score. In short, survival rates for community banks—that is, the chances of them continuing to operate under their original name and ownership—are much higher than for larger banks, but failure rates are about the same.

Regarding survival rates, overall, of the 17,901 bank charters that reported at year-end 1984, 5,372 reported continuously through 2011, for an overall three-decade survival rate of 30 percent. Among institutions that started out in 1984 as community banks, however, the survival rate was 33 percent, compared to only 6 percent for those that began as noncommunity banks. Thus, community banks were more than five times more likely than noncommunity banks to remain in operation for the entire 27-year period.

Regarding failure rates, community banks and noncommunity banks have similar records over time, compared to total number of banks of their size. Overall, nearly 90 percent of all institutions that have failed since 1984 have been community banks. This matches their prevalence among all banks, which varied between 86 percent and 92 percent during the study period.[8]

What are the pros and cons of buying a distressed bank rather than a healthy bank?

On the positive side, the price is likely to be low, due to the distress factor. Also, because bank liquidity and capital are so closely watched by regulators—especially in systemically important financial institutions (SIFIs), the learning curve is likely to be short. Another positive is that the process for insolvency can be fairly smooth due to the FDIC's single receivership. Also, if the FDIC has insured the deposits, that part of the financial difficulties gets resolved without the acquirer's cash.

On the negative side, it is risky to buy a distressed bank—even if the FDIC shares losses. Not every bank has the ability to incorporate the assets that are being brought over in an FDIC-assisted transaction and to raise needed capital.[9] (See Exhibit 11.1 for a comparison of traditional vs. distressed bank M&A.)

What is the technical definition of bank insolvency?

Different authorities define insolvency in different ways.[10] The Bankruptcy Code, which is Title 11 of the United States Code (11 U.S.C.), defines the term *insolvent*, as it applies to a corporation, as a "financial condition such that the sum of [the] entity's debts is greater than all of such entity's property, at a fair valuation."[11] In this definition, debts include contingent liabilities. A fair valuation of an entity's property refers to the amount of cash that could be realized from a sale of the property "during a reasonable

Exhibit 11.1 Traditional versus Distressed Bank M&A

	Traditional M&A	**Distressed M&A**
Diligence	Available and organized data	Detailed data if SIFI
Timing	Quick	Urgent
Valuation	At or above market	Below market
Competition	Relatively high number of bidders	Relatively low number of bidders
Liabilities	Probably need to assume	Probably able to avoid
Legal	Out of court	In court or out of court
Management	Probably retain	Probably replace
Strategy	Grow	Fix

Abbreviation: SIFI, systemically important financial institutions.
Source: Adapted from H. Peter Nesvold, Jeffrey Anapolsky, and Alexandra R. Lajoux, *The Art of Distressed M&A* (New York: McGraw-Hill, 2011).

period of time." A reasonable period of time is an amount of time that "a typical creditor would find optimal: not so short a period that the value of goods is substantially impaired via a forced sale, but not so long a time that a typical creditor would receive less satisfaction of its claim, as a result of the time value of money and typical business needs, by waiting for the possibility of a higher price."

The Uniform Fraudulent Transfer Act (UFTA) also defines *insolvency* as having more liabilities than salable assets, but also deems insolvent any debtor "who is generally not paying his debts when they become due."[12] This is sometimes referred to as the equity definition of insolvency. Most state laws have a definition that resembles that of the Bankruptcy Code, but some states (e.g., New York) follow the equity definition for certain situations other than fraudulent transfers.

Under generally accepted accounting principles (GAAP), a company can be considered solvent if it has sufficient assets to pay its debts as they come due or if it has book assets that are greater than book liabilities. This GAAP definition is more lenient than other definitions because it does not count contingent liabilities. It may be significantly misleading if the market value of the assets declines in a manner that was not predicted by the applicable accounting principles. Therefore, merely examining whether book equity (i.e., the difference between book assets and book liabilities) is positive is usually insufficient to determine whether a company is solvent.

One can also consider distance to default, a market-based assessment on default probability applying a model for assessing credit risk of companies. Recent research has shown that it is a good indicator of bank fragility, by measuring the probability of defaulting within one year if the banks keep their current assets and liabilities.[13]

For banks, however, insolvency and risk of default aren't the only indicators of distress; banking authorities can close a bank for a number of financial reasons not necessarily amounting to insolvency. When the FDIC takes over a bank, the bank need not be insolvent or at risk of defaulting.

BANK CLOSINGS

On what grounds can the FDIC close a bank?

Under the Federal Deposit Insurance Act, the FDIC can close an insured bank or thrift based on a variety of factors, not just insolvency. The grounds for appointing a conservator or receiver (which may be the FDIC) for any insured depository institution, summarized from applicable law, are as follows:[14]

- *Assets insufficient for obligations.* The institution's assets are less than the institution's obligations to its creditors and others, including members of the institution.
- *Substantial dissipation.* Substantial dissipation of assets or earnings due to any violation of any statute or regulation or any unsafe or unsound practice
- *Unsafe or unsound condition.* An unsafe or unsound condition to transact business
- *Cease and desist orders.* Any willful violation of a cease-and-desist order that has become final
- *Concealment.* Any concealment of the institution's books, papers, records, or assets, or any refusal to submit the institution's books, papers, records, or affairs for inspection to any examiner or to any lawful agent of the appropriate federal banking agency or state bank or savings association supervisor

- *Inability to meet obligations.* The institution is likely to be unable to pay its obligations or meet its depositors' demands in the normal course of business.
- *Losses.* The institution has incurred or is likely to incur losses that will deplete all or substantially all of its capital, and there is no reasonable prospect for the institution to become adequately capitalized (as defined in Tite 12, Section 1831o (b)) without federal assistance.
- *Violations of law.* Any violation of any law or regulation, or any unsafe or unsound practice or condition that is likely to cause insolvency or substantial dissipation of assets or earnings, weaken the institution's condition, or otherwise seriously prejudice the interests of the institution's depositors or the FDIC.[15]
- *Consent.* The institution, by resolution of its board of directors or its shareholders or members, consents to the appointment.
- *Cessation of insured status.* The institution ceases to be an insured institution.
- *Undercapitalization.* The institution is undercapitalized[16] and has no reasonable prospect of becoming adequately capitalized; fails to become adequately capitalized when required to do so;[17] fails to submit a capital restoration plan acceptable to the FDIC within a required time frame;[18] or materially fails to implement a capital restoration plan submitted and accepted;[19] or the institution is "critically undercapitalized," or otherwise has substantially insufficient capital.[20]
- *Money laundering offense.* The U.S. Attorney General notifies the appropriate federal banking agency or the corporation in writing that the insured depository institution has been found guilty of a criminal offense.[21]

Of all these reasons for closing a bank, what is the most commonly enforced?

The clearest and most common basis for closing U.S. banks and thrifts is based on how well the bank is capitalized. This is defined in Section 38 of the Federal Deposit Insurance Act, which describes when the FDIC needs to take prompt corrective action to take over a bank.[22] Capital may be defined by the FDIC, but it must include a leverage limit, specifying the ratio of tangible equity to total assets.

Currently, the standard is as follows:

- Well capitalized: 10 percent or higher
- Adequately capitalized: 8 percent or higher
- Undercapitalized: less than 8 percent
- Significantly undercapitalized: less than 6 percent
- Critically undercapitalized: less than 2 percent[23]

Once a bank is defined as "critically undercapitalized," a conservator or receiver must be appointed within 90 days unless the institution can improve its capital ratio or the period is extended.[24]

Is it fair to say that a bank with liabilities greater than its assets is insolvent and should be closed?

According to the FDIC standards for being "critically undercapitalized," it would seem so. However, the importance of income must be noted. On the balance sheet, it is obviously desirable for the bank's assets (e.g., loans) to be larger than their liabilities (e.g., deposits). However, when the income from interest charged for on loans is higher than the income from interest paid on deposits, there can be profits to the bank, despite a high liability-to-assets ratio.[25]

If the FDIC is the one in charge (sole receiver), how does the Bankruptcy Code apply to bank insolvency?

Overall, the Bankruptcy Code contains nine operating chapters:

- Chapter 1 contains general provisions and definitions.
- Chapter 3 describes case administration.
- Chapter 5 explains rules for handling creditors, debtors, and estates.

- Chapter 7 covers liquidation, or the orderly sale of the assets of a debtor by a trustee.
- Chapter 9 applies to the debts of municipalities.
- Chapter 11 addresses reorganization of a debtor.
- Chapter 12 provides relief for family farmers.
- Chapter 13 provides a process by which an individual with regular income may repay all or a portion of his or her indebtedness under a new structure.
- Chapter 15, which became the newest chapter in 2005, covers ancillary and other cross-border cases, enabling a corporate insolvency proceeding outside the United States to gain access to the U.S. court system. Chapter 15 updated and replaced the prior Section 304 of the Bankruptcy Code. Recent cases filed under Chapter 15—all in U.S. Bankruptcy Court—include two Kazakhstani banks, BTA Bank (2010, Southern District of New York) and Alliance Bank (2010, Southern District of New York); Millenium Emerging Credit Fund Limited (2011, Southern District of New York); Interacciones Banking Corporation, Ltd. (2012, Southern District, Texas); and the Irish Bank Resolution Corp. (2013, Delaware District).[26]

The treatment of insolvent banks is based in Bankruptcy Code language and standards.

Under the code, banks are ineligible for bankruptcy, so neither a bank nor its creditors can place the bank in bankruptcy. That is, the Bankruptcy Code clearly designates the FDIC alone as the receiver for banks in financial distress.[27] At the same time, however, the holding companies that own the banks (bank holding companies) can file for bankruptcy. For example, Washington Mutual Bank entered FDIC receivership on September 25, 2008, and the next day its parent Washington Mutual, Inc. along with its affiliated WMI Investment Corp. filed for Chapter 11 reorganization.[28] Lehman Brothers Holdings, which filed for bankruptcy September 15, 2008, is another example of complexity: its failure resulted in more than 100 separate insolvency proceedings around the world, including the United States.[29] Washington Mutual and Lehman both filed under Chapter 11, which requires requiresdetailed disclosures both at filing and in planning reorganization (see Exhibits 11.2 and 11.3).

Another complexity is added by the Dodd–Frank rules addressing SIFIs, as discussed in Chapters 2 and 3. As explained there, large bank holding companies and certain foreign banking institutions—as well as other financial companies deemed systemically important by the Financial Stability Oversight Council—file plans demonstrating that they can be resolved under the Bankruptcy Code in a manner that does not pose a systemic threat to the nation's financial system.[30] These institutions are subject to heightened supervision and higher capital requirements. They are also required to develop and maintain detailed resolution plans ("living wills," discussed below) showing how they can be resolved under the Bankruptcy Code.[31]

Exhibit 11.2 Facts for Disclosure Statements in Chapter 11 Filing

1. The events that led to the filing of a bankruptcy petition
2. A description of the available assets and their value
3. The anticipated future of the company
4. The source of information stated in the disclosure statement
5. A disclaimer
6. The present condition of the debtor while in Chapter 11
7. The scheduled claims
8. The estimated return to creditors under a Chapter 7 liquidation
9. The accounting method utilized to produce financial information and the name of the accountants responsible for such information
10. The future management of the debtor
11. The Chapter 11 plan of reorganization or a summary thereof
12. The estimated administrative expenses, including attorneys' and accountants' fees
13. The collectibility of accounts receivable
14. Financial information, data, valuations, or projections relevant to the creditors' decision to accept or reject the Chapter 11 plan
15. Information relevant to the risks posed to creditors under the plan

(Continued on page 244)

16. The actual or projected realizable value from recovery of preferential or otherwise voidable transfers
17. Litigation that is likely to arise in a nonbankruptcy context
18. Tax attributes of the debtor
19. The relationship of the debtor with affiliates

Source: From H. Peter Nesvold, Jeffrey Anapolsky, and Alexandra R. Lajoux, *The Art of Distressed M&A* (New York: McGraw-Hill, 2011).

Exhibit 11.3 Plan of Reorganization Confirmation Factors

- The plan complies with all applicable provisions of the Bankruptcy Code.
- The plan proponent complies with all applicable provisions of the Bankruptcy Code.
- The plan is proposed in good faith.
- Payments to be made to professionals under the plan are reasonable.
- The plan proponent discloses the identity and affiliations of directors and officers of the reorganized company and its affiliates.
- The plan proponent discloses the identity and compensation of any insiders to be employed by the reorganized company.
- Any regulators with jurisdiction over the rates charged by a debtor have approved of any rate change provided in the plan.
- The plan passes the best interests of creditors' test.
- Unless all classes of claims and interests vote to approve the plan (or are not impaired under the plan), at least one impaired noninsider class has voted in favor.
- Administrative expenses are paid in cash, possibly over time.
- The plan passes the feasibility test.
- All bankruptcy fees are paid.
- If the plan contemplates continuing payments for a pension plan, the payments comply with Bankruptcy Code Section 1114.
- All property transfers comply with applicable nonbankruptcy law.
- The plan satisfies the absolute priority rule.

Source: From H. Peter Nesvold, Jeffrey Anapolsky, and Alexandra R. Lajoux, *The Art of Distressed M&A* (New York: McGraw-Hill, 2011).

About how many commercial banks go into FDIC receivership each year in the United States?

It varies greatly, depending on economic conditions and the attitudes of regulators. Typically, the number is 50 or so, but yearly bank closing totals have been as low as 3 (in 2007) and as high as 158 (in 2010).[32]

The FDIC also maintains a list of "problem" institutions, based on FDIC evaluation of financial and operational criteria, and this number fluctuates.[33] At any given time there are several hundred problem institutions. The current total as we go to press is 553, but the number reached 888 in early 2011.[34]

When the FDIC takes over a bank and inserts money into the bank, where does this money come from?

The FDIC's Deposit Insurance Fund (DIF), currently worth more than $35 billion, receives money from assessments received from insured banks. This covers the costs of the payouts it must make to guarantee (insure) deposits of these banks. The DIF is required to maintain a particular ratio between its own reserves and the amount of deposits it is insuring. The current ratio is only 0.45, but it is required to reach 1.35 by September 30, 2020. The estimated cost from bank failures from 2012 to 2016 is projected to be $12 billion—suggesting the need for significant funding in the DIF.[35]

What happens to banking deposits if a bank is declared insolvent?

As soon as possible after the default of an insured depository institution, the FDIC may organize a new national bank or federal savings association in the same community as the insured depository institution in default to assume the insured deposits of that institution.[36]

As soon as a bank's receiver (whether the FDIC or another bank) is appointed, it has power over the assets and liabilities of the failed bank or thrift. As such, it can arrange an immediate sale of assets and transfer insured deposits to another bank. The receiver for a failed bank has the right to complete a sale as part of the initial resolution or shortly afterward without awaiting court, creditor, or shareholder approval. As a receiver, the FDIC makes failing bank asset information available to potential purchasers through the Internet, including contact information for banks in receivership and an application form for bidding.[37]

There are basically two ways the FDIC can make sure the bank failure does not harm depositors:

- *Purchase and assumption agreement.* Deposits (liabilities) are assumed by an open bank, which also purchases some or all of the failed bank's loans (assets).
- *Deposit payoff.* FDIC as insurer pays the depositors out of its DIF.

Can a depositor of a failed bank expect changes?

Yes. As an FDIC guide to customers' notes, if a customer is doing business with a new bank that acquired the accounts from a bank that failed, the original contract with the failed bank no longer exists. So, the new bank will create a new deposit contract, perhaps with a lower interest rate. Rates on CDs may also be changed. In this case, the failed bank's customers can withdraw their money without an early withdrawal penalty.

LIVING WILLS

What is a "living will" for a bank?

A living will is a plan filed by a large bank with regulators explaining what it would do in the case of financial distress to contain the effects of its failure. The following entities are required to file such a resolution plan (under Dodd–Frank and the final rule): U.S. bank holding companies with assets of $50 billion or more, foreign banks with global assets of $50 billion more,[38] and nonbank financial companies supervised by the FRB. The plans include a description of recovery plans (what assets the bank would sell and to whom), as well as resolution plans (how the bank would be broken up or shut down entirely—hence the "living will" nickname).

Under the final rule,[39] a resolution plan must contain an executive summary, a strategic analysis of the plan's components, a description of the covered company's corporate governance structure for resolution planning, information regarding the covered company's overall organizational structure, information regarding the covered company's management information systems, a description of interconnections and interdependencies among the covered company and its material entities, and supervisory and regulatory information.

The executive summary must summarize the key elements of the covered company's strategic plan, material changes from the most recently filed plan, and any actions taken by the covered company to improve the effectiveness of the resolution plan or remediate, or otherwise mitigate, any material weaknesses or impediments to the effective and timely execution of the plan.[40]

Under the final rule, each resolution plan submitted must also describe the firm's strategy for the rapid and orderly resolution of the covered company in the event of material financial distress or failure of the covered company. This strategic analysis should detail how, in practice, the covered company could be resolved under the Bankruptcy Code.

The strategic analysis should also include the analytical support for the plan and its key assumptions, including any assumptions made concerning the economic or financial conditions that would be present at the time the covered company sought to implement such plan.

How many banks have submitted living wills to date?

Some 29 large banks around the world published their living wills as a result of a Group of 20 agreement to require them to write recovering and resolution plans by the end of 2012. These significant banks, known as G-SIFIs, include banks from the United States, the United Kingdom, Japan, and Continental Europe, as well as one from China. The plans describe what assets or divisions the bank would sell, and what banks might acquire those assets—or might acquire the bank as a whole.

Furthermore, various nations have their own "living wills" regulations. In the United States, Dodd–Frank, Section 165(d), requires large banks (defined under the statute as banks with $50 billion or more in assets) to file plans demonstrating that they can be resolved under the Bankruptcy Code in a way that will not pose a systemic threat to the nation's financial system. The law affects approximately 125 large financial firms in the United States. They are required by the law to submit living wills to the Federal Reserve and the FDIC by the end of 2013. In 2012 in the United States, 11 large banks submitted living wills in July, with a deadline of October the following year for the sequel.

Are banks outside the United States submitting living wills?

Yes. For example, in the United Kingdom, the Banking Act has provided the Bank of England with a way to resolve failing deposit-taking banks. Like the FDIC, the Bank of England has powers to transfer all or part of a failed bank's business to a private sector purchaser or to a bridge bank until a private purchaser can be found. The Banking Act also provides U.K. authorities with an insolvency procedure that protects insured depositors in the course of liquidating a failed bank's assets. To strengthen the ability of regulators to respond to the failure of large, complex, and international financial firms, the United Kingdom has instituted a Prudent Regulation Authority, established April 1, 2013.[41]

D&O LIABILITY

What liability do bank directors and officers (D&O) have for the bank's insolvency?

However, bank directors and officers do have certain protections under the law if they have "fulfilled their fiduciary responsibilities, including the duties of loyalty and care, and who make reasonable business judgments on a fully informed basis and after proper deliberation," according to FDIC policy (see Exhibit 11.4).

Nonetheless, as of June 1, 2013, the FDIC had authorized suits in connection with 114 failed institutions against 921 individuals for D&O liability since January 2009.[42] (See Exhibit 11.5.)

This included 65 filed D&O lawsuits (7 of which have fully settled and 1 of which resulted in a favorable jury verdict) naming 505 former directors and officers. The FDIC also has authorized 52 other lawsuits for fidelity bond, insurance, attorney malpractice, appraiser malpractice,

Exhibit 11.4 D&O Liability in Bank Insolvency: An FDIC Pledge

The FDIC will not bring civil suits against directors and officers who fulfill their responsibilities, including the duties of loyalty and care, and who make reasonable business judgments on a fully informed basis and after proper deliberation.

PROCEDURES FOLLOWED TO INSTITUTE CIVIL LAWSUITS

Lawsuits brought by the FDIC against former directors and officers of failed banks are instituted on the basis of detailed investigations conducted by the FDIC. Suits are not brought lightly or in haste.

The filing of such lawsuits is authorized only after a rigorous review of the factual circumstances surrounding the failure of the bank. In addition to review by senior FDIC supervisory and legal staff, all lawsuits against former directors and officers require final approval by the FDIC Board of Directors or designee.

Source: Statement Concerning the Responsibility of Bank Directors and Officers, Federal Deposit Insurance Corporation, http://www.fdic.gov/regulations/laws/rules/5000–3300.html#fdic5000statementct.

Exhibit 11.5 FDIC D&O Suits Filed

	Authorized D&O Defendants
Authorized in 2009	11
Authorized in 2010	98
Authorized in 2011	264
Authorized in 2012	369
January 2013	46
February 2013	48
March 2013	24
April 2013	28
May 2013	33
June 2013	0
July 2013	41
August 2013	25
September 2013	20
Total	1,007

Abbreviations: D&O, directors and officers; FDIC, Federal Deposit Insurance Corporation.
Source: FDIC, http://www.fdic.gov/bank/individual/failed/pls/index.html?source=govdelivery.

accounting malpractice, and residential mortgage-backed security (RMBS) claims. In addition, 154 residential mortgage malpractice and fraud lawsuits were pending.

In this context, it is worth noting that the Dodd–Frank Act says that the FDIC may recover (or as business slang calls it "claw back") from any current or former senior executive or director "substantially responsible" for a bank failure any compensation received during the two years before the bank went into receivership—though if there has been fraud, no time limit will apply. Nothing in the law prevents shareholders from suing directors and officers for negligence if this clawback is triggered, so this provision of the law could in time increase the liability exposure of bank D&O, despite the protections of FDIC policy.

Recently, United States District Courts in the 7th Circuit (Chicago, Illinois) and the 11th Circuit (Atlanta, Georgia) have opined on jurisdiction for cases against bank D&O. In *FDIC v. Steven Skow, et al.*, regarding Integrity Bank of Alpharetta, Georgia, and *FDIC v. John M. Saphir, et al.*, regarding Heritage Community Bank, of Glenwood, Illinois, the courts defined the legal grounds on which the FDIC's bank failure claims against D&Os may be litigated.[43]

STRUCTURED TRANSACTIONS

What is a so-called structured transaction with the FDIC?

A structured transaction allows the FDIC to retain an interest in bank assets, while transferring day-to-day management responsibility to designated professionals who also have a financial interest in the assets and share in the costs and risks associated with ownership. The following description summarizes the FDIC's Structured Transactions Fact Sheet.[44]

The receiver forms an entity (to date, all limited liability companies [LLCs]) to which assets from one or more failed institutions are conveyed via a contribution and sale agreement. In exchange for contributing assets, the receivership receives all of the equity interest in the LLC.

Since September 2009, all structured transactions have been in the form of partnerships in which the receiver owns an equity interest in the entity. To date, LLCs have been used. The winning bidder (private owner) purchases a portion, typically ranging from 20 to 40 percent, of the equity in the LLC (actual percentage is specific to each LLC). These types of transactions continue to be offered and sold on an "all cash" or leveraged basis. To date all have included some form of seller financing.

What qualifies a bidder to participate in a structured transaction, and what qualifies loans?

Bidders must be prequalified, have demonstrated financial capacity and the expertise to manage and dispose of the asset portfolio, and have certified eligibility to purchase FDIC receivership assets.

To be included in a securitized transaction, loans have to be performing, cannot be more than 60 days delinquent, and must have a maturity date of one month after closing of the securitization transaction. Also, the loans must meet specific loan-to-value requirements at origination and/or modification. For example, a loan cannot exceed 120 percent loan-to-value. There are certain types of loans that do not qualify, such as loans secured by gas stations, churches, or auto repair facilities.[45]

What kind of financing is involved here?

Leveraged LLCs include financing in the form of either amortizing or non-amortizing purchase money notes issued by the LLC as partial payment for the assets conveyed by the receiver, in addition to the cash payment from the private investor for the purchase of its equity interest. The notes may be guaranteed by the FDIC, in its corporate capacity, to facilitate their sale should the receiver decide to sell the notes.

Financing may be offered at various levels and determined based on the risk and cash flow characteristics of the underlying pool of assets. Although these benchmarks are subject to change with changing market conditions, in the past, ranges were typically

- Single family residential: from 1:1 up to 6:1 debt to equity
- Commercial real estate: from 1:1 up to 4:1 debt to equity
- Acquisition, development, and construction loans typically do not exceed 1:1 debt to equity.

Generally, the notes must be paid off before the equity owners receive any distributions. Consent of the FDIC is required to prepay the notes. In certain cases, the receiver may make funding facilities and prefunded accounts available to the LLC to fund construction draws with respect to the assets and working capital needs of the LLC. Advances must be repaid from the cash flow prior to the equity owners receiving any distributions.

The private owner acts as the managing member of the LLC and is responsible for the management and servicing of the assets conveyed to the LLC. The managing member is obligated to enter into a servicing agreement with a qualified servicer to service the assets in a manner consistent with industry standards and to maximize their value to the LLC. Also, the private owner receives a monthly servicing or management fee that is specified prior to the bid date to pay the servicer and other internal expenses incurred in servicing the assets.

Cash flow from the assets, after deducting the monthly servicing fee and advances for such things as taxes, insurance, and property protection expenses, are allocated first to pay off any notes and any other debt outstanding to the receiver and then to the receiver and the private owner, in accordance with their percentage interests.

Transactions may include a provision that provides for a shift in ownership interests once a stated dollar amount of distributions to the receivership, including the sales price received in a competitive bid sale (threshold), is reached. Upon reaching the threshold, the ownership interests of the receiver and private owner change. The threshold and the amount by which the percentage interests change are specific to each transaction and are established and disclosed to bidders prior to the bid date.

What are some additional factors to consider as a participant in a structured transaction with the FDIC?

The private owner acting as the managing partner must adhere to monthly, semiannual, and annual reporting requirements. The FDIC monitors the transactions on a regular basis and conducts an annual review of bank operations—the quid pro quo for the partnership.

CONCLUDING COMMENTS

The potential acquirer of a distressed bank has much of its valuation work already done for it. Of course, regulatory determinations aside, the most important goal for an acquirer is to form its own opinion of the bank's financial health, as well as its strategic fit with the acquirer's goals. This means taking an objective inventory of the bank's assets and liabilities, forming an opinion as to how and why these are under stress, and determining what future financial results will come from consolidation.

CHAPTER 12

Investing in Bank Stocks

The old idea of "permanent investments" exempt from change and free from care is no doubt permanently gone.

—*Benjamin Graham and David Dodd,* Security Analysis[1]

Buying a bank stock is different from buying an entire bank, of course, yet similar principles of analysis apply. As Fidelity's Peter Lynch has famously said, "Behind every stock is a company."[2]

So far this book has conveyed information intended to help buyers of entire banks or bank holding companies in M&A transactions. This chapter will provide additional guidance for partial acquirers—buyers of small, noncontrolling positions in one or more banks, especially banks undergoing mergers or divestitures.

All of the chapters so far can be used to make an investment decision. For example, the discussion of bank growth, valuation, and due diligence can help a stock buyer assess the financial health of a particular bank, and the chapter on integration can help an acquirer assess investment prospects for a recently merged bank. This information, while relevant to bank investing, will not be repeated here. Rather, this chapter will provide additional guidance on buying bank stocks from the unique point of view of a partial investor who is considering buying into a bank initial public offering (IPO), investing in a mutual fund with bank stocks, or making a decision on whether to tender shares in a tender offer.

INVESTING IN BANK INITIAL PUBLIC OFFERINGS

How common are commercial bank IPOs?

Not very. To begin with, IPOs themselves are relatively rare events. As seen in Exhibit 12.1, the level of IPO pricings in recent years has been modest.[3]

Exhibit 12.1 Number of Initial Public Offerings (Pricings), 2004–2013

Year	Number of Initial Public Offerings (Pricings)
2004	217
2005	192
2006	196
2007	213
2008	31
2009	63
2010	154
2011	125
2012	128
2013*	169

*As of October 2013.
Source: Data from Renaissance Capital of Greenwich, Connecticut (renaissancecapital.com).

This list includes IPO pricings at all levels (except for special purpose acquisition companies, closed-end funds, and nonoperating trusts).

When considering IPOs with low starting prices, the level is lower. For the period 2008–2012, counting only IPOs with starting prices of $5 and up, the annual average was only 66.[4]

Who invests in de novo bank IPOs?

Investment dollars for community banks typically come from local individuals who know enough about the new bank's leaders and community. For example, in one recent IPO for a de novo bank, 95 percent of the funds came from the bank's own zip code.[5]

How long does it take to get a return on investment as a de novo bank investor, and what is the typical return?

A fairly typical scenario is for the bank in the first decade after its IPO to take three years to break even, then to grow in per-share value over the next several years while paying no dividends, then to sell for two times book value. Overall, this scenario gives a 15 percent rate of return on average per year.

An experienced banker offers this illustration:

> Let's say you invest in a de novo at $8.00 per share (we'll assume 1 million shares are issued in the IPO). Let's further assume that the bank (1) breaks even at the beginning of year 3 with $6.50 in per share book value remaining, (2) averages a 12% ROE over the following eight years, (3) pays no dividends, and (4) is acquired for 2x book value ten years following its IPO. An investor in the IPO that holds onto their shares until the bank is acquired will have realized an internal rate of return of roughly 15% annually over the 10-year period.[6]

Many investors, however, don't have the patience to wait that long.

INVESTING IN MUTUAL FUNDS WITH BANK STOCKS

What are some general considerations when investing in a mutual fund focused on banks?

When a fund concentrates its investments in a particular industry, performance will usually correlate to performance in the industry. Since many industries are cyclical and/or are affected by regulation, this makes fund performance more volatile than performance of a fund that is diversified across industries.[7] As mentioned in Chapter 4, commercial bank performance is sensitive to economic conditions and interest rates. In addition, banks can be affected by specific events in the financial realm. Events that have impacted commercial bank stock performance in recent years have included the crash of the mortgage market in 2008, the passage of Dodd–Frank in 2010, and the capitalization standards coming from U.S. regulators and international standard setters (Basel Accords). Any prospectus for a bank mutual fund will cite these causes of volatility as risk factors in a bank mutual fund investment.

What are some mutual funds that invest primarily in U.S. commercial bank stocks, and how have they performed?

Mutual funds investing in bank stocks have done relatively well, when considering total return—that is, the increase in the value of a holding in the fund as a percentage of the initial investment. Total return includes both income (in the form of dividends or interest payments) and capital gains or losses (the increase or decrease in the value of a security). Of 79 mutual funds tracked by Morningstar, average annual total returns have been 5.74. Here is a list of some mutual funds that make heavy investments in banks, followed by their three-year returns as of July 2013.[8] (For returns for other periods, refer to Morningstar.) In assessing the returns, consider that the average total shareholder return (TSR) for all funds studied by Morningstar was 12.68 during this same period.[9]

- *Burnham Financial Services Fund.* The fund pursues its goal by investing at least 80 percent of its net assets (including borrowing, if any) in stocks of U.S. companies that are in the financial services sector. It may invest in companies of any size, but, under normal conditions, the fund invests primarily in small capitalization financial services companies. The fund's managers consider companies with market capitalizations of less than $900 million to be small capitalization. The firm has an M&A focus: "We use our own research and expertise in seeking to capitalize on M&A activity in the U.S. banking industry, focusing on smaller cap financial services companies," says portfolio manager Anton Schutz. Holdings (as of mid-2013) include First United Bancorp, ASB Bancorp, and OmniAmerican Bancorp.[10] The three-year TSR as of July 2013 was 12.26.
- *Fidelity Advisor Financial Services Fund.* This fund normally invests at least 80 percent of assets in securities of companies principally engaged in providing financial services to consumers and industry (including some foreign banks). Holdings include Comerica, Bank of America, and Citigroup. The three-year TSR as of July 2013 was 9.23.
- *Fidelity Emerald Banking and Finance Fund Class C.* In this fund, the holdings include both commercial banks and other financial institutions. Investments are widespread, with only

2 to 3 percent of a stake in each bank. Investments focus on smaller cap banks, such as Bank of the Ozarks and Eagle Bancorp, Inc. The three-year TSR as of July 2013 was 17.05.

- *Fidelity Select Banking Portfolio.*[11] In this fund, most of the holdings (94.72 percent as of July 2013) are in bank stocks, with the rest in information technology or cash. By contrast, the Standard & Poor's (S&P) 500 is currently composed of only 16.6 percent bank stocks. The Select Banking Portfolio (founded in 1986 as Select Regional Banks) holds shares in 49 entities, but with half of the portfolio in only 10 banks, including US Bancorp, Wells Fargo, PNC, M&T Bancorp, and Huntington Bancshares. The three-year TSR as of July 2013 was 13.32.
- *Hennessy Small Cap Financial Fund.* The fund employs a consistent fundamental, bottom-up investment process to identify small-cap financial services companies that meet the portfolio's criteria. Holdings include First Bancorp, Bank United, and Popular Inc. The three-year TSR as of July 2013 was 12.36.
- *Icon Financial Fund.* This investment fund seeks long-term capital appreciation. The fund normally invests at least 80 percent of its net assets, plus any borrowings for investment purposes, in equity securities of companies in the financial sector. Holdings include Wells Fargo, JPMorgan Chase, US Bancorp, and Citigroup. The three-year TSR as of July 2013 was 10.37.
- *John Hancock Regional Bank Fund.* The fund normally invests at least 80 percent of its net assets (plus any borrowings for investment purposes) in stocks of regional banks and lending companies, including commercial and industrial banks, savings and loan associations, and bank holding companies. The three-year TSR as of July 2013 was 13.92.
- *Profunds Banks Ultrasector Fund.* This fund refers to itself as an "index" that "measures the performance of the banking sector

of the U.S. equity market." Holdings include JPMorgan Chase, Citigroup, Bank of America, and US Bancorp. The three-year TSR as of July 2013 was 11.67.

- *Rydex Series Trust Banking Fund.* The fund invests substantially all (at least 80 percent) of its net assets in equity securities of banking companies that are traded in the United States and in derivatives, which primarily consist of futures contracts and options on securities, futures contracts, and stock indices. Although its holdings include large bank holding companies such as Bank of America, Wells Fargo, and Citigroup, it will invest to a significant extent in the securities of banks that have small to midsize capitalizations. The three-year TSR as of July 2013 was 8.03.
- *T. Rowe Price Financial Services Fund.* The fund normally invests at least 80 percent of its net assets (including any borrowings for investment purposes) in the common stocks of companies in the financial services industry. In addition, it may invest in companies, such as providers of financial software, that derive substantial revenues (at least 50 percent) from conducting business in the financial services industry. Stocks include JPMorgan Chase, US Bancorp, and PNC Financial Services Group. The three-year TSR as of July 2013 was 14.06.

SELLING IN TENDER OFFERS

What exactly is a tender offer?

A tender offer is a broad solicitation by a company or a third party to purchase a substantial percentage of a company's securities for a limited period of time, as explained recently and authoritatively by the Securities and Exchange Commission (SEC).[12] The tender offer is at a fixed price, usually at a premium over the current market price. It is usually contingent on shareholders tendering a fixed number of their shares or units.[13]

Some tender offers are offers to buy debt securities, and these do not seek control of a company. Other tender offers are attempts to gain control of a publicly trended company. Indeed, it is one of two ways to do so. To gain control over a publicly traded firm, a company must either acquire it or make a tender offer. In an acquisition, the acquirer and the target's board of directors agree on a price, then the target's shareholders vote to approve the transaction. In a tender offer, the acquirer proposes a per-share price directly to the target's shareholders, then the shareholders have the choice to sell their shares at the offer price or keep them.

In a tender offer intended to obtain control, the offer will typically be for more than 5 percent of stock, which is an important regulatory threshold. In this case, certain rules apply. As explained by the SEC, these rules require bidders to

- Disclose important information about themselves
- Disclose the terms of the offer
- File their offering documents with the SEC[14]
- Provide the target company and any competing bidders with information about the tender offer

The SEC's tender offer rules also give investors important protections, including the right to

- Change their minds and withdraw from the transaction while the offer remains open
- Have their shares accepted on a pro rata basis (if the offer is for less than all of the company's outstanding shares and investors tender too many shares)
- Be treated equally by the bidder

None of these rules apply to tender offers for less than 5 percent—so called mini-tender offers. Holders of bank stock who receive offers to sell their stock should be especially cautious when receiving tender offers that do not include the above protections.[15]

How common are tender offers to gain control of a company?

Internationally, JPMorgan Chase says only 5 percent of the transactions seeking control of a company worth more than $100 million between 2002 and 2012 went "hostile." Of these, only a little more than one-quarter (27 percent) were from operating corporations, and one-third were from funds formed from private equity.

What about tender offers for bonds? What can happen there?

Investors in bank bonds can experience volatility in holdings during a disputed tender offer. A case in point is the Bank of America tender for certain MBIA securities in November 2012. Complications ensued, and the two parties wound up suing each other. MBIA claimed that the purpose of the tender offer was not economic but was to manipulate outcomes in the mortgage market. Bank of America claimed that the purpose of its tender offer was "to induce holders of record" of MBIA bonds governed by 2004 legal language to sell their bonds. MBIA had issued Bank of America billions of dollars in policies backing subprime bonds at that time.[16] Both companies' shares dropped in value in the course of the disputes; MBIA shares dropped by some 40 percent in late 2012.[17]

In May 2013, the two parties reached an out-of-court settlement involving this tender offer. "As part of the settlement, Bank of America will pay MBIA, a bond insurer, for approximately $1.6 billion in cash and remit to MBIA all of the outstanding MBIA 5.7 percent Senior Notes due 2034 that Bank of America acquired through a tender offer in December 2012," Bank of America said in a statement. At the same time, Bank of America agreed to provide MBIA with a $500 million credit line and received the right to buy 4.9 percent in MBIA.

Both companies' stock price rose immediately following the settlement—MBIA's by 45 percent and Bank of America by 5.2 percent.

CONCLUDING COMMENTS

Investing in bank stocks, like any investment, is risky. Yet as long as companies continue to employ people, and people continue to support themselves and their families, banks with good reputations will continue to have an indispensable role as providers of financial services, and bank stocks will remain a sensible investment for any portfolio seeking long-term growth in value.

APPENDIX

Landmark U.S. Supreme Court Cases in Banking, 1799–2013[1]

It is the spirit and not the form of the law that keeps justice alive.

—*Chief Justice Earl Warren,* Fortune, *November 1955*

As institutions that hold and process other people's money, banks are highly regulated. Business imperatives drive them forward, but laws apply brakes along the way. The many legal curbs on banking in the United States come from a variety of domains, including constitutional law, federal law, state law, and common law adjudicated in courts of equity.

Yet to understand the principles underpinning U.S. banking law, one need go no further than the highest court of the land—the United States Supreme Court. Describing this treasure of democracy, Massachusetts Representative Edward Everett declared (on February 22, 1851): "If all the labors, the sacrifices, and the waste of treasure and blood, were to give us nothing else than the Supreme Court of the United States . . . I should say the sacrifice was well made."[2]

This appendix summarizes selected Supreme Court banking cases since the first recorded banking case in 1799 through the present year (2013), ordered chronologically and grouped by century. All case summaries are based on original text unless otherwise noted.[3]

The U.S. Supreme Court plays an important role in U.S. law, having ultimate jurisdiction over all other courts in the U.S. legal system. As stated in the U.S. Constitution, the "judicial Power of the United States, shall be vested in one Supreme Court, and in such inferior Courts as the Congress may from time to time ordain and establish" (Article III). Although the

Judiciary Act of 1789 divided the country into 13 judicial districts, the Supreme Court has remained a final arbiter for equal justice under the law, a concept that would become its motto.[4]

From the time the gavel first pounded at the high court on February 2, 1790, to the present day, the U.S. Supreme Court has decided more than 16,000 cases,[5] including a significant number of cases involving banks. Although the list of cases summarized her does not claim to be comprehensive, it is intended to be representative. As such, it represents general trends in high court philosophy. While it is impossible to generalize over such a long stretch of time, one of the main themes of the high court's banking decisions is the clear precedence of federal law over state laws, yet with only limited jurisdiction and scope for any litigation based on an overly narrow interpretation of federal laws and without due attention to the facts of the particular case. As a result, over time the U.S. Supreme Court has tended to make decisions that favor a strong national banking system while at the same time respecting the limits of federal law in rendering decisions under specific circumstances.

THE EIGHTEENTH CENTURY: THE FIRST BANKING CASE

Turner v. Bank of North America, 4 U.S. 8 (1799), considered jurisdiction for a matter involving a promissory note, but the significance is broader. *Turner* interpreted the meaning of Article III, Section 2, Clause 1 of the U.S. Constitution, regarding the power of federal courts. The justices concluded that, unlike the Supreme Court, which derives its judicial powers directly from the Constitution, the federal courts derive their judicial power from Congress, not the Constitution.[6] The practical effect of this decision has been to curb litigation in federal courts; litigants must establish jurisdiction before proceeding with a case.

THE NINETEENTH CENTURY

French's Executrix v. Bank of Columbia, 8 U.S. 141 (1807), explored the rights of a drawer in a bill of exchange, specifically, whether the drawer should receive notice of nonpayment. A bill of exchange is an order from a drawer (someone who draws money) to a drawee (someone whose money is drawn) to pay money to a third party, or payee. In the case of a check, the person who writes the check is both the drawer and drawee. This case and its subsequent history helped form the basis for the modern checking system, in which bank customers receive prompt notice of any check returned without funds.

Young v. Bank of Alexandria, 8 U.S. 384 (1808), delved into the nature of laws of incorporation, distinguishing between the inalienable rights attached to incorporated entities by virtue of incorporation versus additional rights that are bestowed (or not) by law. Justice Marshall wrote, "There is a difference between those rights on which the validity of the transactions of the corporation depends, which must adhere to those transactions everywhere, and those peculiar remedies which may be bestowed on it. The first are of general obligation; the last, from their nature, can only be exercised in those courts which the power making the grant can regulate." The *Young* Court, deciding jurisdiction re a writ of error,[7] decided that the act of incorporation conferred a corporate character on the Bank of Alexandria, but did not imply any other privileges not belonging to it as a corporation unless these had been specifically granted by an act of Congress. This decision had the practical effect of limiting bank powers.

Yeaton v. Bank of Alexandria, 9 U.S. 49 (1809), affirmed the right of a bank to collect from an endorser of a note. In seeking a writ of error regarding a lower court decision, the high court said, "The endorsor is . . . as liable, both in reason and in law, to the claim of the bank, as if he had placed his name on the face instead of the back of the note."

Bank of United States v. Deveaux, 9 U.S. 61 (1809), explored the jurisdiction and constitutionality of a legal claim against a bank. The case involved the principle of "diversity jurisdiction," which gives federal courts jurisdiction over cases involving more than one state. The Bank of the United States wanted to sue a Georgia tax collector named Deveaux, but Deveaux argued that the case could not be argued in federal court because there was no diversity. The Supreme Court sited with Deveaux, basing the citizenship of the Bank of the United States on the identity of its shareholders, some of whom were from Georgia. A later case overruled Deveaux, basing citizenship on state of incorporation, not residence of owners.[8]

Hodgson & Thompson v. Bowerbank, 9 U.S. (5 Cr.) 303 (1809),[9] involved jurisdiction between domestic and foreign entities. Hodgson held that U.S. courts do not have jurisdiction over matters where noncitizens appear as both plaintiffs and defendants, even where a U.S. citizen also appears as a plaintiff or defendant.

Bank of Columbia v. Patterson's Administrator, 11 U.S. 299 (1813), explored the enforceability of a corporate promise made via a putative agent. "Whenever a corporation is acting within the scope of the legitimate purposes of the institution, all parol [spoken] contracts made by its authorized agents are express promises of the corporation." Furthermore

> At length it seems to have been established that though they [the corporations] could not contract directly except under their corporate seal, yet they might, by mere vote or other corporate act, not under their corporate seal, appoint an agent, whose acts and contracts, within the scope of his authority, would be binding on the corporation.[10]

Mandeville v. Union Bank of Georgetown, 13 U.S. 9 (1815), addressed limits on changes to notes, "by making a note negotiable in bank, the maker authorizes the bank to advance on his credit to the owner of the note the sum expressed on its face. It would be a fraud on the bank to set up offsets against this note in consequence of any transactions between the parties."

Union Bank of Georgetown v. Laird, 15 U.S. 390 (1817), opined on the rights and restrictions on transferability of bank shares:

> The shares of any individual stockholder are transferable only on the books of the bank according to the rules established by the president and directors, and all debts due and payable to the bank by a stockholder must be satisfied before the transfer shall be made unless the president and directors should direct to the contrary.

Bank of Columbia v. Okely, 17 U.S. 235 (1819), weighed the rights of a bank versus those of a debtor. The court found that the bank has the right to force a debtor to sell property to satisfy a debt to the bank.

McCulloch v. Maryland 17 U.S. 316, 4 Wheat. 316, 4 L. Ed. 579 (1819) upheld the right of Congress to create a Bank of the United States, ruling that this was a power implied but not enumerated by the Constitution. The case advanced the doctrine of implied powers, condoning an expansive (not merely literal) interpretation of the Constitution. The court, Chief Justice John Marshall wrote, would sanction laws reflecting "the letter and spirit" of the Constitution. This in turn has made possible the concept of federal supremacy. As Justice Ruth Bader Ginsburg wrote in *Watters v. Wachovia* (also in this appendix), "Nearly two hundred years ago, in *McCulloch v. Maryland*, this Court held federal law supreme over state law with respect to national banking."

Mechanics' Bank of Alexandria v. Bank of Columbia, 18 U.S. 326 (1820),[11] relied on a bank's charter to invalidate the signature of a nonofficer. According to this decision, if a charter says a bank's check must be signed by an officer to be valid, this validity does not extend to a private signator who claims to be acting as a bank agent.

Pages Administrators v. Bank of Alexandria, 20 U.S. 7 Wheat. 35 (1822), deals with the timing of an instrument. The court found that a note payable on any number of days after its date is not equivalent to a note that is payable on demand.

Bank of the United States v. Dandridge, 25 U.S. 64 (1827), found that a corporation may be held liable for the action of its agents, even if these actions are not evidenced in writing and/or by a formal vote. This helped build the doctrine of the corporate "person," which implies that corporations, not merely individuals, may be sued.

Bank of Augusta v. Earle, 38 U.S. 13 Pet. 519 (1839), ruled for the first time on the powers a state can wield over a corporation that is incorporated in another state. The bank argued that it could do business in any state, including Alabama. Earle, a provider of financial services in Alabama, argued that states have the right to control who does and does not do business there. The court struck a compromise, ruling that states have a right to impose restrictions on outside ("foreign") corporations, but their policies must be clearly disclosed. In subsequent rulings, the Court would find that states may not unduly restrict interstate commerce.[12]

Bank of Alexandria v. Herbert, 12 U.S. 36 (1846), found that a lender had rights to collateral (land) even though the borrower, due to a defective mortgage, did not. The court stated that "the trustee of an insolvent debtor ... represents the creditors of the insolvent, and can take advantage of a defect in a mortgage of which the insolvent himself could not."

Piqua Branch of State Bank of Ohio v. Knoop, 57 U.S. 369 (1853), protected a state bank's charter from state modification.

> Every valuable privilege given by the charter, and which conduced to an acceptance of it and an organization under it, is a contract which cannot be changed by the legislature, where the power to do so is not reserved in the charter. The rate of discount, the duration of the charter, the specific tax agreed to be paid, and other provisions essentially connected with the franchise, and necessary to the business of the bank, cannot, without its consent, become a subject for legislative action.

Marine Bank v. Fulton Bank, 69 U.S. 2 Wall. 252 (1864), established when a bank is or is not liable for depreciation on notes received as deposits. Money collected by one bank for another, placed by the collecting bank with the bulk of its ordinary banking funds, and credited to the transmitting bank in an account becomes the money of the former. Hence, any depreciation in the specific bank bills received by the collecting bank that may happen between the date of the collecting banks receiving them and the other banks drawing for the amount collected falls upon the former.

Tiffany v. National Bank of Mo., 85 U.S. 409 (1874), pitted the national banking system against state banks. This case limited the liability of national banks, providing some measure of protection from state legislation.[13]

Union Nat'l Bank v. Matthews, 98 U.S. 621, 626 (1878), considered the case of a national bank that loaned money and took a note and a deed of trust secured by real estate. The court held that the deed of trust was not void and that the bank could sell the property. At the same time, it noted the reasons for the restrictions against bank ownership of property, namely, "to keep the capital of the banks flowing in the daily channels of commerce; to deter them from embarking in hazardous real-estate speculations; and to prevent the accumulation of large masses of such property in their hands, to be held, as it were, in mortmain" (held by a "dead hand" of an absentee owner).[14]

Xenia Bank v. Stewart, 114 U.S. 224 (1885), involved an action brought to recover the value of 30 certificates of shares held in a bank and sold by the bank after a customer's death. The Court held that a creditor who has possession of the property of his debtor, as his agent or trustee or bailee, may not sell or otherwise dispose of the property and apply its proceeds to the payment of his debt without either due process or the consent of the debtor. The Court ruled that it is within the scope of authority for a cashier of a national bank to receive offers for the purchase of securities held by the bank and to state whether or not the bank owns the securities the customer wishes to buy. Citing previous law, the Court said, "Whatever an agent does or says in reference to the business in which he is at the time employed and within the scope of his authority is done or said by the principal, and may be proved as if the evidence applied personally to the principal."

THE TWENTIETH CENTURY

National Metropolitan Bank v. United States, 323 U.S. 454 (1945), covered jurisdiction and put the onus on banks, not government, for detection of fraud. The court found that rights and liabilities on commercial paper issued by the government are to be determined by federal, rather than local, law. Regarding forgery, the court found that the government was entitled to recover payments made to a collecting bank on government checks on which the bank had expressly guaranteed prior endorsements but on which the endorsements of the payees were forged. Recovery to the government was not barred even though the government had failed to detect the fraud of a government clerk who, over a period of 28 months, had fraudulently procured issuance of the checks upon forged vouchers.

United States v. Philadelphia Nat'l Bank, 374 U.S. 321 (1963), held that a combination of two banks with a large combined market share (33 percent) was anticompetitive and violated the Clayton Act. The case involved a merger of the third-largest bank in the area, Girard Trust Corn

Exchange Bank, into the second largest, Philadelphia National Bank. The court ruled that if a merger would cause a company to control an undue share of the market, and if there was no evidence, the merger would not be harmful, and the merger could not take place. The court held that a merger that significantly reduces competition is not exempt from the Clayton Act simply because, "on some ultimate reckoning of social or economic debits and credits, it may be deemed beneficial." The Court also stated that growth by internal expansion is "socially preferable to growth by acquisition."

United States v. First National Bank and Trust Co. of Lexington, Kentucky, 376 U.S. 665 (1964), responded to the U.S. Department of Justice's charge that consolidation of First National Bank and Trust Co. of Lexington, Kentucky (First National) and Security Trust Co. of Lexington (Security Trust) to form First Security National Bank and Trust Co. (First Security) could restrain and monopolize trade and commerce in violation of Sections 1 and 2 of the Sherman Act, respectively.

National Bank v. Associates of Obstetrics, 425 U.S. 460 (1976), held that a national bank with a principal place of business in New York and with no office or agent in Utah, and not regularly conducting business in that state, could not be sued in a Utah state court for breach of contract.

Citizens & Southern Nat'l Bank v. Bougas, 434 U.S. 35 (1977), applied U.S. Code, Title 12, Banks and Banking, Section 94 (Venue of Suit), to a bank's conduct of business at an authorized branch within its state. The high court held that the bank's venue need not be restricted to the county where the bank's charter had been issued.

Marquette Nat'l. Bank v. First of Omaha, 439 U.S. 299 (1978), pondered whether the National Bank Act[15] authorizes a national bank based in one state to charge its out-of-state credit card customers an interest rate on unpaid balances allowed by its home state, when that rate is greater than that permitted by the state of the bank's nonresident customers. The Minnesota Supreme Court held that the bank is allowed by Section 85 of the act to charge the higher rate (262 N.W.2d 358 [1977]). The high court affirmed.

Mellon Bank, N.A. v. Southland Mobile Homes of South Carolina, 439 U.S. 900 (1978), declined to hear a case (denied a petition for a writ of certiorari) on the grounds that this was a state, not a federal, matter. At issue was an interpretation of the U.S. Code, Title 12, Banks and Banking, Section 94, Venue of Suits.[16] In his dissenting opinion, Justice Blackmun noted, "The proliferation of branch banking has produced problems of state-court venue with respect to national banks not envisioned when [Section 94]'s predecessor statutes were enacted more than a century ago."

Northeast Bancorp, Inc., et al., v. Board of Governors of the Federal Reserve System 472 U.S. 159 (1985), affirmed the ability of the states to enter into regional reciprocal compacts, paving the way for interstate banking.

Virginia Bankshares, Inc. v. Sandberg, 501 U.S. 1083 (1991), narrowed the applicability of a proxy disclosure rule (Rule 14a–9), finding that misstatements made in a proxy solicitation campaign, although material, did not rise to the level of material misstatements under the rule. The statements were not an "essential link" in the merger process.[17]

Central Bank v. First Interstate Bank, 511 U.S. 164 (1994), a bond underwriting case, concerned Rule 10(b)–5, the insider trading rule that bans buying or selling company securities while in possession of nonpublic information about the company. The Court found that this rule does not extend to aiding and abetting a violation, thus narrowing the application of insider trading laws.

2000 TO THE PRESENT

Director of Revenue of Missouri v. Cobank, ACB, 531 U.S. 316 (2001), affirmed the right of states to tax cooperative banks, noting that federal law (21 U.S.C. 2134 and the Farm Credit Act) does not explicitly exempt them from same.

Franconia Associates v. U.S., 536 U.S. 129 (2002), sided with mortgage holders and against the government in this case involving a statute of limitations. Mortgage holders had tried to prepay their mortgage, which was allowable under the law when they took out the loans. The government, citing later law (Emergency Low Income Housing Preservation Act of 1987) refused to accept the prepayment and release its control over the collateral securing the loan. Mortgage holders then brought suit against the government for breach of contract, but the lower court dismissed their claims, citing a six-year statute of limitations and starting the timeline at 1987. The high court found in favor of the mortgage holders, stating that they had indeed filed their case timely, considering the date of the government's actual breach of contract. The court held that the six-year limitations period began to accrue only when the borrowers tendered prepayment and the government refused to accept the payment, and not at the earlier time cited by the government.

Beneficial National Bank, et al., Petitioners, vs. Marie Anderson et al., 539 U.S. 1 (2003), held that a national bank cannot be sued for usury under state law. The Court held that the National Bank Act preempted the state-law claim and provided the exclusive cause of action for usury claims against national banks.

Household Credit Services Inc. v. Pfennig, 541 U.S. 232 (2004), permitted banks to consider overlimit charges as separate from finance charges. The high court, citing Regulation Z under the Truth in Lending Act, said that when calculating their finance charges (which may be subject to certain limits), banks do not have to include overlimit charges under federal law (15 U.S.C. § 1605).

Koons Buick Pontiac GMC, Inc. v. Night, 543 U.S. 50 (2004), narrowed the applicability of a law involving closed end loans secured by real property. It said that a 1995 amendment to the Truth in Lending Act that raised the minimum and maximum recoveries for such loans did not necessarily apply to all personal-property loans.

Lockhart v. U.S., 546 U.S. 142 (2005), gave the U.S. government the right to offset Social Security benefits to collect a student loan debt that has been outstanding for over 10 years.

Wachovia Bank, Nat'l Ass'n v. Schmidt, 546 U.S. 303 (2006), interpreted a banking law (in Title 28, U.S. Code Section 1348), saying that all national banking associations, for the purposes of all other actions by or against them, will be deemed citizens of the states in which they are located. The court defined location as meaning the state in which its main office, as set forth in its articles of association, is located.

Crédit Suisse Securities (USA) LLC v. Billings, 551 U.S. 264 (2007), ruled against a group of investors who alleged that investment banks, acting as underwriting firms, violated antitrust laws when they formed syndicates to help execute initial public offerings (IPOs) for hundreds of technology-related companies. Federal securities law implicitly precludes the application of the antitrust laws to the conduct alleged in the case, said the Court. Furthermore, the Court stated that "the underwriters' efforts jointly to promote and sell newly issued securities [are] central to the proper functioning of well-regulated capital markets; the law grants the [Securities and Exchange Commission] authority to supervise such activities."

Watters v. Wachovia Bank, 127 S. Ct. 1559, 1565 (2007), showed the long arm of federal law when it comes to mortgages. The high court found that as an activity of a national bank, Wachovia's mortgage business, whether conducted by the bank itself or through the bank's operating subsidiary, is subject to Office of the Comptroller of the Currency's (OCC) superintendence, rather than to more local jurisdictions, such as the licensing and reporting regimes of the several states where its subsidiary operated.

Safeco Insurance Co. of America v. Burr, 551 U.S. 47 (2007), narrowed the applicability of a consumer notification rule under the Fair Credit Reporting Act (FCRA). The notification rule, which requires notice to any consumer subjected to adverse action based in whole or in part on any information contained in a consumer credit report, imposes civil liability only on one who "willfully" fails to provide such notice. In this case, there was no such intent to withhold notice, the Court found.

Morrison et al. v. National Australia Bank Ltd. et al., 130 S. Ct. 2869 (2010)., limited the ability of litigants to sue foreign companies under U.S. law. Although the impact of this decision was blunted by the Dodd–Frank Act of 2010, its arguments could be used in the future to interpret (or even overturn) that law. In the *Morrison* case, an Australian acquirer (National

Australia Bank) purchased a Florida-based mortgages servicing company called Homeside. Three years after the acquisition, the parent had to write down the value of the subsidiary's assets, causing the parent's share prices to fall. Australian investors who purchased the parent company's shares before the write-downs sued National, the subsidiary HomeSide, and officers of both companies under U.S. securities laws, including Section 10(b) of the 1934 Securities Exchange Act, claiming that the subsidiary and its officers had manipulated financial models to make the company's mortgage-servicing rights appear more valuable than they really were, and that the parent company CEO was aware of this deception. The high court held that Section 10(b) does not provide a cause of action to foreign plaintiffs suing foreign and American defendants for misconduct in connection with securities traded on foreign exchanges. Furthermore, said the Court, it is a "longstanding principle of American law 'that legislation of Congress, unless a contrary intent appears, is meant to apply only within the territorial jurisdiction of the United States.'" (Dodd–Frank, by contrast, does apply U.S. national treatment policies to foreign banking organizations that do business in the United States, and to foreign nonbank financial companies engaged in financial activities in the United States. Such banks are considered systemically important and as such are supervised by the Federal Reserve Bank.)[18]

Chase Bank USA, N.A. v. McCoy, Chase Bank USA, N.A. v. McCoy, 131 S. Ct. 871 (2011), affirmed the right of a bank to change an interest rate without giving advance notice to the consumer. The original plaintiff, McCoy, had argued that Regulation Z under the Truth in Lending Act mandates prompt notice of an interest rate change before it takes effect. The high court held that at the time of the transactions at issue, Regulation Z did not require Chase to provide McCoy with a change-in-terms notice before implementing the agreement term allowing it to raise his interest rate, up to a preset maximum, following delinquency or default. The Supreme Court found that the law was ambiguous but based its decision on the Federal Reserve Board's own interpretation of Regulation Z.[19]

Janus Capital Group, Inc., et al. v. First Derivative Traders, 131 S. Ct. 2296 (2011), upheld a private right of action in certain securities cases but distinguished between the liability of an investment fund versus its management company and adviser. Stockholders in Janus Capital Group, Inc. (JCG) filed this private action under Securities and Exchange Commission (SEC) Rule 10(b)-5, which forbids "any person ... [t]o make any untrue statement of a material fact" in connection with the purchase or sale of securities. The complaint alleged JCG and its wholly owned subsidiary, petitioner Janus Capital Management LLC (JCM), made false statements in mutual fund prospectuses filed by Janus Investment Fund—for which JCM was the investment adviser and administrator—and that those statements affected the price of JCG's stock. Although JCG created Janus Investment Fund, it is a separate legal entity owned entirely by mutual fund investors. The high court held that because the false statements included in the prospectuses were made by Janus Investment Fund, not by JCM or its parent, JCG, neither JCM nor JCG can be held liable in a private action under Rule 10(b)-5.

Radlax Gateway Hotel LLC v. Amalgamated Bank, 132 S. Ct. 2065 (2012), considered whether a Chapter 11 bankruptcy plan could be confirmed over the objection of a secured creditor if the plan provides for the sale of collateral free and clear of the creditor's lien but does not permit the creditor to "credit-bid" at the sale. In this case, debtors obtained a secured loan from an investment fund, for which Amalgamated Bank served as trustee. When the debtors became insolvent, they sought relief under Chapter 11 of the U.S. Bankruptcy Code, attempting to confirm a "cramdown" bankruptcy plan over the bank's objection. The Bankruptcy Court and an appeals court had denied the debtors' request, and the high court upheld these decisions, holding that debtors could not obtain confirmation of a Chapter 11 cramdown plan that provided for the sale of collateral free and clear of the bank's lien but did not permit the bank to credit-bid at the sale. Accordingly, the Court affirmed the judgment of the Court of Appeals.

Mims v. Arrow Financial Services, 132 S. Ct. 740 (2012), upheld a plaintiff's standing to sue a bill collector under federal law, staying that the court would "apply the familiar default rule: Federal courts have ... jurisdiction over claims that arise under federal law." The case involved the applicability of a person to sue a telemarketer in federal court under the Telephone Consumer Protection Act of 1991. The high court affirmed that right.

Compucredit Corp. v. Greenwood et al., 132 S. Ct. 665. (2012), considered the case of Greenwood and others, who had a credit card agreement requiring any claims to be resolved by binding arbitration, but who filed a lawsuit against Compucredit and one of its divisions alleging, among other claims, violations of the Credit Repair Organizations Act (CROA). At issue was whether the CROA's assertion of a right to sue could nullify the arbitration agreement and allow a federal lawsuit under CROA to proceed. The Court held that because the CROA was silent on whether claims under the act could proceed via arbitration, the Federal Arbitration Act required the arbitration agreement to be enforced according to its terms.

Bullock v. BankChampaign, NA, 133 S. Ct 1754 (2013), involved the case of Bullock, who filed for bankruptcy under Chapter 7 to discharge debt he had incurred due to fraud and abuse of his fiduciary role. The bank started an adversary proceeding in bankruptcy court, where it argued that debts arising out of fraud or "defalcation" in a fiduciary capacity are not dischargeable by bankruptcy. The Court agreed with the bank that debts arising out of fraud in a fiduciary capacity are not dischargeable in a Chapter 7 bankruptcy proceeding. However, it did not define defalcation so broadly as to jeopardize trustees who act in good faith when serving in their role.

American Express Co. v. Italian Colors Restaurant et. al. 133 S.Ct. 2304 (2013), considered whether a merchant, the Italian Colors Restaurant, that had agreed to abritration of any disputes arising as a bank credit card client, could instead seek legal redress through courts due to the prohibitive cost of arbitation. The high court held that the applicable law, the Federal Arbitration Act (FAA), does not permit courts to invalidate a contractual waiver of class arbitration on the ground that the plaintiff's cost of individually arbitrating a federal statutory claim exceeds the potential recovery.

NOTES

PREFACE

1. David Ciccone, Senior Vice President, Wealth Management, CTH Group, UBS Financial Services, in a client consultation July 14, 2011.
2. Jaron Lanier, *Who Owns the Future?* (New York: Simon & Schuster, 2013).

FOREWORD

1. Financial Services Authority, *List of Banks as Compiled by the FSA on 28 February 2013*, http://www.fsa.gov.uk/static/pubs/list_banks/feb13.pdf; See also Federal Deposit Insurance Corporation, *Statistics at a Glance as of* June 30, 2013. http://www.fdic.gov/bank/statistical/stats/2013jun/industry.html (listing 6,940 FDIC-insured depository institutions, including 5,980 commercial banks and 960 thrifts).
2. *The Shrinking U.S. Banking Sector: On Balance, Who Benefits?*, Knowledge@Wharton, April 27, 2011) (quoting Kenneth H. Thomas of the Wharton School of Business, who noted that the United States is "'over-banked,' with a supply of banking services exceeding demand. . . ."). http://knowledge.wharton.upenn.edu/article/the-shrinking-u-s-banking-sector-on-balance-who-benefits
3. *Understanding the Economics of Large Banks* (New York: The Clearing House Association, LLC, 2011) ("[I]n small-business or commercial-real-estate lending, smaller banks have a relatively higher share of assets; large size is not essential to providing value in these areas.").
4. Michael J. Aiello and Heath P. Tarbert, "Bank M&A in the Wake of Dodd-Frank," *Banking Law Journal,* 127:10, (November/December 2010), pp. 909-916.
5. "2013 Acquire or Be Acquired Conference," *Bank Director,* April 22, 2013, http://www.bankdirector.com/index.php/magazine/archives/2nd-quarter-2013/2013-acquire-or-be-acquired-conference.

6. Press release, Office of U.S. Senator David Vitter, "Sens. Brown, Vitter React to Banking Industry's Flimsy Challenge of 'Too Big to Fail' Subsidy," March 11, 2013; Press release, Office of U.S. Senator Sherrod Brown, "Brown Delivers Major Address on Efforts to End 'Too Big to Fail' Policies," February 28, 2013.
7. Aiello and Tarbert, op cit., note 4.
8. "The midsize banks at $10 billion to $50 billion are in my judgment right in the sweet spot of being large enough to attract and retain good, solid management to a bank where management can still get its arms around everything that is going on. I think there's an inherent efficiency in that." Heather Landy "Standing Out: Why Regional Banks Are the Right Size Right Now," *American Banker,* 5 April 4, 2013, https://www.53.com/resources/pdf/accolades/accolades-american-banker.pdf (quoting William Cooper, chairman and CEO, TCF Financial).
9. Kelsey Weaver, "International M&A: Will China Buy More US Banks?," *Bank Director,* July 4, 2012 (quoting Heath P. Tarbert, partner, Weil, Gotshal & Manges, LLP). http://www.bankdirector.com/board-issues/legal/international-manda-will-china-buy-more-u-s-banks/
10. For example, Canada's TD Bank has successfully pursued community and regional bank acquisitions as part of its overall strategy to become a major player in the U.S. banking sector. Alan Kline, "TD Bank Happy with Footprint, CFO Says," American Banker, September 18, 2013, http://www.americanbanker.com/issues/178_181/td-bank-happy-with-footprint-cfo-says-1062255-1.html;Maria Aspan, "Trained in the USA: Masrani Pick Signals Where TD's Growth Plans Lie," *American Banker,* April 3, 2013 http://www.americanbanker.com/issues/178_64/masrani-pick-signals-where-td-growth-plans-lie-1058022-1.html; Jonathan Berr, "The World According to TD," *American Banker,* June 1, 2012 http://www.americanbanker.com/magazine/122_6/td-bank-us-expansion-strategy-1049447-1.html.11. Catherine Clifford, "4 Insurers Seek Thrift Status, Gaining Bailout Access," *CNN Money,* November. 14, 2008 Catherine Clifford, "4 Insurers Seek Thrift Status, Gaining Bailout Access," *CNN Money,* November. 14, 2008; Joe Adler, "War over Retailer Banks Could Reignite, With or Without Walmart," *American Banker*, April 29, 2013 http://www.americanbanker.com/issues/178_82/war-over-retailer-banks-could-reignite-with-or-without-walmart-1058709-1.html.

CHAPTER 1

1. Also, text of Occupy protest sign in Ogden, Oregon, November 5, 2011.
2. Many sources point to medieval Italy for the origins of modern banking. However, banks can be traced back to an earlier time, to ancient Greece. See Edward Cohen, *Athenian Economy and Society: A Banking Perspective* (Princeton: Princeton University Press, 1996).
3. Connecticut law, in fact, grants thrifts the same powers as commercial banks.

4. The Office of the Comptroller of the Currency (OCC) states that "[n]ational banks may provide financial and transactional advice to customers and assist customers in structuring, arranging, and executing various financial transactions." Activities Permissible for a National Bank (2012), http://www.occ.gov/publications/publications-by-type/other-publications-reports/bankact.pdf.
5. As shown in Chapter 2, most federal regulation from various agencies, such as the Federal Deposit Insurance Corporation [FDIC], the Federal Reserve, and the OCC, as well as regulation from the states (in the case of FDIC-insured but state-chartered banks), stems from the insurance offered by the FDIC. There is an exception for some nonbank financial companies that are considered to be systemically important. Section 113 of the Dodd-Frank Wall Street Reform and Consumer Protection Act authorizes the Financial Stability Oversight Council to determine that a nonbank financial company shall be supervised by the Board of Governors of the Federal Reserve System and shall be subject to prudential standards, if the Council determines that material financial distress at the nonbank financial company, or the nature, scope, size, scale, concentration, interconnectedness, or mix of the activities of the nonbank financial company, could pose a threat to the financial stability of the United States. AIG and GE Capital were so designated in July 2013, with Prudential following in September 2013. See Donna Borak, "Prudential Named as Systematially Important Despite Firm's Objections." *American Banker*, September 19, 2013. (http://www.americanbanker.com/issues/178_182/prudential-named-as-systemically-important-despite-firms-objections–1062292–1.html).
6. Some sources focusing on the most dramatic events refer to the financial crisis of 2007–2008. In retrospect the crisis lasted well into 2009. The time span of the Great Recession, according to the National Bureau of Economic Research, was December 2007 to June 2009. See http://www.nber.org/cycles/sept2010.html. See also 2011 Joint Economic Report: Report of the Joint Economic Committee, Congress of the United States, on the 2011 Economic Report of the President, December 16, 2011. See also Tyler Atkinson, David Luttrell, and Harvey Rosenblum, "How Bad Was It?: The Costs and Consequences of the 2007–2009 Financial Crisis." Federal Reserve Bank of Dallas. No. 20, July 2013. http://dallasfed.org/assets/documents/research/staff/staff1301.pdf.
7. For an authoritative study on the causes of the financial crisis, see *The Financial Crisis Inquiry Report: Final Report of the National Commission on the Causes of the Financial and Economic Crisis in the United States*, January 2011; http://fcic-static.law.stanford.edu/cdn_media/fcic-reports/fcic_final_report_full.pdf. Chapter 2 goes into more detail on government banking regulations and their economic impact. This report notes, among other points, that the FDIC could have asserted more oversight over mortgage lenders, but deferred to the Federal Trade Commission, which had special regulatory turf, along with authorities in the individual states.

8. Ibid., p. 430.
9. See Statement of John Corston, Acting Deputy Director, Complex Financial Institution Branch, Division of Supervision and Consumer Protection, Federal Deposit Insurance Corporation on Systemically Important Institutions and the Issue of "Too Big To Fail" before the Financial Crisis Inquiry Commission; Room 538, Dirksen Senate Office Building September 1, 2010 http://www.fdic.gov/news/news/speeches/archives/2010/spsep0110.html.
10. American Bankers Association, About the American Bankers Association, http://www.aba.com/About/Pages/default.aspx.
11. Bureau of Labor Statistics, February 1, 2013. Employment Situation Summary USDL-12-1531. Table A, Household Data Seasonally Adjusted, showing more than 143 million employed Americans (civilian work force) in January 2013 with an unemployment rate of 7.9. http://www.bls.gov/news.release/empsit.a.htm
12. Small Business Lending in the United States (Washington, DC: U.S. Small Business Administration, U.S. Department of Commerce, 2012 Table A Value of Small Business Loans Outstanding for Depository Lenders by Loan Type and Size, 2007 to 2012). http://www.sba.gov/sites/default/files/files/sbl_12study.pdf.
13. Ibid.
14. Ben Gose et al., "10 Companies that Gave the Most Cash in 2012," The Chronicle of Philanthropy, July 14, 2013. http://philanthropy.com/article/10-Companies-That-Gave-the/140261.
15. As of June 30, 2013, the number of FDIC-insured institutions continued to decline. As of that date, there were 5,980 commercial banks and 960 thrifts, according to the FDIC. By contrast, five years earlier, there were 7,284 banks, and 1,250 thrifts. Source: FDIC, "Statistics at a Glance," as of June 30, 2013. http://www.fdic.gov/bank/statistical/stats/2013jun/fdic.html. See also D. J. Masson, "Commercial Banking in the U.S. versus Canada," *Graziadio Business Review* 10, no. 4 (2007), posted at http://gbr.pepperdine.edu/2010/08/commercial-banking-in-the-u-s-versus-canada/. Masson states that the number of depository institutions was "large" compared to Canada. As mentioned, the trend, however, has been downward.
16. As explained in Chapters 2 and 11, the FDIC's roles as insurer and receiver are separate functionally and legally. "The FDIC as receiver is functionally and legally separate from the FDIC acting in its corporate role as deposit insurer, and the FDIC as receiver has separate rights, duties, and obligations from those of the FDIC as insurer." FDIC, http://www.fdic.gov/bank/historical/reshandbook/ch7recvr.pdf.
17. See U.S. Federal Reserve Bank of Chicago, "U.S. Banks as of June 30, 2012," http://www.chicagofed.org/digital_assets/others/banking/financial_institution_reports/Top_Bank-HC_Listing_June_2012.pdf.
18. "Commercial Banks in the U.S.," Federal Financial Institutions Examination Council, published by the Federal Reserve Bank of St. Louis.

http://research.stlouisfed.org/fred2/series/USNUM. The 1921 figure is from "Mergers of Banking Institutions," Congressional Quarterly, April 29, 1929, http://library.cqpress.com/cqresearcher/document.php?id=cqresrre1929042900.

19. See Kevin Funnell, "Now You See Them, Now You Don't," bankruptcylawyersblog.com, September 11, 2013. For his earlier blog on the topic, see "De Novo a Go Go," September 22, 2010.
20. To see the 39-page application form, estimated to take 250 hours to complete, see http://www.fdic.gov/formsdocuments/InteragencyCharter-InsuranceApplication.doc.
21. Committee on Payment and Settlement Systems, *Statistics on Payment, Clearing and Settlement Systems in the CPSS Countries: Figures for 2011*. Bank for International Settlements, January 2013 and the similar publication for 2004–2008 published December 2009. See also "Commercial Bank Branches per 100,000 Adults." Worldbank http://data.worldbank.org/indicator/FB.CBK.BRCH.P5/countries?page=1&display=default, accessed September 19, 2013. This gives a slightly different trend: 35.4 per 100,000 adults—up from 32.5 in 2004.
22. Ibid, http://www.bis.org/publ/cpss99.pdf.
23. Compared depositors in most other developed countries, U.S. depositors have a low average bank balance. Reasons for this may include greater banking participation by individuals with modest income and a greater tendency to spend or invest rather than save.
24. According to the Fed, the term merger would exclude a purchase of assets and assumption of liabilities in which both the seller and the buyer continue to exist. That is not a merger and does not qualify for merger treatment.
25. Thomson Reuters/Financial Times League Tables January 1, 2013, through June 26, 2013, http://markets.ft.com/investmentBanking/dealMap.asp. See also http://dmi.thomsonreuters.com/Content/Files/2Q2013Global_MA_Financial_Review.pdf.
26. *Mergers and Acquisitions Review, Financial Advisors: Full Year 2012*, http://dmi.thomsonreuters.com/Content/Files/4Q2012_MA_Financial_Advisory_Review.pdf.
27. For a discussion of these relatively new regulations, see Chapter 3.
28. For an overview of commercial banking in the United States and Canada in these respects, see http://gbr.pepperdine.edu/2010/08/commercial-banking-in-the-u-s-versus-canada/#_edn4.
29. The Trust Examination Manual of the FDIC is available at http://www.fdic.gov/regulations/examinations/trustmanual/section_10/section_x.html.
30. *Committee on Payment and Settlement Systems, Statistics on Payment*. The period covered goes through the end of 2010.
31. From *Statistics on Payment, Clearing and Settlement Systems in the CPSS Countries Figures for 2011, Bank for International Settlements*. January 2013 Comparative Tables, Table 3, "Transferable Deposits Held by Banks," p. 432. Does not include $40.83 billion in transferable U.S. balances.

32. Ibid., Table 10, p. 446.
33. Ibid., Table 7, p. 423.
34. As observed by Masson, the U.S. National Automated Clearing House Association (NACHA), in conjunction with the U.S. Federal Reserve, allows retailers, utilities, credit card companies, and so on, to convert a check into an ACH transaction, thus "reducing the number of checks and speeding up the value transfer." See Masson, op. cit., note 15.
35. It is interesting from a historical point of view that the crush of post-Revolutionary debt enabled Alexander Hamilton's vision of a strong central bank to prevail over Thomas Jefferson's advocacy of a decentralized financial system based in the individual states. Some today see their argument as a precursor of the debates now going on in debt-burdened Europe. Whatever one's view then or now, it is clear that the central banking system helped to knit the early United States together from a mere confederation into a real country. See Simon Kennedy and Ian Katz, "Europe Recalls Hamilton as Desperation Turns on the Debt," Bloomberg .com, July 6, 2012, http://www.bloomberg.com/news/2012-07-06/europe-recalls-hamilton-as-desperation-turns-on-the-debt.html.
36. This list is paraphrased from the Federal Reserve Bank of San Francisco, one of the 12 Federal Reserve banks in the U.S. http://www.frbsf.org/publications/federalreserve/fedinbrief/central.html.
37. *Financial Crisis Inquiry Report*, p. 125. For the history of the FCIC, see http://fcic.law.stanford.edu/about/history.
38. Federal National Mortgage Association (Fannie Mae) and the Federal Home Loan Mortgage Corporation (Freddie Mac) share a common mission: to free up capital for mortgage loans by securitizing mortgages (creating mortgage-backed securities that can be traded for cash). Fannie Mae buys its mortgages from banks, and Freddie Mac buys them from thrifts. When large money-center banks began competing for business in the mortgage-lending field, the government-sponsored enterprises lowered their standards for loan quality, contributing to the financial crisis. As loans defaulted, there was a ripple effect throughout the economy.
39. *Financial Crisis Inquiry Report*, p. 125.
40. JPMorgan Chase conducted two internal investigations—one by the board and one by management. *The Report of the Review Committee of the Board of Directors of JPMorgan Chase & Co, Relating to the Board's Oversight Function with Respect to Risk Management*, was released January 15, 2013, and the *Report of JPMorgan Chase & Co. Management Task Force Regarding 2012 CIO Losses* was released January 16, 2013. Federal authorities looking into the matter include Congress (Permanent Subcommittee on Investigations), the Securities and Exchange Commission, and the Federal Trade Commission.
41. See *The Wheatley Review of LIBOR: Final Report, September 2012*, http://cdn.hm-treasury.gov.uk/wheatley_review_libor_finalreport_280912.pdf.

42. The following is from Bank of America (BoA)'s merger agreement with Countrywide, which provided that an MAE shall not be deemed to include effects to the extent resulting from

    (A) changes, after the date hereof, in GAAP [generally accepted accounting principles] or regulatory accounting requirements applicable generally to companies in the industries in which such party and its Subsidiaries operate, (B) changes, after the date hereof, in laws, rules or regulations of general applicability to companies in the industries in which such party and its Subsidiaries operate, (C) actions or omissions taken with the prior written consent of the other party, (D) changes, after the date hereof, in global or national political conditions or general economic or market conditions generally affecting other companies in the industries in which such party and its Subsidiaries operate, or (E) the public disclosure of this Agreement or the transactions contemplated hereby, except, with respect to clauses (A) and (B), to the extent that the effects of such change are *disproportionately adverse* to the financial condition, results of operations or business of such party and its Subsidiaries, taken as a whole, as compared to other companies in the industry in which such party and its Subsidiaries operate. (Emphasis added.)

    The BoA board considered invoking the MAC clause but approved the BoA–Countrywide merger after receiving assurances of government support. See Andrew Ross Sorkin, "The Big MAC," *New York Times*, March 10, 2008. http://dealbook.nytimes.com/2008/03/10/the-big-mac/.
43. Michael Clinton, "Bank of America's $335M Countrywide Settlement Hits Snag," *Jacksonville Business Journal Morning Edition*, December 31, 2012, citing "BofA Settlement Hits Snags: Justice Department Behind Schedule in Resolving Lending-Discrimination Case," *Wall Street Journal*, December 30, 2012. As the Clinton article notes, the settlement is for loans made between 2004 and 2008 by Countrywide Financial. Bank of America acquired Countrywide in 2008.
44. Paul S. Nadler and Richard Miller, *The Banking Jungle: How to Survive and Prosper in a Business Turned Topsy-Turvy* (New York: John Wiley, 1985).
45. *Financial Crisis Inquiry Report.*
46. Michael McKee and Scott Lanman, "Greenspan Says U.S. Should Consider Breaking Up Large Banks," Bloomberg News Service, October 15, 2009, http://www.bloomberg.com/apps/news?pid=newsarchive&sid=aJ8HPmNU fchg.
47. In other countries, it may mean a bank that is owned by the central government. For global definitions, see Chapter 10.
48. In the U.S. Code of federal laws (U.S.C.), see "Definitions," Title 12, Chapter 2, Subchapter XV, Section 214. The jurisdictions that may have a state bank, in addition to a state, are "any Territory of the United States, Puerto Rico, or the Virgin Islands, or which is operating under the Code

of Law for the District of Columbia." Under this section, "the term 'State bank' means any bank, banking association, trust company, savings bank (other than a mutual savings bank), or other banking institution which is engaged in the business of *receiving deposits* and which is incorporated under the laws of any State, any Territory of the United States, Puerto Rico, or the Virgin Islands, or which is operating under the Code of Law for the District of Columbia (except a national banking association)."

49. Title 12, Chapter 2, Subchapters 1 through 17, in the U.S. Code of federal laws (U.S.C.), covers national banks. For more on this and other regulatory matters, see Chapter 2.
50. "For purposes of sections 582 and 584, the term 'bank' means a bank or trust company incorporated and doing business under the laws of the United States (including laws relating to the District of Columbia) or of any State, a substantial part of the business of which consists of receiving deposits and making loans and discounts, or of exercising fiduciary powers similar to those permitted to national banks under authority of the Comptroller of the Currency, and which is subject by law to supervision and examination by State, Territorial, or Federal authority having supervision over banking institutions." U.S. Code Title 26: Internal Revenue Code, Section 581, http://us-code.vlex.com/vid/sec-definition-bank-19209174.
51. A nonbank can make loans but can only accept uninsured deposits. Also, whereas a commercial bank is exclusively engaged in financial activities, the nonbank financial company need only be predominantly engaged in them.
52. http://www.treasury.gov/initiatives/fsoc/Documents/Nonbank%20Designation%20NPR%20-%20Final%20with%20web%20disclaimer.pdf.
53. See Appendix 1A for a summary of this rule.
54. Namely, the Bank Holding Company Act of 1956, Section 4(k), and the Gramm–Leach–Bliley Act of 1999, specifying activities permissible for financial holding companies.
55. Website of Sen. Sherrod Brown (D-OH), http://www.brown.senate.gov/newsroom/press/release/at-senate-banking-hearing-brown-presses-regulators-on-bank-holding-companies-controlling-price-and-supply-of-physical-commodities-effect-on-consumers-and-manufacturers.
56. "Assets and Liabilities of Commercial Banks in the United States," August 2, 2013 (week ending July 24, 2013), http://www.federalreserve.gov/releases/h8/current/. These data are from the chart labeled Assets and Liabilities of Commercial Banks in the United States, not seasonally adjusted, billions of dollars. The chart of seasonally adjusted results showed similar figures: $13.6 trillion in assets, $12.1 trillion in liabilities, and $1.47 trillion in residual. Data include the following types of institutions in the 50 states and the District of Columbia: domestically chartered commercial banks, U.S. branches and agencies of foreign banks, and banks governed by the Agreement Corporation Act of 1916 and the Edge Act of 1919. The Agreement Corporation Act gave national banks

the right to invest a portion of their capital and surplus in state-chartered banks and corporations that would conduct international business,The Edge Act authorized the FRB to charter corporations to engage in international banking. Data exclude international banking facilities.

57. See David C. Wheelock, "Banking Industry Consolidation and Market Structure: Impact of the Financial Crisis and Recession," Federal Reserve Bank of St. Louis Review, 93, no. 6 (November/December 2011): 419–438. The summary of this article states that the number of U.S. commercial banks and savings institutions declined by 12 percent between December 31, 2006, and December 31, 2010, continuing a consolidation trend begun in the mid-1980s. Banking industry consolidation has been marked by sharply higher shares of deposits held by the largest banks—the 10 largest banks now hold nearly 50 percent of total U.S. deposits. http://research.stlouisfed.org/publications/review/11/11/419-438Wheelock.pdf.
58. See "Report to Global 20 Leaders on Basel III Implementation" at http://www.bis.org/publ/bcbs220.htm.
59. More broadly, notes Elliott, the liquidity of a bank often refers to the matching of its obligations with its funding sources. Douglas J. Elliott, "Basel III, Banks, and the Economy," http://www.brookings.edu/research/papers/2010/07/26-basel-elliott.
60. See Regulatory Capital Rules: Regulatory Capital, Implementation of Basel III, Capital Adequacy, Transition Provisions, Prompt Corrective Action, Standardized Approach for Risk-weighted Assets, Market Discipline and Disclosure Requirements, Advanced Approaches Risk-Based Capital Rule, and Market Risk Capital Rule, final rule issued by the Office of the Comptroller of the Currency, Treasury; and the Board of Governors of the Federal Reserve System, July 9, 2013. http://www.federalreserve.gov/bcreg20130702a.pdf.
61. See http://www.fdic.gov/regulations/laws/rules/1000-1260.html
62. This appeared in the Federal Register of June 10, 2013. The text is dated "at Washington, DC, this 4th day of June, 2013. By order of the Board of Directors. Federal Deposit Insurance Corporation. Robert E. Feldman." https://www.federalregister.gov/articles/2012/06/18/2012-14701/definition-of-predominantly-engaged-in-activities-that-are-financial-in-nature-or-incidental-thereto#p-60. The comment period on this definition ended August 17, 2012. Some commenters took strong objection to this definition. In a letter dated August 6, 2012, Tom Quaadman of the Center for Capital Markets of the U.S. Chamber of Commerce, stated that "the Board's 'clarification' exceeds its statutory authority under Title I of the Dodd–Frank Act. In developing the clarification, the Board ignored Congress' clear, unambiguous statutory directive, as embodied in the passage of the Pryor–Vitter Amendment, that, for purposes of defining whether a company is 'predominantly engaged' in 'activities that are financial in nature' under Title I, it must accept that term exactly 'as defined in Section 4(k)' of the Bank Holding Company Act."

CHAPTER 2

1. As stated in an opening quote in Chapter 10 of this book, "Generally speaking, U.S. financial institutions have been much more heavily regulated . . . than their foreign counterparts." Scott Besley and Eugene F. Brigham *Principles of Finance* (Stamford, Conn.: Cengage Learning, 2012). See also James Gwatney, Robert Lawson, and Joshua Hall, *Economic Freedom of the World* (Washington, DC: Cato Institute, 2013) http://www.cato.org/economic-freedom-world. This report gives the United States a score of only 7.34 out of 10 for degree of freedom in domestic credit markets due to a very low score (2) for private sector credit, indicating extensive regulation of this aspect of financial services. Most developed nations score higher in this area. For an explanation of the score see p. 6. For the score see p. 172.
2. "'Federal banking agency' means, individually, the Board of Governors, the Office of the Comptroller of the Currency, and the Corporation." 12 U.S.C. ch. 53 Wall Street Reform and Consumer Protection § 5301 (10)(a). The Wall Street Reform and Consumer Protection language came from the law by that same name sponsored by Christopher Dodd and Barney Frank in 2010 (also known as Dodd–Frank).
3. For the electronic version of the U.S. Code of Federal Regulations (C.F.R.), see http://www.ecfr.gov/.
4. *Financial Regulatory Reform: Regulators Have Faced Challenges Finalizing Key Reforms and Unaddressed Areas Pose Potential Risks,* Report no. GAO-13-195, January 23, 2013. For updates see http://www.davispolk.com/Dodd-Frank-Rulemaking-Progress-Report.
5. Untitled press release of October 25, 2012, http://www.federalreserve.gov/newsevents/press/bcreg/20121025a.htm.
6. For more on the discount rate, see http://www.federalreserve.gov/monetarypolicy/discountrate.htm.
7. *The Federal Reserve Board: Purposes and Functions*, pp. 71–73, http://www.federalreserve.gov/pf/pdf/pf_complete.pdf.
8. 12 U.S.C. § 1828(c)(5)(B).
9. Office of the Comptroller of the Currency, http://www.occ.gov/publications/publications-by-type/comptrollers-handbook/banksupervisionprocess.pdf.
10. Note that the FDIC's role as insurer and receiver are separate functionally and legally. "The FDIC as receiver is functionally and legally separate from the FDIC acting in its corporate role as deposit insurer, and the FDIC as receiver has separate rights, duties, and obligations from those of the FDIC as insurer." FDIC, http://www.fdic.gov/bank/historical/reshandbook/ch7recvr.pdf.

11. *Trust Examination Manual*, http://www.fdic.gov/regulations/examinations/trustmanual/section_10/section_x.html.
12. Safe and sound operation per Sections 802(b) and 804(1).
13. Peter J. Wallison and Arthur F. Burns, *Financial Crisis Inquiry Commission: Dissenting Statement,* http://fcic-static.law.stanford.edu/cdn_media/fcic-reports/fcic_final_report_wallison_dissent.pdf.
14. *The Financial Crisis Inquiry Report: Final Report of the National Commission on the Causes of the Financial and Economic Crisis in the United States,* January 2011, http://fcic-static.law.stanford.edu/cdn_media/fcic-reports/fcic_final_report_full.pdf, p. xxvii.
15. As noted by F. M. Scherer, "A beginning insight is that much commercial banking—notably, the issuance of loans to all but large business firms and the provision of checking account services—is in the present state of technology (ignoring potential internet-based developments such as 'crowd-funding') preponderantly local." F. M. Scherer, "Financial Mergers and Their Consequences," HKS Faculty Research Working Paper Series RWP12-018, May 2012.
16. Community Reinvestment Act Q&A, http://www.ncrc.org.
17. Ibid.
18. Peter J. Wallison and Edward J. Pinto, "Free Fall: How Government Policies Brought Down the U.S. Housing Market," American Enterprise Institute, April 26, 2012, citing a 2007 report from the National Community Reinvestment Coalition.
19. Note, for example, the recent sale by GE Capital Corp. of its $2.51 billion real estate lending unit, Business Property Lending Inc., to EverBank Financial Corp., a newly public commercial bank.
20. *Authority to Require Supervision and Regulation of Certain Nonbank Financial Companies: Final Rule and Interpretive Guidance* (Washington, DC: Financial Stability Oversight Council, Federal Register, April 11, 2012).
21. See Heath P. Tarbert, "Systemic Risk Regime," a part of a Weil, Gotshal & Manges series entitled "Dodd-Frank Two Years Later," published October 2012. See also http://www.metrocorpcounsel.com/articles/20915/dodd-frank-act-two-years-later.
22. Risk management protocols include enhanced capital and leverage requirements, additional liquidity provisioning, mandatory contingent capital, resolution plans (commonly called "living wills"), credit exposure reports, concentration limits, supplemental public disclosures, and periodic stress testing.
23. For a rule on risk management under Sections 805(a) and 806(e) of Dodd-Frank, see https://www.federalregister.gov/articles/2012/08/02/2012-18762/financial-market-utilities, passed August 2, 2012.
24. See 78 Fed. Reg. 20756 (April 5, 2013) (adding Regulation PP, 12 C.F.R. Part 242: Definitions Relating to Title I of the Dodd—Frank Act).

25. See Ronald D. Orol, "Ally Only Bank Below Federal Standard in Stress Test," *Wall Street Journal,* March 7, 2013. See also Federal Reserve's Stress Test Results, http://www.marketwatch.com/stress-test-results-march–2013?siteId=.
26. *Application of the Revised Capital Framework to the Capital Plan and Stress Test Rules: Interim Final Rules with Request for Comment.* September 24, 2013. http://www.federalreserve.gov/newsevents/press/bcreg/bcreg20130924b2.pdf For regulations impacting smaller banks, see *New Capital Rule: Community Bank Guide*. Federal Deposit Insurance Corporation, July 2013. https://www.fdic.gov/regulations/capital/Community_Bank_Guide.pdf
27. See Antitrust Division, Workload Statistics FY 2003–2012, chart entitled "Participation in Bank Merger Proceedings." In Fiscal 2012 (ending September 30, 2012), the division conducted. http://www.justice.gov/atr/public/workload-statistics.html.
28. Twenty-seven acquirers in fiscal 2012 were classified as providers of depository credit intermediation, which was 1.9 percent of all Hart–Scott–Rodino filings.
29. DOJ press release, November 10, 2011, First Niagara Bank N.A. acquisition of HSBC Bank USA N.A.
30. More technically, it "increased by 2.5 to 2.9 times, depending upon difficult inclusion and exclusion choices, to somewhere between 46 and 53 percent in 2010." Scherer, "Financial Mergers and Their Consequences."
31. This figure is from 2006. Scherer, "Financial Mergers and Their Consequences."
32. http://www.justice.gov/atr/public/press_releases/2011/269239.htm.
33. For more on this topic and the *Chevron* deference, see the following resource from the Department of Justice: http://www.justice.gov/eoir/vll/benchbook/resources/sfoutline/agency_deference.html.
34. *National Cable & Telecommunications Assn.* v. *Brand X Internet Services*, 545 U.S. 967, 980 (2005).
35. *Christopher et al. v. SmithKline Beecham Corp.,* 132 S. Ct. 2156 (2012), citing *Auer v. Robbins*, 519 U.S. 452 (1997).
36. *Descriptions of laws prior to 2004 are taken from "Major Statutes Affecting Financial Institutions and Markets," Congressional Research Service, July 7, 2004, http://www.fdic.gov/regulations/laws/important/.*
37. See Appendix 10-A in this book.
38. "History of Anti-Money Laundering Legislation," Federal Deposit Insurance Corporation, http://www.fdic.gov/regulations/examinations/bsa/bsa_3.html.
39. For a detailed review of the banking sections of Dodd-Frank, see "Financial Regulatory Reform:An Overview of The Dodd-Frank Wall Street Reform and Consumer Protection Act, 2010." http://www.weil.com/files/upload/

Weil%20Dodd-Frank%20Overview.pdf See also Heath Tarbert and Sylvia A. Mayer, "'Living Wills' Present an Opportunity for Banks," *American Banker*, July 3, 2012. http://www.weil.com/news/pubdetail.aspx?pub=10922.

40. See Michael J. Aiello and Heath P. Tarbert, "Bank M&A in the Wake of Dodd-Frank." *Banking Law Journal November/December* 2010, pp. 909 ff., http://www.weil.com/files/Publication/35981ae3-04bd-4f89-9578-1741d252c0d6/Presentation/PublicationAttachment/3d142d62-d063–421d-abe8–1e83c36be049/Bank_MA_in_Wake_of_Dodd-Frank.pdf.

CHAPTER 3

1. Amanda Alix, "Citgroup Makes Work for Itself: The Perks of Being a Bank Holding Company," *The Motley Fool,* August 6, 2013, http://www.fool.com/investing/general/2013/08/06/citigroup -makes-work-for-itself-the-perks-of-being.aspx.
2. See the Bank Holding Company Act of 1956, 4(c)(8).
3. *The Federal Reserve Board: Purposes and Functions*, http://www.federalreserve .gov/pf/pdf/pf_complete.pdf.
4. Information per Federal Reserve Bank of Chicago. As of June 2012, the precise numbers were 4,679 institutions reporting $17,142 billion in assets. http://www.chicagofed.org/digital_assets/others/banking/financial_institution_reports/Top_Bank-HC_Listing_June_2012.pdf. The total number of banks is reported for mid-2012 for comparability purposes. As of mid-2013, as reported in Chapter 1, the total number of commercial banks was 6,048.
5. Ibid.
6. http://www.ffiec.gov/nicpubweb/nicweb/Top50Form.aspx.
7. See Dafna Avraham, Patricia Selvaggi, and James Vickery, "A Structural View of Bank Holding Companies," *FRBNY Economic Policy Review* July 2012, http://www.newyorkfed.org/research/epr/12v18n2/1207avra.pdf.
8. See, for example, the invitation for comments at https://www.federalregister.gov/articles/2012/06/14/2012-14578/formations-of-acquisitions-by-and-mergers-of-bank-holding-companies#p-1.
9. *A User's Guide to the Bank Holding Company Performance Report,* http://www.federalreserve.gov/boarddocs/supmanual/bhcpr/UsersGuide12/s32.pdf.
10. Some holding companies exclude internal loss data by "omitting losses from merged or acquired institutions mergers or acquisitions due to complications in collection and aggregation." Source: Capital Planning at Large Bank Holding Companies: Supervisory Expectations and Range of Current Practice. Board of Governors of the Federal Reserve System, August 2013, p. 27. http://www.federalreserve.gov/bankinforeg/bcreg20130819a1.pdf
11. http://www.ffiec.gov/nicpubweb/content/BHCPRRPT/BHCPR_Peer.htm

12. http://www.federalreserve.gov/apps/h2a/h2aindex.aspx.
13. This section is based on the knowledge of the authors and expert reviewer, as well as several publications at federal reserve.gov, including *The Federal Reserve System: Purposes and Functions,* http://www.federalreserve.gov/pf/pdf/pf_complete.pdf.
14. Acquisition refers to a purchase of 5 percent or more of the bank's stock.
15. Ibid.
16. "The term 'State member bank' means any State bank which is a member of the Federal Reserve System." http://www.fdic.gov/regulations/laws/rules/1000-400.html.
17. 12 U.S.C. § 24a, Financial Subsidiaries of National Banks, http://www.law.cornell.edu/uscode/text/12/24a, preliminary release current as of January 27, 2013.
18. Exceptions are noted in section 302 or 303(c) of the Gramm–Leach–Bliley Act (15 U.S.C. § 6712 or 6713 (c)).
19. Specifically, income that is taxable under 26 U.S.C., § 72, re annuities, endowments, and life insurance.
20. For example, approval would be granted if the national bank meets standards of creditworthiness established by the OCC, and the national bank has received the approval of the OCC for the financial subsidiary to engage in such activities.
21. 12 U.S.C. § 24a, Ibid. note 17.
22. See Etyan Avriel, "It's the End of the Wall Street Era," Haaretz, September 16, 2008, quoting Israeli investor Eddy Shalev; and Julie Creswell and Ben White, "Wall Street R.I.P, The End of an Era, Even at Goldman." *New York Times*, September 27, 2008. As summarized by financial author Michael Lewis, in "The End." Portfolio, December 2008, "The era that defined Wall Street is finally, officially, over."
23. This section on merchant banking is based on Title 12, Code of Federal Regulations, Section 225, Subpart J—Merchant Banking Investments, http://www.law.cornell.edu/cfr/text/ 12/225/subpart-J.
24. See also Heath Tarbert, Shukie Grossman, and David Wohl, "Federal Reserve Issues Final Rule on Volcker Rule Conformance Periods" at the Weil Gotshal Financial Regulatory Reform Center. http://financial-reform.weil.com/commercial-banks/federal-reserve-issues-final-rule-volcker-rule-conformance-periods/#axzz2MmKxEXVP. See also http://financial-reform.weil.com/commercial-banks/federal-reserve-issues-final-rule-volcker-rule-conformance-periods/#ixzz2MmLNe8SY.
25. Bank Holding Company Act, 12 U.S.C. § 1843.
26. An exception applies in the case of a subsidiary that is a small business investment company (SBIC) and that is held in accordance with the Small Business Investment Act; such a subsidiary may routinely manage or operate a portfolio company in which an affiliated company owns or controls an interest.

27. Dodd–Frank at http://www.gpo.gov/fdsys/pkg/PLAW–111publ203/pdf/PLAW–111publ203.pdf.
28. For an explanation of prudential standards, see Chapter 2 of this book.
29. Daniel K. Tarullo, speech on "Financial Stability Regulation," October 10, 2012, University of Pennsylvania Law School, http://www.federalreserve.gov/newsevents/speech/tarullo20121010a.htm#f38.
30. See Jack Milligan, "Is the Game Over?" *Bank Director,* January 22, 2013, http://www.bankdirector.com/board-issues/manda/big-bank-mergers-is-the-game-over/.
31. http://www.federalreserve.gov/pubs/feds/2012/201251/201251pap.pdf.
32. Proposed bank mergers in 1998 were so large that the Department of Justice became concerned. See J. Robert Kramer II, chief, Litigation II Section, Antitrust Division, Department of Justice, "Megamergers in the Banking Industry," address before the American Bar Association, April 14, 1999. Today Kramer heads the division's Office of the General Counsel.
33. As Milligan ("Big Bank Mergers," op. cit., note 27) states, SNL Financial, JPMorgan, and Wells Fargo are close to the 10 percent nationwide cap on bank deposits—and Bank of America actually exceeds that by 2.62 percent.
34. Louise Bennetts, "Thanks to Dodd-Frank, America's Community Banks Are Too Small to Survive." American Banker, November 9, 2012. www.americanbanker.com.
35. Board of Governors of the Federal Reserve, Capital One Financial Corporation, McLean, Virginia, Order Approving the Acquisition of a Savings Association and Nonbanking Subsidiaries (PDF), FRB Order No. 2012-2 (Feb. 14, 2012), p. 30.
36. For a thoughtful discussion of antitrust considerations, see Ira M. Millstein, "Unfinished Business: Should Regulation Supplant the Applicability of Competition/Antitrust Principles in Dealing with Systemic Risk?" outline of remarks at a Conference on Financial Risk and Regulation at Columbia Business School on March 27, 2012, http://www.youtube.com/watch?v=kMSIOJkfScY and http://www7.gsb.columbia.edu/richman/sites/default/files/files/Ira%20Millstein.pdf.

CHAPTER 4

1. John Medlin was CEO of Wachovia from 1977 to1993, when its assets grew to $35.3 billion from $3.6 billion. He made this observation in a 1999 oral history interview. Interview with John Medlin, May 24, 1999. Interview I-0076. Southern Oral History Program Collection (#4007). John Medlin, interviewee; Joseph Mosnier, interviewer, http://docsouth.unc.edu/sohp/I-0076/I-0076.html.
2. Cody Boyte, "Small Banks Merging to Save Themselves." August 22. 2013, blog noting a rise in small bank acquisitions in 2013.

3. See Table 2.1, "Deposit reporting categories, September 2013? September 2014," in the Federal Reserve Board's *Reserve Maintenance Manual*, http://www.federalreserve.gov/monetarypolicy/rmm/june–2013/Chapter_2_Reporting_Requirements.htm#CE496A08f5r.
4. Governor Daniel K. Tarullo, Board of Governors of the Federal Reserve System. "Industry Structure and Systemic Risk Regulation," December 4, 2012, speech at Brookings Institution. http://www.federalreserve.gov/newsevents/speech/tarullo20121204a.htm#fn3.
5. See David B. McNab, CA, "Deposit Growth: Measure What You Manage," Internet blog accessed April 13, 2013. http://www.flowtrackeranalytics.com/index.php? module=pagemaster&PAGE_user_op=view_page&PAGE_id=31.
6. Ibid.
7. See *Banking 2016: Accelerating Growth and Optimizing Costs in Distribution and Marketing,* http://www.accenture.com/us-en/Pages/insight-banking–2016-next-generation-banking-summary.aspx.
8. *Risk Management Manual of Examination Policies*, http://www.fdic.gov/regulations/safety/manual/section2–1.html#evaluation.
9. Paul Kedrosky and Dane Stangler, "Financialization and Its Entrepreneurial Consequences," Kauffman Foundation, March 2011, http://www.kauffman.org/research-and-policy/Financialization-and-Its-Entrepreneurial-Consequences.aspx.
10. http://www.forbes.com/sites/billconerly/2013/01/11/bank-problems-in–2013-and-strategies-to-overcome-them.
11. For a general explanation, see FAQ "What is inflation and how does the Federal Reserve calculate changes in the rate of inflation?" http://www.federalreserve.gov/faqs/economy_14419.htm. For a more detailed explanation with graphs, see Brent Meyer, Guhan Venkatu, and Saeed Zaman, "Forecasting Inflation? Target the Middle," April 11, 2013, an economic commentary posted at http://www.clevelandfed.org/research/commentary/2013/2013-05.cfm.
12. Sensitivities to inflation vary significantly across industries and tend to be lower for cyclical industries. See Inflation and Industry Returns–A Global Perspective," http://papers.ssrn.com/sol3/papers.cfm?abstract_id=1321440Another study, by Mike McElroy of Batterymarch Financial Management however, showed that banks only do well when inflation is stable (not rising or falling). See Mike McElroy, Protecting Assets with an Inflation-Sensitive Equity Portfolio, December 2012. (https://www.batterymarch.com/PDF/BFM_InflationSensitiveEquity.pdf.)
13. At the Annual Monetary/Macroeconomics Conference: The Past and Future of Monetary Policy, sponsored by Federal Reserve Bank of San Francisco, San Francisco, California, March 1, 2013. http://www.federalreserve.gov/newsevents/speech/bernanke20130301a.htm.
14. See Mike McElroy, op. cit., note 12.

15. John H. Boyd and Bruce Champ, "Inflation, Banking, and Economic Growth." http://www.clevelandfed.org/research/Commentary/2006/0515.pdf.
16. John H. Boyd, Ross Levine, and Bruce D. Smith. 2001. "The Impact of Inflation on Financial Market Performance." *Journal of Monetary Economics*, vol. 47, pp. 221–48.
17. John H. Boyd, "The Impact of Inflation on Financial Sector Performance." http://faculty.haas.berkeley.edu/ross_levine/Papers/2001_JME_Inflation%20Fin%20Sector.pdf http://www.fdic.gov/news/conferences/communitybanking/community_banking_by_the_numbers_clean.pdf.
18. See http://www.bls.gov/data/inflation_calculator.htm.
19. Calculation of Reserve Balance Requirements, Reserve Maintenance Manual, June 2013. Federalreserve.gov/monetarypolicy/rmm/June2013/chapter_3_calculation_of_reserve_balance.
20. http://www.fdic.gov/news/conferences/communitybanking/community_banking_by_the_numbers_clean.pdf. See also http://www.fdic.gov/regulations/resources/cbi/report/cbi-full.pdf.
21. Richard Brown, "Lessons Learned from the Financial Crisis Regarding Community Banks. Testimony before the Senate Committee on Banking, Housing, and Urban Affairs," June 13, 2013, http://www.fdic.gov/news/news/speeches/spjun1313.pdf.
22. A December 2012 report by the FDIC showed 6,526 community banks in the United States as of January 1, 2011, http://www.fdic.gov/news/conferences/communitybanking/community_banking_by_the_numbers_clean.pdf. This was a special study; the FDIC does not routinely publish the number of community banks. In general, however, these banks still comprise a majority of U.S. banks and have a major impact on the economy. As stated during a fall 2013 conference,"Despite the challenges facing community banks, they continue to play a unique and important role in the U.S. economy. Community banks provided 46 percent of small loans to farms and businesses, 16.1 percent of residential mortgage lending, 65.8 percent of farm lending, and 34.5 percent of commercial real estate loans, while accounting for 19.4 percent of all retail deposits at U.S. banks as of 2011 (FDIC, 2012). In 2011 community banks also made up 92 percent of FDIC-insured banks and 95 percent of U.S. banking organizations." Charles Kelly, Mohammed Khayum,and Curtis Price, "Equipment Lease Financing: The Role of Community Banks," white paper dated http://www.stlouisfed.org/banking/community-banking-conference/PDF/Community_Banking_Conference_Kelly_Khayum_and_Price.pdf. October 2–3, 2013, conference: Federal Reserve System and the Conference of State Bank Supervisors Community Banking in the 21st Century: Also preliminary research at this same conference by Yan Y. Lee and Smith Williams, "Do Community Banks Play a Role in New Firms' Access to Credit," indicates that increasing firms' distance to their nearest bank decreases their likelihood of receiving any bank credit. http://www.stlouisfed.org/banking/community-banking-conference/PDF/Lee_williams.pdf

23. Christine Harper, "Too Big to Fail Rules Hurting Too Small to Compete Banks," February 28, 2013, http://www.bloomberg.com/news/2013-02-28/too-big-to-fail-rules-hurting-too-small-to-compete-banks.html.
24. See http://www.fdic.gov/regulations/resources/cbi/report/cbi-full.pdf.
25. A news article about a BB&T bank acquisition stated that the North Carolina–based institution "operates each of its 36 regions as a community bank, with local decision-making to nurture local ties, plus 'national infrastructure that gives you economies of scale.'" Doreen Hemlock, "Big Banks Prompt Concerns," *Sun Sentinel*, August 1, 2012. http://articles.sun-sentinel.com/2012-08-01/business/fl-bankatlantic-trend–20120801_1_bigger-banks-community-reinvestment-act-community-bank.
26. See Matthias Rieker, "Demand for Business Loans Lifts Regional Banks' Profits," *Wall Street Journal,* January 16, 2013. http://online.wsj.com/article/BT-CO-20130116-714252.html.
27. FDIC Community Banking Study, December 2012, http://www.fdic.gov/regulations/resources/cbi/report/cbi-full.pdf.
28. Chelsey Levingston "Bank's Growth 'Good for County': CEO of First Financial Renews Commitment to Area as Bank Moves Headquarters," *Hamilton Journal-News*. June 13, 2011.
29. See "On Being the Right Size," speech given by Andrew G Haldane, Executive Director, Financial Stability, and member of the Financial Policy Committee, Institute of Economic Directors, Pall Mall, October 20, 2012, http://www.bankofengland.co.uk/publications/Documents/speeches/ 2012/speech615.pdf.
30. See note 1.
31. In the 113th Congress, as of October, there was draft legislation called the Too Big to Fail, Too Big to Exist Act, in the House (H.R. 1450) and Senate (S. 685), to require all U.S. banks to hold 10 percent equity capital and subject banks with more than $400 billion in total assets to additional capital surcharges based on the size of the institution. If the legislation passes, the U.S. would no longer be in compliance with the voluntary Basel III international capital accord (see Chapter 6). See also "Study and Recommendations Regarding Concentration Limits on Large Financial Companies," Financial Stability Oversight Council, January 2011, http://www.treasury.gov/initiatives/Documents/Study%20on%20Concentration%20Limits%20on%20Large%20Firms%2001-17-11.pdf.
32. "Shareholders may force boards to study more carefully whether such banks should be broken up into stand-alone pieces," says Sheila Bair, the former FDIC chair. "They may well be worth more if they're broken up into smaller, easier-to-manage, more-specialized pieces." Bair quoted in Harper, "Too Big to Fail Rules," op cit., note 23.
33. FDIC Community Banking Study, December 2012, http://www.fdic.gov/regulations/resources/cbi/report/cbi-full.pdf.

34. Deloitte. Rethinking Retail Banking Growth. http://www.deloitte.com/assets/Dcom-UnitedStates/Local%20Assets/Documents/us_rethinkingretailbankinggrowth_080411.pdf.
35. FDIC Community Banking Initiatives Summary of Roundtable Findings and Examination and Rulemaking Review Activities (summarizing discussions held throughout 2012). Source FDIC. http://www.fdic.gov/regulations/resources/cbi/rtreport.html#FullReport.
36. Ibid.
37. This paragraph is from the 2012 BB&T annual report published in 2013. http://www.bbt.com/sites/bbtdotcom/about/investor-relations/reports/bbt_2012ar10k.pdf.

CHAPTER 5

1. From an advertisement at http://banksmartusa.com/acquisition-smartkit.htm.
2. The most commonly used definition of a community bank is one with less than $1 billion in assets. However, some authorities prefer to define community banks by qualitative factors, such as geographical scope and the degree of local source of core deposits. The FDIC uses a hybrid definition. See http://www.fdic.gov/news/conferences/communitybanking/community_banking_by_the_numbers_clean.pdf.
3. Fair value is also often used as a statutory standard of value in dissenting shareholder cases where some level of oppression or unfairness is alleged.
4. See http://www.snl.com/Sectors/Fig/BanksAndThrifts.aspx.
5. The median price to tangible book value was 115.91 percent in 2012 for 135 deals with disclosed terms, compared to 106.74 percent in 2011 for 91 deals with disclosed terms. See http://www.ababj.com/briefing/snl-report-bank-m-a–2013-the-years-deals-begin–3663.html.
6. Monthly Bank Stock Performance, at http://www.smslp.com/investment-banking/bank-stock-performance-july–3/#.UB6hZ6CEXKQ.
7. These perennials are among more than a dozen measures tracked by SNL Financial for the financial institutions it profiles. See http://www.snl.com/Sectors/Fig/BanksAndThrifts.aspx. Other data points tracked are regulatory leverage ratio, book value, tangible book value, last twelve months (LTM) return on average equity, LTM return on average common equity, LTM net interest margin, non-performing assets/assets, LTIM/loans, and LTM efficiency ratio. On this last measure, see http://www.americanbanker.com/magazine/122_4/efficiency-ratios–1047522–1.html.
8. Only tangible equity capital should be counted in the denominator; the intangible parts, like goodwill, are excluded. See Thomas Siems, "The So-Called Texas Ratio," November 28, 2012. http://www.dallasfed.org/assets/documents/banking/firm/fi/fi1203.pdf.
9. Ibid.

10. "Most Efficient Bank Holding Companies," American Banker, September 2012. http://www.americanbanker.com/tools/ranking-the-banks.html.
11. Bartlett Naylor, "Business as Usual," December 2012, http://www.citizen.org/documents/banks-unaffected-by-volcker-rule-financial-reform-report.pdf.
12. The standard for fair value is Accounting Standards Codification (ASC) 820 (formerly Financial Accounting Standard 157). For a general discussion, see Floyd Norris, "Distortions In Baffling Financial Statements," *New York Times*, November 11, 2011. For historic background see *Report and Recommendations Pursuant to Section 133 of the Emergency Economic Stabilization Act of 2008: Study on Mark-To-Market Accounting*, http://www.sec.gov/news/studies/2008/marktomarket123008.pdf.
13. *Report and Recommendations Pursuant to Section 133 of the Emergency Economic Stabilization* Act of 2008: Study on Mark-To-Market Accounting, http://www.sec.gov/news/studies/2008/marktomarket123008.pdf.
14. The standard is ASC 820 (formerly FAS 157). See note 12.
15. Extraordinary items and other adjustments are factored out prior to annualization, but then added back to the annualized numerator.
16. A number of state bank examiners stipulate 1 percent ROA as good. According to the FDIC, at the end of the first quarter of 2012, the average ROA rose above the 1 percent threshold for only the second time since second quarter 2007 (third quarter 2011 ROA was 1.03 percent). See Quarterly Banking Profile, First Quarter 2012. http://www2.fdic.gov/qbp/2012mar/qbp.pdf.
17. Extraordinary items and other adjustments are factored out prior to annualization, but then added back to the annualized numerator.
18. "Statistics at a Glance." FDIC. http://www.fdic.gov/bank/statistical/stats/2013mar/industry.html.
19. For the second quarter of 2013, the ratio of noninterest income to average assets nationwide for all institutions insured by the FDIC was 1.86. See *Quarterly Banking Profile* Second Quarter 2013. FDIC, June 2013. http://www2.fdic.gov/qbp/2013jun/qbp.pdf.
20. For example, provisions for loan and lease losses, realized losses on securities, and income taxes should not be included in noninterest expense.
21. For the second quarter of 2013, the ratio of noninterest expense to average assets nationwide for all institutions insured by the FDIC was 2.83. See *Quarterly Banking Profile* Second Quarter 2013. FDIC, June 2013, op. cit., note 21, according to the FDIC.
22. See the "CFO Report: The New Era of Banking Regulation." Ernst & Young, 2011. http://www.ey.com/GL/en/Industries/Financial-Services/Banking—Capital-Markets/CFO-report—the-new-era-of-banking-regulation.
23. The interest a bank pays on its deposits is not counted under the expense part of the income statement; it is already subtracted from interest

revenue, so it is not considered an expense in this part of the income statement.

24. Some members of the 112th Congress attempted to improve federal bank examination standards by proposing the Financial Institutions Examination Fairness and Reform Act (H.R. 3461), sponsored by Rep. Shelley Moore Capito (R-WV). This bill died in committee but was reintroduced in the 113th Congress (as H.R. 1553 in the House and S. 727 in the Senate) in April 2013 and is back in committee as we go to press.
25. For a good discussion of banking risks, see http://www.calculatedriskblog.com/2009/04/bank-balance-sheet-liquidity-and.html – WkRz2379MeXJrtBP.99.
26. Consider the Heath–Jarrow–Morton Framework based on the work of researchers such as Robert A. Jarrow and others. See Martin Haugh, "The Heath-Jarrow-Morton Framework," http://www.columbia.edu/~mh2078/HJM_models.pdf. Accessed March 27, 2013.
27. For a list of all the credit rating services recognized as nationally recognized statistical rating organizations, see *Report to Congress on Assigned Credit Ratings: As Required by Section 939F of the Dodd-Frank Wall Street Reform and Consumer Protection Act* (Washington, DC: Division of Trading and Markets of the U.S. Securities and Exchange Commission, 2012). http://www.sec.gov/news/studies/2012/assigned-credit-ratings-study.pdf.
28. The use of the mark-to-market approach in this context should not be confused with the technique of the same name used to value a bank's securities investments. In the case of a "mark-to-market" approach to credit risks, the analysis considers credit ratings. In the case of mark-to-market analysis for securities held in the bank's portfolio considers security prices.
29. *Principles for the Management of Credit Risk,* September 2000, http://www.bis.org/publ/bcbs75.pdf.
30. Ibid.
31. See debt clock at http://www.usdebtclock.org.
32. See Jose A. Lopez "Stress Tests: Useful Complements to Financial Models" Federal Reserve Board of San Francisco (June 24, 2005). http://www.frbsf.org/economic-research/publications/economic-letter/2005/june/stress-tests-useful-complements-to-financial-risk-models.
33. Nassim Nicholas Taleb, *The Black Swan: The Impact of the Highly Improbable* (New York: Random House, 2007).
34. See Board of Governors of the Federal Reserve System Federal Deposit Insurance Corporation, Office of the Comptroller of the Currency. *Guidance on Stress Testing for Banking Organizations with Total Consolidated Assets of More Than $10 Billion*, May 14, 2012. http://www.federalreserve.gov/bankinforeg/srletters/sr1207a1.pdf.

35. Bank of America Dodd–Frank Act Mid-Cycle Stress Test Results BHC Severely Adverse Scenario, September 15, 2013. See "Bank of America Provides Mid-Cycle Stress Test Results." Bank of America, September 16, 2013. http://investor.bankofamerica.
36. The *Commercial Bank Examination Manual* is a massive document (1,847 pages as of this writing) that has been updated over time. See http://www.federalreserve.gov/boarddocs/supmanual/cbem/cbem.pdf. For a sample of an FDIC exam, see http://www.fdic.gov/regulations/safety/manual/section17-1.pdf.
37. Federal Financial Institutions Examination Council, https://cdr.ffiec.gov/CDR/public/download/UserGuide/v36/FFIEC%20UBPR%20User%20Guide%20Summary%20Ratios—Page%201_2012-09-26.pdf.
38. See Mark DeCambre, "Citi's Stress Mess," *New York Post,* March 14, 2012. http://www.nypost.com/p/news/business/citi_stress_mess_mUcLpIbw2lHqqnmNwNNq7J#ixzz1p68BCDcM.
39. Vincent Ryan, "The Hedge That Wasn't." *CFO,* August 1, 2012, http://www3.cfo.com/article/2012/8/risk-management_jp-morgan-hedging-credit-risk–2-billion-loss-cio?currpage=2.
40. Report of the Review Committee of the Board of Directors of JP Morgan Chase and Co. Relating to the Board's Oversight Function with Respect to Risk Management, January 15, 2013, http://files.shareholder.com/downloads/ONE/2619903093x0x628655/752f9610-b815–428c–8b22-d35d936e2ed8/Board_Review_Committee_Report.pdf.; Report of JPMorgan Chase & Co. Management Task Force Regarding 2012 CIO Losses, http://files.shareholder.com/downloads/ONE/2619903093x0x628656/4cb574a0–0bf5–4728–9582–625e4519b5ab/Task_Force_Report.pdf.
41. Institutions Examination Council. https://cdr.ffiec.gov/CDR/public/download/UserGuide/v36/FFIEC%20UBPR%20User%20Guide%20Summary%20Ratios—Page%201_2012-09-26.pdf; Most recently updated September 26, 2012.

CHAPTER 6

1. See U.S. Department of Justice Antitrust Division, *Antitrust Division Policy Guide to Merger Remedies*, June 2011, http://www.justice.gov/atr/public/guidelines/272350.pdf.
2. For example, in connection with its proposed merger with Hudson City, M&T filed a registration statement on Form S–4 that included a joint proxy statement of M&T and Hudson City and a prospectus of M&T, as well as other relevant documents concerning the proposed transaction. See http://ir.mandtbank.com/releasedetail.cfm?releaseid=702425.
3. The SEC's *Filing and Effectiveness of Registration Statement Involving Formation of Hold-Companies; Requests for Confidential Treatment* spells the conditions out in detail, but may be summarized as being a

matter of mere structuring—e.g., the 20-day fast track applies as long as "the transaction in connection with which securities are being registered involves the organization of a bank or savings and loan holding company for the sole purpose of issuing common stock to acquire all of the common stock of the company that is organizing the holding company." In essence, the new legal structure takes over the old legal structure with no change to the underlying assets. http://www.sec.gov/about/forms/forms-4.pdf.

4. Ibid.
5. The Group of 10 countries that agreed to participate in the General Arrangements to Borrow (GAB) are Belgium, Canada, France, Germany, Italy, Japan, the Netherlands, Sweden, the United Kingdom, and the United States. They were later joined by Switzerland, but the name "Group of 10" was kept. For other global groups see Chapter 10.
6. The number of commercial banks insured by the FDIC as of , June 30, 2013, was 5,980. In addition, the FDIC insures 960 thrifts. See "FDIC: Statistics at a Glance," http://www.fdic.gov/bank/statistical/stats/2013mar/industry.html. For the current capital requirements, see http://www.fdic.gov/regulations/laws/rules/2000–4400.html.
7. The Society for Human Resource Management (SHRM) has a competency model that can be used as a due diligence checklist for assessing human capital and its management. See http://www.shrm.org/HRCompetencies/Documents/Competency%20Model%207%203.pdf. SHRM works with a number of standards organizations; see http://www.shrm.org/HRStandards/StandardsBodies/Pages/default.aspx. One of these is the American National Standards Institute, Inc. (ANSI). The SHRM-ANSI Performance Management Standard approved November 30, 2012, is available at http://www.shrm.org/HRStandards/Documents/Performance%20Management%20ANS%20(2012).pdf.
8. For a classic book on this topic—one well ahead of its time—see Brian Friedman, James Hatch, and David M. Walker, *Delivering on the Promise* (New York: Free Press, 1999).
9. Heath P. Tarbert, the Allen & Overy partner who wrote the foreword to this book, heads the firm's bank regulatory practice.
10. See, for example, the description of litigation practice areas for financial services clients at http://www.allenovery.com/expertise/practices/financial-services/Pages/financial-services-regulation.aspx.
11. See Department of Justice, Antitrust Division, *Policy Guide to Merger Remedies,* June 2011, http://www.justice.gov/atr/public/guidelines/272350.pdf.
12. See Federal Trade Commission, 2013 Revised Thresholds under the HSR Act, effective February 2013, http://www.ftc.gov/os/2013/01/130110claytonact7afrn.pdf.
13. Hart–Scott–Rodino Annual Report, Fiscal Year 2012 (released June 2013), http://www.ftc.gov/os/2013/04/130430hsrreport.pdf. The fiscal year covers the period of October 1, 2011, through September 30, 2012.

14. "First Niagara's Acquisition of HSBC Branches Receives OK," *Albany Business Review*, April 9, 2012. http://www.bizjournals.com/albany/news/2012/04/09/first-niagaras-acquisition-of-hsbc.html.
15. See United States Securities and Exchange Commission Industry Guides, "Statistical Disclosure by Bank Holding Companies, General Instructions," pp. 6–13, http://www.sec.gov/about/forms/industryguides.pdf.
16. See Robert A. G. Monks and Alexandra R. Lajoux, "Appendix J: Monte Carlo Simulation for Security Investments," from *Corporate Valuation for Portfolio Investment: Analyzing Assets, Earnings, Stock Price, Governance, and Special Situations* (New York: John Wiley & Sons, 2011). http://onlinelibrary.wiley.com/doi/10.1002/9781118531860.app10/summary.
17. See FDIC Bank Examinations, http://www.fdic.gov/regulations/examinations.
18. See "Statistical Disclosure by Bank Holding Companies," *Guide 3, Securities Act Industry Guides (Washington, DC: Securities and Exchange Commission,* pp. 5–12. http://www.sec.gov/about/forms/industryguides.pdf.

CHAPTER 7

1. Matthew Kish, *Portland Business Journal*. January 18, 2013. http://www.bizjournals.com/portland/print-edition/2013/01/18/merged-banks-face-pressure-to-match.html?page=all.
2. The Antitrust Division of the Department of Justice can challenge a merger, and banks can make divestitures (euphemistically called restructure) in response. See Hart–Scott–Rodino Annual Report: Fiscal Year 2012, Section 7A of the Clayton Act, Hart-Scott-Rodino Antitrust Improvements Act of 1976. (35th Annual Report), by Edith Ramirez, Chairwoman, Federal Trade Commission, William J. Baer, Assistant Attorney General, Antitrust Division of the Federal Trade Commission and the Department of Justice. http://www.ftc.gov/os/2013/04/130430hsrreport.pdf. For a guide to this process, see Department of Justice, Antitrust Division, *Antitrust Division Policy Guide to Merger Remedies,* June 2011, http://www.justice.gov/atr/public/guidelines/272350.pdf.
3. According to the Fed, the term *merger* would exclude a purchase of assets and assumption of liabilities in which both the seller and the buyer continue to exist. That is not a merger and does not qualify for merger treatment.
4. This section is based on guidance from "Effect of Mergers on Reserve Balance Requirements," *Reserve Maintenance Manual,* June 2013, http://www.federalreserve.gov/monetarypolicy/rmm/june–2013/Chapter_6_Effect_of_Mergers_on_Reserve_Balance_Requirements.htm.
5. The consolidated FR 2900 will be filed weekly if either the survivor or the nonsurvivor filed the FR 2900 weekly prior to the merger. If both the survivor and the nonsurvivor filed the FR 2900 quarterly prior to the merger, the consolidated FR 2900 report will be filed quarterly after the

merger. The Federal Reserve will review the merged institution's reporting status as part of the annual reporting category reassignment process (effective each September).

6. "The amount of an institution's reservable liabilities that are subject to a 0-percent reserve requirement is used to make the distinction between detailed reporting and reduced reporting. In general, institutions with net transaction accounts greater than the exemption amount over prescribed periods are not exempt from reserve requirements and are subject to detailed reporting (categories one and two). Institutions with net transaction accounts equal to or less than the exemption amount over prescribed periods are exempt from reserve requirements and are subject to reduced reporting (categories three and four)." See Federal Reserve System, *Reserve Maintenance Manual,* June 2013, http://www.federalreserve.gov/monetarypolicy/rmm/june–2013/pdf/RMM_final_june2013.pdf.
7. As mentioned in Chapter 2, the Fed sets bank reserve requirements, meaning how much cash banks must have on hand to satisfy any demands made by their depositors. (Regular bank accounts are called "demand deposits" for this reason.) The reserve is set as a percentage of deposits, determined in groups or tranches. Under current U.S. regulations, banks with more than $12.4 million and up to and including $79.5 million must set aside 3 percent of their capital, and banks with more than $79.5 million must set aside 10 percent. Banks with $12.4 million in capital or less are exempt from these requirements. To make sure they meet the reserve requirements, banks have accounts with the Fed and may take out loans from the Fed to make up any shortfall between cash on hand and cash needed by their demand depositors.

   Source: Untitled press release of October 25, 2012. http://www.federalreserve.gov/newsevents/press/bcreg/20121025a.htm.
8. Federal Financial Institutions Examination Council, *User's Guide for the Uniform Bank Performance Report: Technical Information*. Board of Governors of the Federal Reserve System, Federal Deposit Insurance Corporation, Office of the Comptroller of the Currency, 2012.
9. This answer is based on one provided in Stanley Foster Reed, H. Peter Nesvold, and Alexandra R. Lajoux, *The Art of M&A: A Merger/Acquisition/Buyout Guide* (New York: McGraw-Hill, 2007) and updated to reflect current rules as of mid-2013.
10. 12 USC #ST 36, Branch Banks, covers the conditions upon which a national banking association may retain or establish and operate a branch or branches. See http://www.law.cornell.edu/uscode/text/12/36.
11. See http://www.law.cornell.edu/uscode/text/12/29.
12. *Union Nat'l Bank v. Matthews*, 98 U.S. 621, 626 (1878).
13. From 1995 to 2005, the number of banking institutions declined from 11,631 to 7,982,the average number of branches per bank increased from 6:03 to 10:63, and buyer banks tended to have more branches than their peers that grew internally. See Oktay Akkus, J. Anthony Cookson, and

Ali Hortac, "The Determinants of Bank Mergers: A Revealed Preference Analysis," January 31, 2012, https://webspace.utexas.edu/ja8294/www/eco393/hortascu/hw/assignment2_RevealedPreferenceMergers013112.pdf. However, in more recent times, the trend toward branch closings has accelerated. Overall, banks closed 2,267 branches in 2012 and opened only 1,149, according to research firm SNL Financial. That resulted in a total loss of 1,118 branches nationwide. See SNL Financial cited in "Say Goodbye to More Bank Branches," CNN Money, January 2013. http://money.cnn.com/2013/01/25/pf/banks-online-mobile-banking/index.html.

14. The Antitrust Division of the Department of Justice can challenge a merger, and banks can make divestitures (euphemistically called restructure) in response. See Hart–Scott–Rodino Annual Report: Fiscal Year 2012 Section 7A of the Clayton Act Hart-Scott-Rodino Antitrust Improvements Act of 1976 (35th Annual Report), by Edith Ramirez, Chairwoman, Federal Trade Commission, William J. Baer, Assistant Attorney General, Antitrust Division of the Federal Trade Commission and the Department of Justice. http://www.ftc.gov/os/2013/04/130430hsrreport.pdf For a guide to this process, see Antitrust Division Policy Guide to Merger Remedies. Antitrust Division of the Department of Justice June 2011. http://www.justice.gov/atr/public/guidelines/272350.pdf. See DOJ Press Release, "First Niagara Bank N.A. acquisition of HSBC Bank USA N.A," November 10, 2011. See p. 13 of the annual report cited in note 14, at http://www.ftc.gov/os/2013/04/130430hsrreport.pdf.
15. "From our empirical exercise, the mergers we study were primarily motivated by efficiencies, cost reductions, or reducing inefficiencies from previous regulations rather than merging to market power or merging to acquire great performing banks." Akkus et al., "The Determinants of Bank Mergers," op. cit.
16. "Although Wells Fargo has 6,293 branches, the most of any U.S. bank, it has closed 425 brick-and-mortar buildings during the last five years, and most of these (about 75 percent) were related to the company's 2008 takeover of Wachovia." See Frank Bass and Dakin Campbell, "Predator Targets Hit as Banks Shut Branches Amid Profits," May 2, 2013, http://www.bloomberg.com/news/2013-05-02/post-crash-branch-closings-hit-hardest-in-poor-u-s-areas.html.
17. See http://www.pacbiztimes.com/2013/06/07/243m-merger-comes-with-fine-branch-closures/.
18. The law requires an insured depository institution to give notice of any proposed branch closing to the appropriate federal banking agency no later than 90 days prior to the date of the proposed branch closing. The required notice must include the following: identification of the branch to be closed, the proposed date of closing, a detailed statement of the reasons for the decision to close the branch, and statistical or other information in support of such reasons consistent with the institution's written policy for branch closings.

19. The law defines a customer of a branch as "a patron of an institution who has been identified with a particular branch by such institution through use, in good faith, of a reasonable method for allocating customers to specific branches." An institution that allocates customers based on where a customer opened his or her deposit or loan account will be presumed to have reasonably identified each customer of a branch. See http://www.gpo.gov/fdsys/pkg/FR-1999-06-29/html/99-16471.htm.
20. See http://www.fdic.gov/regulations/laws/rules/5000-3830.html.
21. Office of the Comptroller of the Currency (OCC) and Office of Thrift Supervision regulations specify distances considered short-distance relocations. See 12 CFR 5.3(l) (national banks) and 12 CFR 545.95(c) (thrifts).
22. Conditional Approval No. 612, November 21, 2003, http://www.occ.gov/publications/publications-by-type/other-publications-reports/bankact.pdf.
23. OCC's Corporate Decision No. 2000–11, June 24, 2000, http://www.occ.gov/publications/publications-by-type/other-publications-reports/bankact.pdf.
24. See Deloitte & Touche, "Human Capital Merger, Acquisition, Restructuring, and Organization Design," 2010, http://www.deloitte.com/assets/Dcom-UnitedStates/Local%20Assets/Documents/Consulting%20MOs/us_consulting_mo_HCMARestructuringandOrganizationDesign_111810.pdf. Deloitte & Touche is part of the global firm Deloitte Touche Tohmatsu.
25. "Form of Brochure for Employees of Frequently Asked Questions." Exhibit 99.2. November 2, 2012 http://www.sec.gov/Archives/edgar/data/785024/000078502412000019/e992nov12a.htm. This brochure was filed with the Securities and Exchange Commission prior to the merger as part of its disclosures to the agency.
26. Ibid.
27. Ibid.
28. Ibid.
29. *Horizontal Merger Guidelines*, Department of Justice and Federal Trade Commission August 19, 2010. http://www.justice.gov/atr/public/guidelines/hmg–2010.html.
30. Akkus et al., "The Determinants of Bank Mergers" op. cit.
31. See BPC Group Banking Technologies and Smart Vista "The Effect of Mergers and Acquisitions on Banking Systems," 2007. http://www.bpcbt.com/upload/information_system_115/2/4/1/item_2412/information_items_property_15777.pdf. This document was used as the main source for this section of the chapter.
32. Ibid.
33. Matthew Kish, "Merged Banks Face Pressure to Merge Technologies." *Portland Business Journal,* January 20, 2013, http://www.bizjournals.com/portland/print-edition/2013/01/18/merged-banks-face-pressure-to-match.html?page=all.

34. This answer is based in part on Ken Smith and Alexandra Lajoux, *The Art of M&A Strategy* (New York: McGraw-Hill, 2011).
35. For example, after Bank of Montreal (BMO) bought banks in Wisconsin, its customer rating dropped sharply. "After any large merger it is not uncommon to see temporary declines in customer satisfaction," a BMO spokesman said in an email. See http://www.chicagobusiness.com/article/20130418/NEWS01/130419776/bmo-harris-customer-ranking-plummets-after-merger.
36. *Beyond Day One: Minimizing Customer Attrition During Bank Mergers and Acquisitions* http://www.deloitte.com/assets/Dcom-UnitedStates/Local%20Assets/Documents/FSI/us_fsi_BS_Beyond_Day_One_APR2010updated.pdf.
37. Ibid.
38. The source of this section is "If Your Bank Is Merging," *FDIC Consumer News*. Spring 2013. http://fdic.gov/consumers/consumer/news/cnspr13/bankmerging.html.
39. Frank Bass and Daiken Campbell, "Banks Disappear from Poor Neighborhoods Like Longwood, Bronx," *Bloomberg BusinessWeek*, May 9, 2013.
40. Interagency Bank Merger Act Application http://www.fdic.gov/formsdocuments/bma-fapp.pdf Paperwork Reduction Act notices omitted. See Appendix.
41. Ibid.
42. Long after the leveraged buyout era, M&A financing continues to concern regulators. Today "highly leveraged transactions" (HLTs) are called "higher-risk commercial and industrial loans and securities" (higher-risk C&Is). *Interagency Guidance on Leveraged Lending*, published by the Fed March 21, 2013, cites as a prime example of such lending "proceeds used for buyouts, acquisitions, or capital distributions." See http://www.federalreserve.gov/bankinforeg/srletters/sr1303a1.pdf. Re impact on the bank's balance sheet, see final FDIC rule on Assessments, Large Bank Pricing, October 31, 2012. http://www.fdic.gov/deposit/insurance/2012_10_31_rule.pdf.
43. Board composition may or may not change following a merger, depending on the extent to which the parent company consolidates its boards. For pertinent regulations, see the *Bank Holding Company Supervision Manual* (July 2013), on Supervision of Subsidiaries (Section 2010) at http://www.federalreserve.gov/boarddocs/supmanual/bhc/bhc.pdf.

CHAPTER 8

1. Regarding community protests, see testimony of Peter Skillern, Executive Director, Community Reinvestment Association of North Carolina, before the Financial Institutions and Consumer Credit Subcommittee (of the House Committee on Financial Services), March 3, 2011. http://financialservices.house.gov/media/pdf/030211skillern.pdf. See also Peter Skillern, "When Your Bank Leaves Town," National Housing Institute, November/December 2002. http://www.nhi.org/online/issues/126/bankclosings.html.

2. For example, one study showed that "our evidence from a sample of more than 3,000 commercial borrowers from banks involved in large mergers indicates that the wealth effects on these borrowers are highly negative, statistically significant, and economically important." Donald R. Frasier, James W. Kolari, Seppo Pynnõnen, and T. Kyle Tippens, "Market Power, Bank Mergers, and the Welfare of Bank Borrowers," *Journal of Financial Research* (last revised December 19, 2011). http://onlinelibrary.wiley.com/doi/10.1111/j.1475-6803.2011.01305.x/full.
3. "On average, shareholders of the acquiring bank fail to benefit from the merger," states Varini Sharma in "Do Bank Mergers Create Shareholder Value? An Event Study Analysis," December 17, 2009, http://www.minneapolisfed.org/mea/contest/2010papers/sharma.pdf. For details on a shareholder lawsuit alleging this point, see "New Info Settles Shareholder Lawsuit against Ongoing Bank Merger," posted at Competition Policy International, May 6, 2013, https://www.competitionpolicyinternational.com/us-new-info-settles-shareholder-lawsuit-against-ongoing-bank-merger/.
4. To review the bank's Uniform Bank Performance Report from the Federal Financial Institutions Examination Council, see https://cdr.ffiec.gov/public/SearchResultsUbprReports.aspx?reportType=283.
5. Trustmark 2012 annual report, https://www.snl.com/interactive/lookandfeel/100464/TRMK_2012AR032213.pdf.
6. As explained in Chapter 4, $10 billion is generally the maximum level of deposits a bank can have to be considered a community bank (among other qualifiers), according to the Federal Deposit Insurance Corporation. In its 2013 proxy statement, Trustmark states, "[F]ollowing the closing of the merger with BancTrust on February 15, 2013, Trustmark had assets greater than $10.0 billion." (By comparison, consider that Synovus Financial Corp. of Columbus, Georgia,, the smallest of the nation's 50 largest bank holding companies, had $26.7 billion in assets as of listed as of June 2013.) Source: Federal Financial Institutions Examination Council, National Information Center. http://www.ffiec.gov/nicpubweb/nicweb/top50form.aspx.
7. Steven J. Pilloff, "Performance Changes and Shareholder Wealth Creation Associated with Mergers of Publicly Traded Banking Institutions," *Journal of Money, Credit and Banking,* 28:3 (August 1996): 383–417.
8. See "BancTrust, Trustbank, Talked More Than a Year Before Merger Deal," *Alabama Business News,* May 31, 2012, http://bamabusinessnews.com/banctrust-trustmark-talked-for-a-year-before-merger-deal-4.
9. Order Approving the Acquisition of a Bank Holding Company and the Merger of Bank Holding Companies, Board of Governors of the Federal Reserve System, January 24, 2013. http://www.federalreserve.gov/newsevents/press/orders/order20130124.pdf. The order notes that the the Office of the Comptroller of the Currency ("OCC") has approved the proposed merger pursuant to the Bank Merger Act and the National Bank Act.
10. "To the extent not already provided, please describe the community outreach efforts (e.g., credit needs ascertainment, marketing/advertising,

product development), if any, by Trustmark National Bank to make home mortgage credit available to borrowers throughout the bank's assessment areas, including to Hispanics and African Americans." Letter of October 11, 2012, re Application by Trustmark Corporation to Acquire BancTrust Financial Group, Inc., signed by Richard Kim of Wachtell, Lipton, Rosen, and Katz. Posted at http://www.innercitypress.com/trustmark1cra10112.pdf.

11. Letter of October 11, 2012, re Application by Trustmark Corporation to Acquire BancTrust Financial Group, Inc., op. cit., note 10.
12. Ibid.
13. Order Approving the Acquisition of a Bank Holding Company and the Merger of Bank Holding Companies, op. cit., note 9.
14. Ibid.
15. For example, "the bank's percentage of originations to African American applicants was higher than the aggregate's in the bank's combined assessment areas in 2011." The report also noted that "examiners highlighted qualified investments, grants, and donations totaling $36.3 million in the bank's full-scope assessment areas in Mississippi. Most of those investments provided for the construction, repair, and expansion of schools serving primarily LMI [low- to moderate-income] students; funding home ownership and rental housing for LMI households; and a project to revitalize and stabilize a low-income area." Order Approving the Acquisition of a Bank Holding Company and the Merger of Bank Holding Companies, op. cit., note 9.
16. Ibid.
17. See Trustmark earnings call transcript, July 24, 2013, http://seekingalpha.com/article/1568512-trustmark-corp-trmk-ceo-discusses-q2–2013-results-earnings-call-transcript.

CHAPTER 9

1. Ana Botin, CEO, Santander, "Building a Customer-Driven, Best in Class Service Commercial Bank," June 29, 2011, speech at British Bankers' Association, Annual International Banking Conference.
2. See *Survey of Professional Forecasters: Data Sources and Descriptions,* Updated as of July 11, 2013, http://www.phil.frb.org/research-and-data/real-time-center/survey-of-professional-forecasters/spf-data-sources.pdf. Forecasters predictions are based on 11 primary indicators: gross domestic product (GDP), prices (GDP chain-weighted price index), corporate profits after tax, civilian unemployment rate, nonfarm payroll employment, industrial production index, housing starts, Treasury bill rates, AAA and BAA corporate bond yield, and Treasury bond rate. In addition, they look into GDP in nine specific areas, ranging from real GDP to real net exports of goods and services. They also include the consumer price index (CPI) and three related measures: core consumer price index (CPI minus food and energy, which are relatively volatile), personal consumption expenditure (PCE) chain price index, and PCE less food and energy chain price index. Thus, 23 measures are forecast.

3. Currently the chained consumer price index is the subject of controversy because it tends to report the rate of inflation as lower than the traditional consumer price index. For commentary and a link to several articles in the popular press, see Doug Short, "Chained CPI vs. Standard CPI: Breaking Down the Numbers," blog posted September 18, 2013 at dshort.com. For the original paper introducing the chained CPI, see Robert Cage, John Greenlees, and Patrick Jackman, "Introducing the Chained Consumer Price Index," U.S. Department of Labor, U.S. Bureau of Labor Statistics, presented at the Seventh Meeting of the International Working Group on Price Indices, Paris, France, May 2003, http://www.bls.gov/cpi/super_paris.pdf.
4. "Given the time lag inherent in implementing monetary policy, we generally think of policy as being effective if it achieves its goal(s) in one to two years." See Narayana Kocherlakota, "Achieving the Dual Mandate, Together," a column published June 10, 2012, by the Federal Reserve of Minneapolis. http://www.minneapolisfed.org/publications_papers/pub_display.cfm?id=5111.
5. Federal Reserve Board Press Release, July 31, 2013. http://www.federalreserve.gov/newsevents/press/monetary/20130731a.htm.
6. Federal Reserve Chairman Ben Bernanke, "Outstanding Issues in the Analysis of Inflation," June 9, 2008, http://www.federalreserve.gov/newsevents/speech/bernanke20080609a.htm. As of October 2013, as the President nominates Janet Yellen to succeed Mr. Bernanke after he steps down January 31, 2014, these issues are still outstanding.
7. George Soros, *The Alchemy of Finance*, Second Edition with a Foreword by Paul A. Volcker (New York: John Wiley & Sons, 2003).
8. George Soros, "The Theory of Reflexivity," lecture delivered April 26, 1994, MIT Department of Economics World Economy Laboratory Conference, Washington, DC.
9. See http://www.federalreserve.gov/newsevents/press/monetary/20130731a.htm.
10. See http://www.occ.treas.gov/publications/publications-by-type/other-publications-reports/semiannual-risk-perspective/semiannual-risk-perspective-spring-2013.pdf.
11. The Treasury's yield curve uses a quasi-cubic hermite spline function. A spline is a smooth polynomial, that is, a mathematical expression composed of variables and constants using addition, subtraction, and multiplication, including exponents (several multiplications by the same value). The hermite aspect means that there are variables with an orthogonal relationship (x- and y-axis); the "quasi" modifer means more than one dimension and being somewhat irregular—a condition captured by the nonuniform rational B-spline, or NURBS. The inputs to the spline are close of business (COB) bid yields for the on-the-run securities. On-the-run securities are the most recently issued U.S. Treasury bond or note of a particular maturity; they are the opposite of off-the-run) Treasuries (securities that have been issued before the most recent issue and are still outstanding). On-the-run securities are used because their trading value is typically close to their par value.

12. David B. Moore, *Analyzing and Investing in Community Banks: Introduction to Banks and Bank Investing.* (New York: Icarus Publishing, 2005). He explains: "More specifically, banks take in funds, in the form of deposits and borrowings, at one interest rate and lend those funds out or invest them at (presumably) higher rates in the form of loans and investment securities." Posted at http://www.scribd.com/doc/37801388/Analyzing-Thrifts-Primer-08-06-10.
13. According to one study of yield curves and recessions from 1970 to 2009, "yield spread is indeed important and has significant predictive power when forecasting industrial production growth over a one-year time horizon," but the results deteriorate when forecasting growth two years ahead. See Menzie D. Chinn and Kavan J. Kucko, "The Predictive Power of the Yield Curve Across Countries and Time." National Bureau of Economic Research, September 2010. http://www.ssc.wisc.edu/~mchinn/w16398.pdf. See also Joseph G. Haubrich, "Yield Curve and Predicted GDP Growth" August 20, 2013. http://www.clevelandfed.org/research/data/yield_curve.
14. By size of GDP, the top five nations are the United State, China, Japan, Germany, and France, with the United States well in advance of the other four top rankers. For growth rate, however, the top five are Sierra Leone, Mongolia, Turkmenistan, Sri Lanka, and Panama. See http://search.worldbank.org/data?qterm=gdp%20growth%20rate&language=EN.
15. See National Income and Product Accounts, Gross Domestic Product, second quarter 2013 (advance estimate), Comprehensive Revision: 1929 through 1st quarter 2013, published July 31, 2013, http://www.bea.gov/newsreleases/national/gdp/gdpnewsrelease.htm.
16. See "Real Gross Domestic Product—Forecasts,"*Economics: Key Tables from OECD*, No. 4, http://www.oecd-ilibrary.org/economics/real-gross-domestic-product-forecasts_gdp-kusd-gr-table-en.
17. *U.S. 2013 Mid-Year Economic Outlook, Securities Industry and Financial Markets Association* (SIFMA), July 25, 2013, http://www.sifma.org/econoutlook20132h. The survey was conducted from June 27, 2013, to July 11, 2013. The forecasts discussed in the text are the median values of the individual member firms' submissions, unless otherwise specified.
18. The economic world arguably operates according to multiple interrelated laws (however imperfectly participants may be in discovering them), whereas the policy world may be less susceptible to prediction. It is difficult to prove or disprove this statement, though, as it is illegal to bet on political elections.
19. See *The Budget and Economic Outlook, Fiscal Years 2012 to 2022,* http://www.cbo.gov/sites/default/files/cbofiles/attachments/01–31–2012_Outlook.pdf.
20. See Susan Lund et al., *Game Changers: Five Opportunities for U.S. Growth and Renewal*, July 2013. http://www.mckinsey.com/insights/americas/us_game_changers.

21. Semiannual Risk Perspective, From the National Risk Committee, Figure 19: Commercial Loan Growth by Industry for Select Banks, http://www.occ.treas.gov/publications/publications-by-type/other-publications-reports/semiannual-risk-perspective/semiannual-risk-perspective-spring-2013.pdf.
22. For case studies of sustainable business practices at the Cooperative Bank, Fleet Boston, and Van City, see http://www.iisd.org/business/banking/sus_banking.aspx.
23. David Rowe, "The False Promise of Expected Shortfall," *Risk Magazine,* November 2012, http://www.dmrra.com/publications.
24. "Both community and noncommunity banks headquartered in nonmetro areas outperformed their counterparts headquartered in metro areas on the basis of pretax return on assets (ROA) for the study period as a whole and for each five-year interval for which the comparison was made. Even the 1,091 community banks headquartered in depopulating rural counties in 2011 outperformed their counterparts headquartered in metro areas over the past decade. Instead, the disparities between metro and nonmetro counties are reflected in the growth rates of the institutions headquartered there." FDIC Community Banking Study, December 2012. http://www.fdic.gov/regulations/resources/cbi/report/cbi-full.pdf.
25. As defined by the Office of Management and Budget, a metropolitan statistical area (MSA) contains a core urban area of 50,000 or more in population.
26. Meredith Gunther, "UVA Releases First National and State Population Projections" July 23, 2013. https://news.virginia.edu/tags/united-states-demography.
27. *Insights into the Financial Experiences of Older Adults: A Forum Briefing Paper,* July 2013, http://www.federalreserve.gov/newsevents/conferences/older-adults-forum-paper-20130717.pdf.
28. Samuel R. Summers, "On Racial Diversity and Group Decision Making: Identifying Multiple Effects of Racial Composition on Jury Deliberations," *Journal of Personality and Social Psychology*, 90, no. 4 (2006): 597–612. The author found "specific advantages of racial heterogeneity for group decision making."
29. See Bank of America's landing page on "Global Diversity and Inclusion Partnerships and Recruiting Strategy," at http://careers.bankofamerica.com/learnmore/recruitingevents.asp.
30. "Conversation with Eric Schmidt hosted by Danny Sullivan," Search Engine Strategies Conference, August 9, 2006. http://www.google.com/press/podium/ses2006.html.
31. "Who Coined Cloud Computing?" MIT Technology Review, October 2011. http://www.technologyreview.com/news/425970/who-coined-cloud-computing.
32. Ibid.

33. Peter Mell and Timothy Grance. "The NIST Definition of Cloud Computing: Recommendations of the National Institute of Science and Technology." September 2011. http://csrc.nist.gov/publications/nistpubs/800-145/SP800-145.pdf.
34. Ibid.
35. "Top 10 Technology Trends Impacting Information Infrastructure," February 9, 2013, http://my.gartner.com/portal/server.pt?open=512&objID=270&mode=2&PageID=3862698&resId=2340315#t-N66258.
36. "Gartner Says Worldwide Mobile Payment Transaction Value to Surpass $235 Billion in 2013." Press Release, June 4, 2013. http://www.gartner.com/newsroom/id/2504915. See also Brian Finn, "Mobile Technology: Banking and Beyond." *Wired*. September 9, 2013. http://insights.wired.com/profiles/blogs/mobile-technology-banking-and-beyond#axzz2gFnsrsWb.
37. See questions and answers at http://bitcoin.org/en/press. For independent commentary, see Steve Faktor, "10 Reasons Bitcoin is the MySpace of Money and What Might Save It." *Forbes* August 2013. http://www.forbes.com/sites/stevefaktor/2013/08/30/10-reasons-bitcoin-is-the-myspace-of-money-and-what-might-save-it.
38. See explanation of "Bank Accounts" at paypal.com. https://www.paypal.com/webapps/helpcenter/article/?articleID=94040&m=SRE#link_your_bank_accounts.
39. See Alexandra R. Lajoux, "The Debate Over Cyberthreats." *NACD Directorship* (May/Jun 2013), Vol. 39 Issue 3, p. 22.
40. See Trends in the Global Banking Industry, Cap Gemini, 2012. http://www.capgemini.com/sites/default/files/resource/pdf/trends_in_the_global_banking_industry_2012_0.pdf. A more detailed forecast appears in *Global Banking Industry: Trends, Profits, and Forecast Analysis* prepared by the research firm Lucintel and available at http://www.researchandmarkets.com/reports/2183749/global_banking_industry_20122017_trends.
41. For guidance from the Fed on how to incorporate the Basel III regulatory capital reforms into capital and business projections, see the untitled Fed press release issued September 24, 2013 on this topic. http://www.federalreserve.gov/newsevents/press/bcreg/20130924b.htm.

CHAPTER 10

1. Sir Mervyn King, chair of the Bank of England July 2003 to June 2013, and currently the chair of the International Integrated Reporting Council, is the most widely quoted source of this phrase, which has also been attributed to Bank of England consultant Charles Goodhart. For a source that cites King, see "U.S. Cannot Pay for Europe's Capital Sin," *Financial Times* editorial, April 23, 2013, http://www.ft.com/intl/cms/s/0/84fc2c4e-ac28–11e2-a063–00144feabdc0.htmlt. For a source that cites Goodhart, see Simon Johnson, "Tarullo Telegraphs Fed's Plans to Cap Bank Size."

December 9, 2012, posted at bloomberg.com. http://www.bloomberg.com/news/2012-12-09/tarullo-telegraphs-fed-s-plans-to-cap-bank-size.html.

2. Scott Besley and Eugene F. Brigham, *Principles of Finance* (Cengage Learning, 2012).
3. Harvey R. Miller "A Better Solution Is Needed for Failed Financial Giants," *Dealbook,* October 9, 2012. http://dealbook.nytimes.com/2012/10/09/a-better-solution-is-needed-for-failed-financial-giants/?_r=0.
4. Ibid.
5. The Basel Committee's charter is found at http://www.bis.org/bcbs/charter.pdf.
6. The Basel Committee's 27 members are Argentina, Australia, Belgium, Brazil, Canada, China, France, Germany, Hong Kong SAR, India, Indonesia, Italy, Japan, Korea, Luxembourg, Mexico, the Netherlands, Russia, Saudi Arabia, Singapore, South Africa, Spain, Sweden, Switzerland, Turkey, the United Kingdom, and the United States.
7. The G20 comprises Argentina, Australia, Brazil, Canada, China, France, Germany, India, Indonesia, Italy, Japan, Mexico, Russia, Saudi Arabia, South Africa, South Korea, Turkey, the United Kingdom, and the United States of America. The European Union is also a member, represented by the European Commission and the European Central Bank. For an informative article, see G7/G8, G20 at the website of the European Commission, http://ec.europa.eu/economy_finance/international/forums/g7_g8_g20/.
8. For a critique of this approach, see David Rowe, "The False Promise of Expected Shortfall," *Risk Magazine,* November 2012, http://www.dmrra.com/publications.
9. The United States, Germany, and Spain have enacted stricter capital requirements, some of which may conflict with Basel III. See Walter A. Eubanks, "The Status of the Basel III Capital Adequacy Accord," *CRS Report for Congress*, prepared for Members and Committees of Congress, October 28. 2010, http://www.fas.org/sgp/crs/misc/R41467.pdf. See also Douglas J. Elliott, "Basel, the Banks, and the Economy," Brookings Institute, July 23, 2010, http://www.brookings.edu/~/media/research/files/papers/2010/7/26%20basel%20elliott/0726_basel_elliott.pdf.
10. The number of banks insured by the FDIC as of June 30, 2013, was 6,940. See "FDIC: Statistics at a Glance," http://www.fdic.gov/bank/statistical/stats/2013jun/industry.html. See "Federal Reserve Board Issues Interim Final Rules Clarifying Basel III Reforms Into Capital and Business Projections." http:www.federalreserve.gov/newsevents/press/bcreg/20130924b.htm.
11. See Benoit Coeuré, member of the executive board of the European Central Bank, "Global Liquidity and International Risk-Sharing in the Post-Crisis Environment," speech June 3, 2013, at the Bank of Korea International Conference 2013, "Assessing Global Liquidity in a Global Framework," Seoul, South Korea, http://www.ecb.europa.eu/press/key/date/2013/html/sp130603_1.en.html. See also Viral V. Acharya Gara Afonso, and Anna

Kovner, "How Do Global Banks Scramble for Liquidity? Evidence from the Asset-Backed Commercial Paper Freeze of 2007," Federal Reserve Bank of New York Staff Reports, March 18, 2013, http://www.bc.edu/content/dam/files/schools/csom_sites/finance/Kovner–032013.pdf. http://www.newyorkfed.org/research/staff_reports/sr623.pdf.

12. Commitments such as irrevocable letters of credit should not be included in outstandings; however, where such items are material, the amounts should be separately disclosed. See http://www.sec.gov/about/forms/industryguides.pdf.
13. See http://www.sec.gov/about/forms/industryguides.pdf.
14. "In 2007, 76% of global banking revenue came from developed markets; banks' price-to-book ratio in these markets was 1.6. By the trough of the crisis in 2009, developed market banks accounted for 44% of global revenues, while their price-to-book had fallen to 1.0." See Stefano Visalli, Charles Roxburgh, Toos Daruvala, Miklos Dietz, Susan Lund, and Anna Marrs., *The State of Global Banking: In Search of a Sustainable Model*. McKinsey & Company, September 2011. http://www.mckinsey.com/clientservice/Financial_Services/Knowledge_Highlights/Recent_Reports/~/media/Reports/Financial_Services/McKGlobalBanking.ashx. Accessed December 15, 2011.
15. Accenture, July 25, 2011. http://www.accenture.com/us-en/Pages/insight-cross-border-banking.aspx.
16. Angel Liao and Jonathan Williams, "Do Win-Win Outcomes Exist? A Study of Cross-Border M&A Transactions in Emerging Markets," July 16, 2006. http://www.fin.ntu.edu.tw/~conference/conference2006/proceedings/proceeding/10/10–1(A65).pdf. The authors state: "Between 1998 and 2005, we identify 74 cross-border M&A transactions in which international banks acquired ownership stakes in 46 listed banks in emerging market economies (EME). Whereas abnormal returns to targets are mostly positive and significant, they tend to be offset by negative returns to acquiring banks." The authors suggest that this is an unusual finding, "inconsistent with evidence from the non-financial sector." However, based on the authors' own research and experience, this is a typical pattern in postmerger returns.
17. Shaghil Ahmed and Andrei Zlate, "Capital Flows to Emerging Economies: A Brave New World?" http://www.federalreserve.gov/pubs/ifdp/2013/1081/ifdp1081.pdf.
18. Example provided by Accenture. See note 15. Also see page 203 for a quote by Santander CEO Ana Botin.
19. See McKinsey & Company, *The State of Global Banking: In Search of a Sustainable Model*. The first McKinsey annual review of the banking industry, September 2011, based on data spanning 79 countries and the world's 300 largest banks. This is the firest in the McKinsey series. It is currently posted only at http://www.brandchannel.com/images/papers/530_mckinsey_wp_sustainble_banking_0911.pdf.
20. This information is based on McKinsey's service called a Global Banking Pool, with more than 4 million data points on different banking markets and individual banks. See *The Triple Transformation: Achieving a*

Sustainable Business Model, McKinsey, October 2012. This is the second McKinsey annual review of the banking industry; see note 19 for the first in the series.

21. See *Banking in 2050: How the Financial Crisis Has Affected the Long-Term Outlook for the Global Banking Industry,* May 2011, http://www.pwc.com/en_us/gx/world–2050/assets/pwc_banking_in_2050_-_may.pdf.
22. Ibid.
23. Bruce Kience, David W. Helin, and Brad Eckerde, *Cross-Border Banking: A Study of Cross-Border Mergers and Acquisitions in Banking* (2011). http://www.accenture.com/SiteCollectionDocuments/Accenture.Cross-Border-Bankering.pdf.
24. See http://www.iosco.org/library/pubdocs/pdf/IOSCOPD154.pdf.
25. For a recent article on the Edge Act, (12 U.S.C. § 632), see Mark G. Hanchet and Christopher J. Houpt, "The Edge Act Confers Federal Jurisdiction According to U.S. District Court for the Southern District of New York, March 20, 2013, posted at http://www.martindale.com/banking-law/article_Mayer-Brown-LLP_1715398.htm.
26. Ibid.
27. Am. Int'l Grp., Inc. v. Bank of Am. Corp., 820 F. Supp. 2d 555, 556 (S.D.N.Y. 2011).
28. See http://www.pwc.com/us/en/financial-services/regulatory-services/publications/assets/closer-look-fbo-fnfc.pdf. See also Randall Guynn, Mark Plotkin and Ralph Reisner, *Regulation of Foreign Banks and Affiliates in the United States,* 6th ed. (Eagan, MN: West, 2012).
29. For the report instructions, see www.bea.gov/surveys/pdf/be605.pdf.
30. Under Regulation S-X, section 201 9.05.
31. A significant geographic area is one in which assets or revenue or income before income tax or net income exceed 10 percent of the comparable amount as reported in the financial statements.
32. The Federal Reserve consulted with other members of the Financial Stability Oversight Council in developing the proposal. See http://www.federalreserve.gov/newsevents/press/bcreg/20121214a.htm. For all comments on the proposal, which is still pending as of mid-October 2013, see http://www.federalreserve.gov/apps/foia/ViewComments.aspx?doc_id=R-1438&doc_ver=2.
33. See comment letter of April 30, 2013, from the Institute of International Bankers, http://www.federalreserve.gov/SECRS/2013/May/20130517/R–1438/R–1438_043013_111113_555179652070_1.pdf.
34. See 12 C.F.R. §§ 243, 381. A separate resolutions plan rule applies to FDIC-insured banks with $50 billion or more in assets. See 12 C.F.R. § 360. The Board of Governors of the Federal Reserve System has also separately proposed (but not yet adopted) rules that will require foreign banks with $50 billion or more in global assets to submit risk management, liquidity, and certain other plans, and impose certain other

risk management and planning requirements on all foreign banks with a U.S. branch, agency, subsidiary U.S. bank, or Edge corporation. See http://www.arnoldporter.com/resources/documents/Advisory-Deadline_Approaching_for_Foreign_Banks_on_Living_Wills.pdf. The term *U.S. nonbank assets* generally refers to assets held outside the foreign bank's U.S. branch, agency, U.S. commercial lending company, or depository institution subsidiary. See Arnold Porter, op. cit.

35. "FDIC Approves Final Rule on the Definition of Deposit at Foreign Branches of U.S. Banks to Clarify That These Deposits Are Not Insured by the FDIC." Press release of September 10, 2013. http://fdic.gov/news/news/press/2013/pr13081.html.
36. See http://www.aicpa.org/InterestAreas/Tax/Resources/International/DownloadableDocuments/5472-Guide–2012-%20FINAL-w-Appendices.pdf.

CHAPTER 11

1. Jaron Lanier, *Who Owns the Future?* (New York: Simon & Schuster, 2013). Lanier, a computer programmer and futurist, is credited as the leading pioneer of virtual reality technology.
2. See the FDIC's Failed Bank List, http://www.fdic.gov/bank/individual/failed/banklist.html. For a map showing all failed banks from 2007 to the present, see http://research.stlouisfed.org/maps/failed_banks.php. See also Dennis Wheelock, "Have Acquisitions of Failed Banks Increased the Concentration of U.S. Banking Markets?" *Federal Reserve Bank of St. Louis Review,* 93, no. 3 (May/June 2011: 155–168). As reported by Wheelock, "During 2007–10, failures eliminated 318 U.S. commercial banks and savings institutions, about 4 percent of the total number of banks operating at the end of 2006. The assets and deposits of many failed banks were acquired by institutions that already had offices in markets served by the failed banks."
3. Ibid.
4. According to a paper by economists at the U.S. Department of the Census, the one-year survival rates for establishments started in 2004 was 76.4 percent, and the five-year survival rates for establishments started in 2000 was 50.7 percent. See Brian Headd, Alfred Nucci, and Richard Boden, "What Matters More: Business Exit Rates or Business Survival Rates?" May 25, 2010. http://www.census.gov/ces/pdf/BDS_StatBrief4_Exit_Survival.pdf.
5. As mentioned in Chapter 2, the FDIC's role as insurer and receiver are separate functionally and legally.
6. *Banking Conditions As-of June 2013*. Federal Reserve Bank of Kansas City, June 2013. http://www.kansascityfed.org/publicat/banking/districtbankingconditions/DistrictConditionsSlides.pdf.
   See FDIC Quarterly Banking Profile, Second Quarter 2013. http://www2.fdic.gov/qbp/2013jun/qbp.pdf. For a report on general economic

conditions, see http://www.federalreserve.gov/monetarypolicy/beigebook/files/Beigebook_20130717.pdf.

7. Ibid., p. 6.
8. A more comprehensive measure of relative failure rates between community and noncommunity banks is a failure index that measures the frequency of failures within each group relative to their prevalence. Results from this are mixed. See http://www.fdic.gov/regulations/resources/cbi/report/cbi-full.pdf.
9. As the consulting firm McGladrey notes, "Even the healthiest banks may have a tough time raising capital that is non-dilutive to ownership or earnings per share." See "Distressed Bank Acquisition Strategies," March–April 2011, http://mcgladrey.com/Bank-Notes/Distressed-Bank-Acquisition-Strategies.
10. This answer (except for the last sentence) is excerpted verbatim from H. Peter Nesvold, Jeffrey M. Anapolsky, and Alexandra R. Lajoux, *The Art of Distressed M&A: Buying, Selling, and Financing Troubled and Insolvent Companies* (New York: McGraw-Hill, 2011).
11. 11 U.S.C. § 101(32)(A).
12. Uniform Fraudulent Transfer Act, Sections 2(a) and (b).
13. Wenting Song, "Were Bank Mergers Following the 2008 Financial Crisis Efficient? Three Case Studies," Senior Honors Thesis advised by Professor Costas Azariadis, Department of Economics, St. Louis University, March 20, 2012, http://economics.wustl.edu/files/economics/imce/song-thesis.pdf.
14. See U.S. Title 12, Section 1821, Section 1821. http://www.law.cornell.edu/uscode/text/12/1821.
15. Legal violations can be litigated by a variety of plaintiffs, including the U.S. Department of Justice. For a list of Department of Justice actions against bank frauds, see http://www.justice.gov/accomplishments/accomplishments.pdf.
16. As defined in U.S.C. Title 12, Section 1831o (b). See http://www.law.cornell.edu/uscode/text/12/1821.
17. Under U.S.C. Title 12, Section 1831o (f)(2)(A). See http://www.law.cornell.edu/uscode/text/12/1821.
18. Under U.S. C. Title 12, Section 1831o (e)(2)(D). See http://www.law.cornell.edu/uscode/text/12/1821.
19. Under U.S.C. Title 12, Section 1831o (e)(2). See http://www.law.cornell.edu/uscode/text/12/1821.
20. As defined in U.S.C. Title 12, Section 1831o (b). See http://www.law.cornell.edu/uscode/text/12/1821.
21. For prohibitions on money laundering, see U.S.C. Title 18, Section 1956–1957; or U.S.C. Title 31, Section 5322–5324. Seehttp://www.law.cornell.edu/uscode/text/18/1956 and http://www.law.cornell.edu/uscode/text/31/5322.22.

22. For more on FDIC "prompt corrective action," see http://www.fdic.gov/regulations/laws/rules/1000-4000.html.
23. Also, "not more than 65 percent of the required minimum level of capital under the leverage limit," at http://www.fdic.gov/regulations/laws/rules/1000-4000.html.
24. For a good explanation of how the recovery process works, see Michael H. Krimminger, "Deposit Insurance and Bank Insolvency in a Changing World: Synergies and Challenges," International Monetary Fund Conference, May 28, 2004, http://www.imf.org/external/np/leg/sem/2004/cdmfl/eng/mk.pdf. See also Sylvia A. Mayer, Heath P. Tarbert, and Sunny Singh, "The Hidden Value in Recovery and Resolution Planning," *The American Banker*, Vol. 122, No. 12. December 7, 2012. http://www.americanbanker.com/bankthink/the-hidden-value-in-recovery-and-resolution-planning–1055000–1.html.
25. For a sensible, pre-Dodd–Frank essay about the liability-to-assets ratio, see a blog by James Surowiecki, "What Does Insolvency Mean for a Bank?" *New Yorker* blog, January 20, 2009, http://www.newyorker.com/online/blogs/jamessurowiecki/2009/01/what-does-insol.html.
26. For a general discussion of this and other Bankruptcy Code chapters, see Peter H. Nesvold, Jeffrey M. Analpolsky, and Alexandra R. Lajoux, *The Art of Distressed M&A, Buying, Selling, and Financing Troubled and Insolvent Companies* (New York: McGraw-Hill, 2011), op. cit., note 10, at pp. 38–43.
27. Richard M. Hynes and Steven D. Walt, "Why Banks Are Not Allowed in Bankruptcy," *Washington & Lee Law Review,* Vol. 67:3 (Summer 2010), pp. 985–1051.
28. See report on Wamu by Kurzman Carson Consultants at http://www.kccllc.net/wamu.
29. For U.S. update, see http://dm.epiq11.com/LBH/Project.
30. See Statement of Federal Deposit Insurance Corporation by James R. Wigand, Director, Office of Complex Financial Institutions, and Richard J. Osterman, Jr., Acting General Counsel, "Who Is Too Big To Fail?" Examining the Application of Title I of the Dodd?Frank Act before the Subcommittee on Oversight and Investigations, Committee on Financial Services, U.S. House of Representatives, April 16, 2013.
31. See Steve J. Lubben, "Transaction Simplicity," *Columbia Law Review Sidebar,* 112:194 July 2012, citing Hollace T. Cohen, "Orderly Liquidation Authority: A New Insolvency Regime to Address Systemic Risk," *University of Richmond Law Review,* 45:4 (May 2011): 1143, 1151; and "Does the Dodd? Frank Act End Too Big to Fail?" Hearing before the Subcommittee on Financial Institutions and Consumer Credit of the House Committee on Financial Services, 112th Congress, 2011 (statement of Micha (on file with the *Columbia Law Review*) (describing mechanisms for resolving financial institutions through bankruptcy and the Orderly Liquidation Authority).

32. See the FDIC's Failed Bank List, op. cit., note 2. See also http://research.stlouisfed.org/maps/failed_banks.php.
33. According to a glossary posted at its website, the FDIC assigns a composite rating between 1 and 5 to each financial institution, based on financial and operational criteria. The higher the number, the greater the concern. The rating is based on a scale of 1 to 5 in ascending order of supervisory concern. "Problem" institutions are those institutions with financial, operational, or managerial weaknesses that threaten their continued financial viability. Depending upon the degree of risk and supervisory concern, they are rated either a "4" or "5." http://www2.fdic.gov/qbp/Glossary.asp?menuItem=GLOSSARY.
34. http://www2.fdic.gov/qbp/2013jun/qbp.pdf. See also Remarks by Martin J. Gruenberg Chairman, FDIC Third Annual American Banker Regulatory Symposium Arlington, VA, September 23, 2013. http://fdic.gov/news/news/speeches/spsep2313.pdf.
35. See Arthur J. Murton's Memorandum to the Board of Directors, FDIC, re Update of Projected Deposit Insurance Fund Losses, Income, and Reserve Ratios for the Restoration Plan, October 2, 2012. http://www.fdic.gov/deposit/insurance/memo_2012_10_02.pdf.
36. See http://www.fdic.gov/regulations/laws/rules/1000-4000.html, op. cit., note 22.
37. For contact information see http://www2.fdic.gov/drrip/cs/index.asp. For a sample bidder qualification sheet see http://www.fdic.gov/buying/financial/BidderQualApp072012Sample.pdf.
38. This applies if the banks are treated as BHCs under § 8(a) of the International Banking Act of 1978. See chapter 10 on global bank M&A.
39. Final rule on "Resolution Plans Required," Board of Governors of the Federal Reserve System (Board) and Federal Deposit Insurance Corporation (Corporation). http://www.gpo.gov/fdsys/pkg/FR-2011-11-01/html/2011-27377.htm.
40. Ibid.
41. *Resolving Globally Active, Systemically Important, Financial Institutions*, a joint paper by the Federal Deposit Insurance Corporation and the Bank of England, December 10, 2012, http://www.fdic.gov/about/srac/2012/gsifi.pdf.
42. See http://www.fdic.gov/bank/individual/failed/pls/index.html?source=govdelivery. See also Chapter 11 of "Managing the Crisis: The FDIC and RTC Experience," http://www.fdic.gov/bank/historical/managing/history1–11.pdf.
43. *FDIC, as receiver of Integrity Bank v. Skow, et. al.,* Civil Action No. 1:11-CV-0111-SCJ (N.D. Ga. Feb. 27, 2012) and *FDIC, as receiver of Heritage Community Bank v. Saphir*, 2011 WL 3876918, No. 10 C 7009 (N.D. Ill. Sept. 1, 2011) (Pallmeyer, J.). For a discussion see "FDIC Failed Bank Director and Officer Claims: Recent Court Decisions Better Define the Landscape." Jones

Day client letter, http://www.jonesday.com/files/Publication/6b79bcc6–36e0-42a5-aebe-942f730f4774/Presentation/PublicationAttachment/14bf3054-0b63-4a5c-a272-a5af40459744/FDIC%20Failed%20Bank%20Director%20and%20Officer%20Claims%20Commentary.pdf.

44. The largely verbatim source of this answer is the FDIC Structured Transaction Fact Sheet posted on the FDIC website: http://www.fdic.gov/buying/financial/factsheet.html. The authors inserted the questions.
45. See http://www.fdic.gov/regulations/laws/rules/5000-1000.html.

CHAPTER 12

1. Benjamin Graham and David L. Dodd, *Security Analysis* (New York: Whittlesey House/McGraw-Hill, 1934) special reprint edition.
2. Peter Lynch. *Beating the Street* (New York: Simon & Schuster, 1994).
3. See http://www.renaissancecapital.com/IPOHome/Press/IPOPricings.aspx. For total number of filings see http://www.renaissancecapital.com/IPOHome/Press/IPOFilings.aspx.
4. J. R. Ritter, "Initial Public Offerings: Updated Statistics," June 2013. http://bear.warrington.ufl.edu/ritter/IPOs2012Statistics.pdf. The author samples IPOs with an offer price of at least $5.00, excluding American depositary receipts (ADRs), unit offers, closed-end funds, real estate investment trusts (REITs), partnerships, small best efforts offers, banks and savings and loans, and stocks not studied by the Center for Research in Security Prices (CRSP). CRSP has historical data for NYSE (from December 1925), NYSE-Amex (from July 1962), NYSE-Arca (from March 2006), and and NASDAQ (from December 1972). The total number of IPOs, including some of these excluded categories, is higher.
5. See Bank Capital Group. http://www.bankcapitalgroup.net/services-capital-raising.php.
6. Source: David B. Moore, Analyzing and Investing in Community Bank Stocks, http://csinvesting.org/wp-content/uploads/2012/07/analyzing_and_investing_in_community_bank_stocks.pdf.
7. A good source of insights on industry cyclicality is Morningstar, which divides all industries into three categories: cyclical, sensitive, and defensive. Cyclical industries are significantly impacted by economic shifts, expanding during times of economic prosperity and shrinking during downturns; sensitive industries also move with the economy but to a lesser degree; defensive industries are relatively immune to these trends. https://corporate.morningstar.com/us/documents/Indexes/SECTOR_PRISM_2011YB.pdf pdf.
8. See http://poweredby.morningstar.com/selectors/funds/FundRank.html?fundCategory=SpecFin&screen=tr5yr&CN=NSC124&x=35&y=8.
9. See http://poweredby.morningstar.com/selectors/funds/FundRank.html?fundCategory=SpecFin&screen=tr3yr&CN=NSC124&x=50&y=7.

10. All holdings reported in this section are for mid-2013 and are subject to change.
11. Select Banking Portfolio, https://fundresearch.fidelity.com/mutual-funds/performance-and-risk/316390640.
12. The Securities and Exchange Commission (SEC) definition specifies "Section 12 registered equity shares or units," referring to Section 12 of the Securities Act of 1933, which sets forth requirements for registering shares with the SEC—the step necessary to become a public company and to participate in public company markets. See "Tender Offer," http://www.sec.gov/answers/tender.htm.
13. Ibid.
14. For example, under the Securities Exchange Act of 1934, parties who will own more than 5 percent of a class of the company's securities after making a tender offer for securities registered under the Exchange Act must file a Schedule TO with the SEC. The SEC also requires any person acquiring more than 5 percent of a voting class of a company's Section 12–registered equity securities directly or by tender offer to file a Schedule 13D.
15. See http://www.sec.gov/investor/pubs/minitend.htm.
16. Melodie Warner, "MBIA Recommends Note Holders Reject Bank of America's Hostile Tender Offer," Dow Jones News, November 20, 2012. http://www.djnewsplus.com/rssarticle/SB135343057813932210.html.
17. Ibid.

APPENDIX

1. Unless otherwise indicated, case summaries written by Alexandra R. Lajoux are based on the text of the decisions, as cited. Cases before 1882 were identified by "Dates of Supreme Court Decisions and Arguments," *United States Reports, Volumes 2–107 (1791–1882),* prepared by Anne Ashmore, Library, Supreme Court of the United States, August 2006. The full text of these early cases is available at http://www.supremecourt.gov/opinions/datesofdecisions.pdf. Full case details were located through http://supreme.justia.com/us.
2. Edward Everett, speech of February 22, 1851, cited in Charles Warren, *History of the Harvard Law School and of Early Legal Conditions in America* (New York: Lewis, 1908).
3. For original text of the cases, see http://supreme.justia.com/.
4. For the history of how this became the court's motto, see the U.S. Supreme Court brochure titled *The West Pediment*: *Information Sheet* at http://www.supremecourt.gov/about/westpediment.pdf.
5. This estimate of "more than 16,000" cases is made in good faith based on data provided by the Supreme Court on its website. Although the Court has nearly 10,000 cases on the docket each year as petitions for a writ of certiorari—up from only 1,440 on the docket in 1945—the Court hears oral

argument in only about 75–80 per year. Multiplying the number of years the Supreme Court has been deciding cases (223 years) by 75 as the annual estimate for formal cases yields 16,725. For the annual numbers, see http://www.supremecourt.gov/faq.aspx#faqgi9 and http://www.supremecourt.gov/about/justicecaseload.aspx.

6. For a discussion of Supreme Court jurisdiction, see *CSR Annotated Constitution,* http://www.law.cornell.edu/anncon/html/art3frag51_user.html.
7. A writ of error is a formal written order in which an appellate court asks a lower court to send the record of its legal action for review by the appellate court for possible correction or reversal.
8. For a good discussion of this case, see Kermit L. Hall, *The Oxford Companion to the Supreme Court of the United States* (New York: Oxford University Press, 1992).
9. *Hodgson & Thompson v. Bowerbank*, 9 U.S. (5 Cr.) 303 (1809). Full case is not available, but a discussion is available at http://supreme.justia.com/constitution/article–3/31-controversies-involving-foreigners.html.
10. Other early decisions on enforceability of contracts include *Farmers and Mechanics' Bank of Pa. v. Smith,* February 12, 1821, re retroactivity of a law (an act of a state legislature pertaining to debts did not nullify the standing of the contracts entered into prior to the act), and *Union Bank v. Hyde,* March 14, 1821/March 16, 1821, re interpretation of a contract (a promise not to protest a note was considered out of place and ambiguous).
11. See also *Mechanics' Bank of Alexandria v. Withers,* 19 U.S. 106 (1821), finding that cases may still be pled on day of adjournment.
12. For a good discussion of this case, see Hall, *Oxford Companion to the Supreme Court,* op. cit., note 8.
13. This case was cited in *Beneficial National Bank, et al., Petitioners, v. Marie Anderson, et al.* 539 U.S. 1 (2003).
14. This case is cited in the Office of the Comptroller of the Currency's Interpretive Letter no. 1034, July 2005. 12 U.S.C. § 29.
15. National Bank Act, Rev. Stat. 5197, as amended, 12 U.S.C. § 5.
16. Cited as Rev. Stat. 5198, 12 U.S.C. § 94. At the time of this case, the Section read as follows: "Actions and proceedings against any association under this chapter may be had in any district or Territorial court of the United States held within the district in which such association may be established." In 1982 the section was amended to refer specifically to the Federal Deposit Insurance Corporation as a receiver.
17. For more on this case, see Chapter 3.
18. For more on this topic, see Chapter 2.
19. Note that not all case law defers to agencies' own interpretations of their laws. For a discussion of this matter, see Chapter 2.

INDEX

ABOUT THE AUTHORS

Alexandra Reed Lajoux is chief knowledge officer of the National Association of Corporate Directors and the author or coauthor of all titles to date in McGraw-Hill's Art of M&A Series. A past editor of *Mergers & Acquisitions magazine*, she is a regular contributor to business and professional periodicals. Dr. Lajoux serves on the advisory boards of several organizations, including *Campaigns & Elections* magazine, the Caux Round Table, E-Know, and the M&A Leadership Council. She is based in Fairfax, Virginia.

Dennis J. Roberts is the chairman of the McLean Group, an M&A investment bank with multiple U.S. offices. He is the author of the internationally selling and highly acclaimed *Mergers and Acquisitions: An Insider's Guide to the Purchase and Sale of Middle Market Business Interests* (John Wiley & Sons, 2009). He is the former chairman and CEO of a bank holding company with a multistate branch presence. He lectures, teaches, and writes on M&A, business valuation, and corporate finance to national and international audiences. Mr. Roberts is a contributor to numerous professional and business journals. He is based in McLean, Virginia.